D1402307

ASSERTING YOURSELF

A Practical Guide for Positive Change

SHARON ANTHONY BOWER

GORDON H. BOWER

Addison-Wesley Publishing Company

Reading, Massachusetts · Menlo Park, California

London · Amsterdam · Don Mills, Ontario · Sydney

Library of Congress Cataloging in Publication Data

Bower, Sharon Anthony, 1934-
  Asserting yourself.

  Bibliography: p. 243
  1. Assertiveness (Psychology) — Problems,
exercises, etc. I. Bower, Gordon H., joint author.
II. Title.
BF575.A85B68   158'.1   76-5077
ISBN 0-201-00837-8
ISBN 0-201-00838-6 pbk.

Text copyright © 1976 by Addison-Wesley Publishing Company, Inc., Philippines copyright
1976 by Addison-Wesley Publishing Company, Inc.

Illustrations copyright © 1976 by Tom Durfee, Philippines copyright 1976 by Tom Durfee.

All rights reserved. No part of this publication may be reproduced, stored in a retrieval
system, or transmitted, in any form or by any means, electronic, mechanical, photocopying,
recording, or otherwise, without the prior written permission of the publisher. Printed in the
United States of America. Published simultaneously in Canada. Library of Congress Catalog
Card No. 76-5077.

ISBN 0-201-00837-8-H
ISBN 0-201-00838-6-P
ABCDEFGHIJ-MA-79876

We dedicate this book
with love and thanks to our parents,
Lois and Lorenzo Anthony, and Mabelle and the late Clyde Bower,
and with love and hope to our children,
Lori, Tony, Julia

Preface

From time to time, many of us feel uneasy in social situations; often we feel put down or cheated. Phrases like "a nation of sheep" and "the Great Silent Majority" characterize our inability to speak up for our legitimate rights.

We have written this book to help remedy this situation. We want people to gain self-esteem and confidence in expressing themselves effectively and forthrightly. We want readers to be able to stand up for their rights and negotiate productively with others who put them down.

The goal we stress in this book is better self-management. We promote the values of personal growth and fulfillment for everyone. The self-managed life style rests upon humanistic values, particularly the idea that each person must take responsibility for the quality of his relationships with others. Assertiveness training is a process that can make it possible to achieve this goal of self-management.

We believe that this book represents a unique approach to helping people become more assertive. The techniques that we introduce and use here have come from our experiences. Sharon, a former actress and director, studied behavior-change techniques while working toward a master's degree in counseling and guidance at Stanford University. During her clinical training, Sharon started to do assertiveness training with middle-aged women, typically housewives who were trying to reenter the working world. Drawing upon her experience in theatre, Sharon helped her students develop assertive "scripts" — DESC scripts — for various interpersonal conflicts in their lives. She also taught her students how to rehearse their scripts and deliver them with expressive voice and body language. She has continued to expand these methods in the many workshops she conducts for colleges, business, industry, and government.

Gordon, a professor of psychology at Stanford University, specializes in experimental studies of human learning and memory. He has helped formulate some of the behavior modification concepts and exercises in this book. Also, he has helped in explaining the learning theory under-pinnings for the step-by-step program which Sharon has used in her work-shops and which forms the basis of this book.

We hope that you will find the information and techniques in this book helpful in designing your own personal program for positive change. Leaders of workshops will also be interested in the *Instructor's Manual* that has been written to accompany the book.

Asserting Yourself can be an important first step to a better life. We hope that you will take it.

Stanford, California   S.A.B.
July 1976   G.H.B.

Acknowledgments

We express our appreciation to Dr. Beverly Potter for her continuous encouragement and suggestions. We also thank Ms. Georgia Meredith, Coordinator of Continuing Education for Women, Foothill College; Ms. Vicky Katz, Coordinator of SLS-90 and Short Courses, De Anza College; Dr. Richard Henning, Director of Short Courses, Foothill College; Ms. Judy Moss, Personnel and Training, Stanford University; Mr. Gale Fullerton, Employee Trainer and Developer, Western Region, U.S. Geological Survey; Ms. Donis Wellman, Civil Service Commission, San Francisco Branch; and Ms. Meredith Moore, Ames Research, Moffet Field, Mountain View, California. They have provided Sharon with continuous support as well as settings where she could teach assertiveness classes in college and governmental settings. We are grateful also for the encouragement received from Professors John D. Krumboltz and Carl E. Thoresen, both of Stanford University's Educational Psychology Department. Our special thanks to Joyce Lockwood for her warm interest and for her determined typing of the manuscript. Thanks to Tom Durfee, our illustrator, for his special talent. Thanks also to the assertiveness students who have offered their scripts as illustrations. Finally, we thank the authors who have permitted us to quote from their writings. These are acknowledged in the notes at the end of the book.

Contents

5. DESC Scripting: A New Approach for Dealing with Conflicts   87

6. Sample Scripts for Standard Situations   106

Introduction

An anthropologist interviewing the average person would come to a startling conclusion: in the midst of great economic abundance, cultural opulence, and technological sophistication, many people think they aren't getting enough satisfaction out of life.

When asked what is wrong, they say they are dissatisfied with many things, from their personality to their physical appearance to their social adjustment. A recent survey found that 90 percent were unhappy in some way with their appearance. People felt they were too fat, or too thin, or that their ears, nose, mouth, waistline, or figure deviated too much from some mythical standard of beauty. People similarly complained of unhappiness in their social and personal lives. They felt they were either too passive or too aggressively hostile in dealing with interpersonal problems.

All kinds of people experience feelings of personal inadequacy, from housewives and students to movie stars and politicians. They feel unhappy that they're unable to get along with others or even with themselves. They often feel put down, stifled, upset, and exploited. These feelings come to the surface in various forms: as loneliness, as depression, as a sense of helplessness, and perhaps most of all as shyness. In another survey,[1]* 82 percent of the American college and high school students interviewed felt that they had been disturbingly shy for a substantial part of their lives. Significantly, 42 percent considered their shyness a current personality defect; that is, they wanted counseling to help them overcome their shyness and passivity.

---

*Notes for all chapters are grouped at the end of the book.

We were led to write *Asserting Yourself* by two basic beliefs. First, we have concluded that lack of assertiveness is a major cause of the feelings of uneasiness and inadequacy that millions of people experience. Second, we believe that assertiveness is the product of a set of learned attitudes and communication skills that can be changed for the better.

The program suggested in this book comes from behavior-change psychology, speech and communications, and acting. A large part of our behavior, undesirable as well as desirable, depends on the learning experiences we have had, and our learning continues as we constantly adjust to our changing environment. Believing that behavior can be changed, psychologists suggest that we can learn new behaviors to replace older, less productive ones. And that is the purpose of this book — to help you learn to change your behavior in a positive way, to relate to others more effectively, to help you speak up appropriately when you feel put down.

This process of change involves some systematic work.

First, you need to estimate how assertive you are now and identify situations in which change is both an important and a realistic goal. To help you with this assessment, we have provided several self-tests in Chapter 1.

Second, you will work on improving your self-esteem. Many people who feel inadequate report a negative self-concept. Throughout their lives, they have learned to think of themselves as shy or inept or passive. They constantly berate themselves with, "I'm too weak," or "I'm stupid," or "I could never talk in front of all those people." In Chapter 2, we provide a number of examples and exercises to help you replace negative self-statements with more positive ones. With a systematic approach to thinking positively about yourself, you can begin improving your self-image *and* your assertive actions.

Third, we will offer some tips on coping with stress. Chapter 3 provides information on progressive relaxation and coping skills exercises that can help you deal more systematically with the fear or anxiety you may feel in a stressful confrontation.

Finally, you can learn specific skills for relating to others more assertively. The main part of this book (Chapters 4 to 10) is devoted to helping you acquire and practice these skills. You can learn to:

- Become more objective in observing what you and others are doing in upsetting situations.
- Plan a campaign to "contract" for favorable behavior changes from yourself and others in upsetting situations.
- Speak up with assertive language, voice quality, and body movements.
- Follow through on the consequences of the contract you have negotiated with the other person.
- Learn to deal with the occasional, one-shot put-down situations where you interact with an offensive person only once.

Also, since nonassertive people often have trouble developing friendships, in Chapter 11 we have included exercises to help widen your circle of acquaintances and develop more rewarding and meaningful friendships.

Our assertiveness training program is *action oriented,* so we provide many exercises for you to develop your assertiveness. You don't need to do every single one, but the more you do, the more you can help yourself. At first you may feel a little awkward learning the skills of assertiveness. But it is like learning to ride a bicycle or to ski — the more you practice carefully, the more skilled you become. It won't always be easy. But it will be worth your time and effort, because you will be able to develop more balanced relationships with other people. Chances are you'll feel less stifled and put down when you have developed the skills needed to speak up positively. You can gain in confidence and self-esteem just knowing that you can assert yourself to solve interpersonal problems and enrich the quality of your life.

1

How Assertive Are You Now?

*Behavior is a mirror in which
everyone shows his image.*

GOETHE

Assertiveness has many forms. It is the ability to express your feelings, to choose how you will act, to speak up for your rights when it is appropriate, to enhance your self-esteem, to help yourself develop self-confidence, to disagree when you think it is important, and to carry out plans for modifying your own behavior and asking others to change their offensive behavior. The dictionary defines *assertiveness* as "the disposition to bold or confident assertion without need for proof," and *assertion* as "confident declaration or affirmation of a statement." To *assert oneself* is "to compel recognition of one's rights or position."

This book presents a step-by-step program for becoming a more assertive person. We have combined a number of techniques from behavior-change psychology, speech, communications, and acting to create a strong, practical program. With this program, you can work on confidently declaring and affirming yourself with others, and you can learn to stand behind what you say and do.

As an assertive person, you can do the following:[1]

- *Use feeling-talk.* You can express your personal likes and interests spontaneously rather than stating things in neutral terms. You say "I like this soup or "I love your blouse" rather than "This soup is good." You can use the phrase "I feel" or "I think" when it is appropriate.

- *Talk about yourself.* If you do something worthwhile and interesting, you can let your friends know about it. You don't monopolize the conversation, but you can mention your accomplishments when it is appropriate.

- *Make greeting-talk.* You are outgoing and friendly with people you want to know better. You smile brightly and sound pleased to see them. You say,

"Well, Hello! How good to see you again" rather than softly mumbling "H'lo" or nodding silently or looking embarrassed.

- *Accept compliments.* You can accept compliments graciously ("Yes, I like this shirt, too") rather than disagreeing with them ("Oh, this old thing?"). You reward rather than punish your complimenter.

- *Use appropriate facial talk.* Your facial expressions and voice inflections convey the same feelings your words are conveying. You can look people directly in the eye when conversing with them.

- *Disagree mildly.* When you disagree with someone, you do not pretend to agree for the sake of keeping the peace. You can convey your disagreement mildly by looking away, or grimacing, or raising eyebrows, or shaking your head, or changing the topic of conversation.

- *Ask for clarification.* If someone gives you garbled directions, instructions, or explanations, you can ask that person to restate them more clearly. Rather than going away confused and feeling dumb, you can say, "Your directions were not clear to me. Would you please go over them again?"

- *Ask why.* When you are asked to do something that does not seem reasonable or enjoyable, you can ask, "*Why* do you want me to do that?"

- *Express active disagreement.* When you disagree with someone and feel sure of your ground, you can express your disagreement by saying things like "I have a different view of that matter. My opinion is . . ." or "I think your opinion leaves out of consideration the following factors . . ."

- *Speak up for your rights.* You do not let others take advantage of you when you feel put upon; you can say no persistently without feeling guilty. You can demand your rights and ask to be treated with fairness and justice. You can say, "I was next in line," or "Excuse me, but you will have to leave as I have another appointment now," or "Please turn down your radio," or "You're half an hour late for our appointment." You can register your complaints firmly without blowing up.

- *Be persistent.* If you have a legitimate complaint, you can continue to restate it despite resistance from the other party until you get satisfaction. You do not allow one or two no's to cause you to give up.

- *Avoid justifying every opinion.* In discussion, if someone continually argues and asks you why, why, why, you can stop the questioning by refusing to go along, or by reflecting it back to the other person. You can state simply, "That's just the way I feel. Those are my values. I don't have to justify everything I say. If justifying is so important to you, you might try justifying why you're disagreeing with me so much."

Above all, as an assertive person you can learn to negotiate mutually satisfactory solutions to a variety of interpersonal problems — from dealing with your neighbor whose dog likes to march over your marigolds to adjusting an unsatisfactory relationship with a friend or relative.

You may have trouble handling such situations now because of your habitual ways of acting toward a spouse, a child, a teacher, a friend, a co-worker, a boss, an employee, or a parent. A situation recurs over and over in which some other person frustrates you, "misbehaves," takes advantage of you, hurts and upsets you. We call these persisting situations "put-down" scenes, and we call the other person — your "antagonist" in any specific put-down situation — the "Downer." You may have several Downers — perhaps a demanding child, an overweaning parent, a nosy neighbor, a ridiculing friend, an overly dependent employee.

Your goal is to change the way you and your Downer interact in that old put-down situation so you *both* derive more satisfaction from it. Achieving many such goals is the aim of assertiveness training and it's what this book is all about.

DO YOU HAVE A RIGHT TO BE ASSERTIVE?

Some people believe that assertiveness training must turn a nice person into a constant irritant, a rebel, a complainer, and a general, all-around pain. Others charge that assertiveness training teaches people to be calculating and manipulative, and helps them control others for selfish ends. Views like these are based on a misunderstanding of the goals of assertiveness training, or reflect a distorted sense of humanistic values.

To be sure, adopting more assertive habits will "make waves" and disturb the relations that passive people had with their Downers. But only a misguided form of humanism would say you cannot under any circumstances create unpleasantness or discomfort for someone else. One of your basic human rights is self-defense when your rights are being stepped on. When being exploited and mistreated by a Downer, it is your basic right to object and to change that exploitive relationship. Of course, your legitimate rebellion may cause the exploiter some discomfort! To draw an analogy, slave masters used to gain many advantages from slaves, so they tried to squelch "slave revolts" to protect those advantages. But few people would argue that slaves should not have revolted because it displeased the slave masters.

Our human rights flow from the idea that we are all created equal in a moral sense and we are to treat one another as equals. In social relations between two equals, neither person has exclusive privileges, because the needs and goals of each person are to be equally valued. As equals, two people (say, a husband and wife) may work out — or "fall into" — a diverse set of agreements, compromises, and rules to "govern" themselves. Such agreements, often inexplicit, allow the day-to-day business of the relationship to proceed without daily arguments and negotiations about who is to do what and when. There is no universally correct form for these social accommodations; any arrangement or division of labor is okay provided both parties are satisfied with it and the arrangement doesn't infringe on the rights of others. But whatever the agreement, it rests on the premise that we are equals with the same rights. This means that each party has a moral right to renegotiate what he thinks is an unfair or inequitable arrangement.

As for the charge that assertiveness training teaches people how to manipulate others for their own gain, it simply does not apply. "Manipulate" is a negative term meaning to control someone by devious or underhanded means, perhaps without his awareness and for selfish motives. Rather than using devious methods, assertiveness training promotes explicit above-board "contracts" setting out for the Downer exactly what "rewards" will be provided for changing specified behaviors. Moreover, this assertiveness training program recommends taking account of the Downer's needs and interests, and trying to negotiate a behavior-change contract agreeable to both parties. The aim is mutual satisfaction, not "turning the tables" so that the newly assertive person becomes the dominant member in the relationship. The object is to speak up for one's rights without aggressively putting down other people and trampling on their rights.

Assertiveness training aims to help you (1) get control of yourself, to be less shy and more expressive (or less aggressive and hostile), with the result that (2) you can influence the way others behave towards you, particularly those who mistreat you. To object that it is immoral to try to influence anyone is just plain silly. Interpersonal influence through rewards and punishments is a fact of life just like the law of gravity; you can't turn it off. It pervades all areas of our life — the wages we earn for our work, the disapproval we show our children's or mate's bad actions, the good (or bad) "example" we set for our children or co-workers. Everyone uses many social rewards and punishments every day, often unwittingly and in destructive, self-defeating ways. We suggest that you use behavior-change methods consciously and ethically, with concern for the other person, to foster positive behavior change in yourself as well as in the Downers in your life.

Of course, there are alternative approaches to trying to alter an unjust, exploitive relationship — for example, "moral persuasion" or arguments about the "fairness" of the current relationship. But these are simply weaker methods of trying to influence a Downer. They typically produce only arguments, not behavior change. Few real Downers are ever at a loss to rationalize their behavior! So to get a satisfactory behavior change from your Downer in a put-down situation, you need some more powerful methods, which this book suggests.

Remember, you are starting from the observation that you are unhappy about the way several areas of your life have been going: you are the one who is feeling indignant, downtrodden, put-upon, mistreated. You have a basic right to rectify these situations, to ask for equal treatment, to search after more personal satisfaction. One goal of assertiveness training is to equalize the balance of power between two parties, redressing the former "master-slave" relation, so that both parties win something in resolving their conflict.

Assertiveness training, then, is concerned with speaking up about interpersonal conflicts, and very often with getting problems resolved. To

WHICH IS YOUR STYLE?

clarify what assertiveness is, let's contrast it with two opposite but self-defeating behavior patterns — inhibited passivity on the one hand and excessive aggressiveness on the other hand.

THE PASSIVE, THE AGGRESSIVE, AND THE ASSERTIVE STYLES OF BEHAVIOR

The differences among passive, aggressive, and assertive styles of behavior show up in the way a particular problem would be handled by a "script" which typifies that style. Let us begin with a simple problem: suppose a woman wants to get her Downer (say, her partner) to cooperate in planning some improvements in the garden. This is important to her but not to him. For a setting, suppose the Downer is reading the evening newspaper.

The Passive Scene

She Uh, excuse me but I wonder if you would be willing to take the time to decide about the garden?
Downer [Looking at paper] Not now, I'm busy.
She Oh, okay.

That's a pretty short script, but it illustrates several points. The passive person starts by asking permission to even broach the subject. This in itself conveys timidity, along with the impression that the Downer probably does not want to waste time on this problem. The Downer's answer is a standard put-off, evading the issue and postponing action. The "I'm busy" justification is empty; it is equivalent to saying "I am doing something that I don't want to stop in order to deal with your request." People are always busy doing something. This particular "I'm busy" means "I like reading more than making garden decisions."

The "Oh, okay" reply only rewards the Downer's put-off. The passive person will now go off somewhere and suffer silently a little. She may run some other dialogues through her head, such as "I should have said . . ." or "If only he would . . ." But we can be reasonably sure that the next time the scene occurs she won't say it, and he won't do whatever it was she wished he would.

A person who reacts passively plays that kind of scene hundreds of times. And like drips of water slowly wearing away a rock, those experiences wear away confidence and self-esteem. Whenever you react passively by retreating when you feel you should assert yourself, you lose some self-respect.

Passive people are likely to blame other people more than themselves for their unhappy lot. They do not take responsibility for what is happening, for the quality of their life. They become silent martyrs. But that position is a mistake and a delusion: often they are just as responsible as their Downers for the poor situation.

Passive people have quiet ways of punishing their Downers. The passive wife may accidentally burn her husband's bacon or forget to buy him some beer; the passive husband may sabotage sexual relations by getting too eagerly engrossed in a book to come to bed when expected. The most frequent punishment is for the injured person to withdraw from the Downer, to sulk or to cry. Sulking and crying are classic manipulations by which injured passive people call forth sympathy and guilt, and hence "get their own way." But such manipulative behaviors (sometimes referred to as "passive aggression" or "indirect aggression") are an emblem of inadequacy, the sole form of aggression left for the person who feels helpless.

The Aggressive Scene

She Listen, I'm sick and tired of you putting off deciding about this damn garden. Are you going to help?

Downer [Looking at paper] Not now, I'm busy.

She Why can't you look at me when you're turning me down? You don't give a damn about the garden or the house or me! You just care about yourself!

Downer That's not true. I do care.

She No, you don't. You never pay any attention to your household or to me. I have to do everything around here myself!

Downer For God's sake, are we back to that again! Leave me in peace! Just stop nagging at me!

She You don't care two cents for me or for anything around here except watching those childish football games on TV and getting fat drinking beer.

Downer Oh shut up, you nag! You only want a handyman around the house to fix the plumbing and pull the weeds. When the hell do I ever get any peace and pleasure from coming back to this sweat shop you call a home?

Although the script builds up the aggression faster than might be realistic, it nonetheless illustrates the main points. What is happening in this scene of household warfare? First, the opening line is an attack. The woman may intend it only as a statement that she wants help in planning garden improvements, but her voice is loud, harsh, demanding. The Downer naturally resists. She interprets the Downer's resistance as a put-down, which calls up all the old memories of his unhelpful evasions. For good measure, she includes herself in the list of things he supposedly does not care about. She replays the angers of earlier irritations with him. He denies her charges, but she comes back with more. He demands that she leave him alone. Interpreting this as an insult, she downgrades his simple pleasures as laziness. Finally, he fires off the curtain-closing salvo, one usually followed by the slamming of doors.

Such scenes have no winner: both parties storm away from it feeling miserable, ready to flee. He becomes increasingly lazy, unconcerned, diffident; she becomes increasingly bossy, shrewish, nagging. Her aggression shows in the way she immediately puts her partner on the defensive, trying to make him feel guilty. Angered by her accusations, he counterattacks with insults. If passive aggression is more his style, he might withdraw to a mistress, a poker club, or a whisky bottle. But such escapes are self-defeating; in particular, they avoid the immediate problem, which is the quality of the marriage relationship. The partner seems not to be looking at and listening enough to her, whereas she seems to ask too many questions and make too many insulting remarks. Both partners are hurt because they too quickly leap to generalities about the other's personality rather than concentrating on the issue of planning the garden. Each person blames the other for being selfish, for "not listening." Each tries to hurt the other. If this battle continues, it could even break out into physical violence, with pots and pans being thrown.

In most cases a domestic battle doesn't develop into a physical one; instead it becomes a psychological tug-of-war, sometimes of grotesque dimensions. But regardless of the form it takes, aggressive behavior aims at hurting another person, physically or emotionally. The two parties adopt a fighting posture: one person must win and the other lose in the conflict. Aggressive behavior thus serves to exalt oneself at the expense of another's self-esteem; it aims at domination of one person by another.

In the long run, aggressive interactions have only unfavorable consequences; both players lose. Of course, during childhood, beating up our playmates may have gotten us the small treasures of childhood — the marbles, the gumdrops, the football, or the first place in line. But as our social conscience matures, we develop more altruistic goals. We come to realize that some of our happiness depends upon having the significant people around us be happy and feel friendly toward us. The aggressive person is fixated at the old kindergarten level, saying "I want all the marbles" rather than "Let's share the marbles." But at the same time, having mistreated the other person, he or she suffers from feelings of guilt and dejection. Aggressive people are often as conscience-stricken and concerned as shy people are about their poor record in making friends and solving interpersonal conflicts satisfactorily.

The Assertive Scene

While aggressive behavior injures in order to win, assertive behavior focuses, not on winning as such, but on negotiating reasonable changes in the way both parties behave so as to equalize the balance of social power. The purpose of assertive speaking-up is usually to solve an interpersonal problem. But assertiveness is not just expressing feelings, laying down the law to someone, and then walking away. In general, to solve problems you must do more than talk back or express feelings; you must be very clear about what you want to accomplish by asserting yourself. You must attend to your feelings, decide what you want, and then use some specific verbal skills to negotiate for the changes you want. Assertive problem-solving involves the ability to plan, "sell," and implement an agreeable contract between yourself and the other person without sounding like a nag, a dictator, or a preacher. In other words, an assertive person can express feelings in a manner that is both personally satisfying and socially effective.

Let us see how the garden problem gets solved when the person is prepared for assertive negotiation.

She It's spring and time to make plans for our garden.
Downer [Looking at paper] Oh, c'mon — not *now!* It's only April.
She I feel that the garden is more enjoyable if we've planned it carefully together, in advance.
Downer I'm not sure I'm going to have the time for that.
She I've already drawn up and budgeted two alternative plans — will you look at them? I'd like to get your decisions about them, say, tonight after supper.
Downer [With indignation] I have to look at these tonight?
She Is there some other time that's better for you?
Downer Oh, I don't know.
She Well, then let's discuss the plans after supper for half an hour. Is that agreed?
Downer I guess so.
She Good! It won't take more than half an hour, and I'll feel relieved when we get this planning finished.

This person knows how to negotiate. First, she has scaled down her request to a small one. Ideally, she wants her partner to be passionately concerned about their garden; but realistically, she knows strong interests develop gradually from doing small jobs successfully. Thus, she makes the smaller request, that he merely help decide between two plans for the garden. Small requests are likely to be accepted by the other party. Second, she has done her homework by preparing two specific plans with itemized costs. Third, she deals with attempts to evade or put off the decision by sticking to the point and asking for a commitment to a definite time when the decision can be made. Fourth, she rewards her partner for contracting, that is, she notes her satisfaction when he agrees to look over the plans.

The most striking difference between the assertive script and the passive and aggressive scripts is that it succeeded in solving the problem for which it was intended, whereas the other scripts failed miserably. Ideally, both parties come away from the assertive scene feeling better about themselves and each other. This is the sort of goal toward which you will be working.

GETTING STARTED

To get started with your assertiveness program, you need to find out how assertive you are now and how you react to mildly threatening situations. The worksheets in the rest of this chapter can help you to focus on your strengths as well as to identify some of your weaknesses; they can also help you to select tasks and set priorities for your own assertiveness program.

Worksheet #1 asks you to examine your interactions with other people. It is a general but useful guide to help you assess your own behavior.

WORKSHEET #1
ASSERTIVENESS QUESTIONNAIRE

In answering the questions below, think of complaints or conflicts with others that you have had in the last few weeks or months. Decide how well each statement characterizes your behavior and fill in the blank as follows.

  5   if the behavior *almost always* occurs (90-100 percent)
  4   if the behavior occurs about *three-fourths of the time* (60-90 percent)
  3   if the behavior occurs *half of the time* (40-60%)
  2   if the behavior occurs about *one-fourth of the time* (10-40%)
  1   if the behavior *almost never* occurs (0-10%)

When I have had specific complaints, I have:

_____ stated my complaint.
_____ momentarily stopped and decided upon the most productive course of action.
_____ considered the possible consequences of my actions before I spoke up.
_____ questioned the other person about the problem situation to avoid misunderstanding it.
_____ objectively described the annoying behavior of the other person or the annoying situation.

_____ expressed my feelings with restraint.

_____ not put down or blamed the other person.

_____ not made guesses about the other person's motivations or attitudes.

_____ worked out a specific solution to the problem when necessary.

_____ communicated concern for the other person.

_____ made my message to the other person short and clear.

_____ expressed myself in a firm voice.

_____ looked directly at the other person.

_____ used appropriately forceful gestures.

_____ Total score

Now, add your score; it will fall between 14 and 70. If you scored near 14, you consider yourself only rarely assertive. If you scored near 70, you consider yourself consistently assertive — at least with respect to the 14 behaviors surveyed. Adults who come to Sharon's assertiveness training classes usually score between 25 and 50 on this test. Most people have a few 1's mixed with some 2's, 3's and 4's. Look over your answers again. Check those you rated as 1, 2, or 3; they are the weaker behaviors you may want to strengthen in your own program.

PALS: THE PHASES IN
LEARNING ASSERTIVE BEHAVIORS

The other worksheets in this chapter and in the rest of the book correspond to four phases of developing more assertive behaviors.

PROJECT Here, you remember and project yourself into past conflict situations in which you failed to assert yourself, to see what situational features are commonly present.

ANALYZE Now, you analyze the degree of threat and upset you felt in those put-down situations, and select a specific "medium-threat" scene as an immediate focus for your self-improvement planning.

LOOK Next, you look at your behavior critically to see what emotions, negative sentences, and self-images are maintaining your nonassertiveness in the problem scene and what you might do to change them.

SPEAK UP Finally, you plan a negotiating script or message to remedy your problem situation and learn to express yourself in an affirmative manner.

We will be looking at the first three phases in this chapter, and deal in later chapters with the fourth phase.

PROJECT: Identifying the Who, When, and What

To begin, try to remember past experiences in which you felt nonassertive or inadequate. PROJECT yourself into each remembered scene, and relive your feelings and actions. Pin down the details of each experience or scene in terms of the people, the setting, and the events that took place — the who, when, and what of the scene. Who are you uncomfortable with? Who is your Downer? What is the situation or setting? What topics or discussion subjects bother you? When does this scene occur? When do you get uptight or upset?

In Worksheet #2, check those who's, what's, and when's causing you difficulty. Don't try to figure out *why* you feel inadequate with a particular person, topic, or situation; simply respond to the items on the checklist with "Yes, I feel some discomfort" ($\checkmark$) or "No, I feel no discomfort" (no mark).

WORKSHEET #2
PROJECT: IDENTIFYING THE WHO, WHEN, AND WHAT

In the first (left-hand) blank, check ($\checkmark$) the items that apply to you. You will be filling in the second blank when you get to the ANALYZE phase.

A. WHO are the people with whom you behave nonassertively or inadequately?

— — acquaintance? neighbor?
— — authority figure such as a doctor, teacher, etc.?
— — child? children?
— — employer? employee?
— — friend? friends?
— — members in a club or organization?
— — relative?
— — repairman? gardener? hired help?
— — sales clerk? waiters? waitresses?
— — solicitor? bill collector?
— — spouse? mate?
— — strangers?
— — work colleague?
— — any other?

Name: _____

B. WHEN do you behave nonassertively or inadequately?

When you are:

— — accepting or giving a compliment?
— — asserting a difference of opinion?

__ __ being interviewed?
__ __ clarifying your idea?
__ __ dealing with a nonnegotiator?
__ __ establishing your independence?
__ __ expressing negative feelings verbally?
__ __ expressing positive feelings verbally?
__ __ giving instructions or commands?
__ __ participating in group discussion?
__ __ proposing your idea or solution?
__ __ protesting a "rip-off"?
__ __ protesting an emotional outburst?
__ __ protesting annoying habits?
__ __ protesting excessive or unjust criticism?
__ __ protesting attempts to make you feel guilty?
__ __ protesting unnecessary violence?
__ __ returning merchandise?
__ __ saying no to requests of your time, money, efforts?
__ __ any other?

Name: _____

When you are requesting:

__ __ action from authority figures (doctors, teachers, etc.)?
__ __ adjustment of a bill? or refund?
__ __ approval?
__ __ a raise?
__ __ clarification of instructions or an idea?
__ __ cooperation?
__ __ date or appointment?
__ __ favors?
__ __ help (donation of time, money, work)?
__ __ information?
__ __ negative criticism about yourself?
__ __ participation?
__ __ reconciliation?
__ __ service?
__ __ any other?

Name: _____

When you are using facial expressions, gestures, expressive voice, and body language to show:

__ __ positive feelings: approval, joy, liking?
__ __ negative feelings: annoyance, dislike, anger, resentment?
__ __ physical caring and loving: physical closeness?

C. WHAT TOPICS cause you to behave nonassertively or inadequately?

___ ___ achievements of yours?
___ ___ achievements of others?
___ ___ anatomy and its function?
___ ___ artistic merits of art, plays, movies, etc.?
___ ___ child-rearing practices?
___ ___ choice of work, career?
___ ___ death? illness in others?
___ ___ differing tastes in foods, architecture, music, etc.?
___ ___ divorce? separation?
___ ___ educational issues?
___ ___ finances? use of money, etc.?
___ ___ generation gap viewpoints?
___ ___ hobbies?
___ ___ home management problems?
___ ___ marriage? life styles?
___ ___ medical problems?
___ ___ mistakes you make?
___ ___ mistakes others make?
___ ___ personal appearance (yours or others')?
___ ___ politics?
___ ___ prejudice and racial issues?
___ ___ recreational activities (use of free time)?
___ ___ religion? philosophical viewpoints?
___ ___ sex?
___ ___ societal problems: crime, drugs, housing, land use, overpopulation, poverty, taxes, unemployment, welfare?
___ ___ women's rights? men's rights?
___ ___ any other?

Name: _____

D. How does the SIZE of the audience affect you? Did the situation involve you and:

___ ___ one other familiar person?
___ ___ one stranger?
___ ___ a group of familiar persons?
___ ___ a group of strangers?

For an overall estimate of your strengths and weaknesses, look over the pattern of your answers on Worksheet #2. The answers will be valuable in helping you analyze the following.

- *Your self-image.* Many people begin assertiveness training believing overblown, negative generalizations about themselves: "I'm always passive" or "I can never speak up." When they consider their behavior with specific people or situations, they make the illuminating discovery that they are passive (or aggressive) in only a few situations or with only a few people. Their poor self-image is fostered by dwelling on their failures rather than on their many successes. Realizing that your problem is probably related to a few specific situations is the first step in overcoming your passivity.

- *What topics or subjects bother you.* See whether the topics which upset you fall into a pattern. Perhaps no subjects bother you when you know your views agree with your listener's. But what if his or her views conflict with yours, and you must defend your opinion? Which topics would then cause difficulty? For instance, one woman was unable to talk about legalizing abortion without working herself into a terrible anger. She assumed that almost everyone held an opinion opposed to hers; she felt attacked and compelled to argue the immorality of her opponent's views. Also, people with many accomplishments and honors often are embarrassed to talk about themselves because they have been taught to consider this conceited and egotistical.

- *What situations threaten you.* Is there something in common to those situations which upset you? Is it when you have to place yourself in explicit conflict with someone you like? With a stranger? Are you afraid to "speak up" with any authority figure? Are you embarrassed only when you have to ask for help, because you feel you are "imposing" on the other person?

- *How sensitive you are to the size of the group you are in.* Most people would be uptight at the prospect of addressing a large, unfriendly crowd of "experts" who were evaluating them. That scene becomes less threatening as you imagine removing various elements of it — suppose they are not experts, or they are not unfriendly, or you are not expected to be an expert, or the crowd in fact is only two people. As you change these aspects, the situation becomes less anxiety-provoking. Try to find where it is along this scale of speech-situations you would feel relaxed, at what point you would feel uncomfortable, and where you would feel so terrified as to be totally incapable of performing.

Many passive people fear public speaking situations. If that is a problem for you, assertiveness training might help you reduce some of your fear, at least in low-threat situations. To become a good public speaker, however, requires much training and practice; assertiveness training cannot substitute for speech training. People who have extreme anxiety about speaking to a group of people require special kinds of skills that will reduce their anxiety.[2]

ANALYZE: Assessing Your Discomfort in Threatening Situations

You have now identified some situations in which you feel uncomfortable about asserting yourself. The next step is to analyze those situations in order to find where you can best focus your efforts to become more assertive. This involves making some judgments about the degree and kind of discomfort that each situation holds for you. Do this now by filling out Worksheet #3.

WORKSHEET #3
ANALYZE: ASSESSING YOUR DISCOMFORT IN THREATENING SITUATIONS

THREAT SCALE

A. First, read the entire scale carefully. Note that each tier describes the factors that determine the severity of a particular threat item.

(5)

VERY
THREATENING SCENE

causes you to feel hostility or total helplessness;
occurs almost daily
or
you *think* of it daily

B. Look over the situations you checked on Work-sheet #2 and rate each one for the degree of dis-comfort or threat it involves. Assign a 1 for weak, infrequent annoyances, assign a 3 for moderately strong annoyances occurring more frequently, and assign a 5 for strong threats or frequent assaults on your self-esteem.

(3)

MODERATELY
THREATENING SCENE

causes you to feel discomfort, inadequacy, or frustration;
occurs at least once a week
or
you *think* of it at least once a week

(1)

SLIGHTLY
THREATENING SCENE

causes you to feel uneasy;
occurs at least once a month
or
you *think* of it about every two weeks

C. Put your numerical rating of 5, 3, or 1, on the *second* space provided on Worksheet #2, beside those items you have checked as causing you concern and discomfort.

After completing your rating of items on Worksheet #2, continue analyzing these threatening scenes by answering the questions below.

D. What area causes you the most concern — the who's, the what's, or the when's?

E. What is the most important factor causing you to rate an item as 5 (highly threatening)? (Check all those that apply.)

_____ Is it the *intensity* of your feeling (Do you recall the scene vividly?)

_____ Is it the *duration* of your emotional reaction (Does it cause an "all-day" upset?)

_____ Is it the *frequency* of your emotional reaction (Does it cause daily or weekly upsets?)

_____ Any other factors (How important is the other person to you? Does the size of the audience affect you?)

F. Consider situations you rated as very threatening and upsetting (5). What *physical reactions* do you experience in these highly threatening situations? (Check all those that apply.)

__ blushing

__ increased pulse

__ "butterflies in stomach"

__ tingling sensations

__ heart pounding

__ weakness

__ hot flashes

__ dry mouth

__ tremors

__ perspiration

__ fatigue, weariness

__ others (specify below)

_____

_____

G. What are the *overt behaviors* you engage in during these threatening situations? (Check all those that apply.)

__ low speaking voice

__ silence

__ stuttering

__ cursing, obscenity

__ inability to make eye contact

__ slouching posture

__ disorganized speech

__ tensing muscles of jaw, face, or fists

__ crying

__ others (specify below)

_____

_____

H. In such highly threatening situations, what are the *specific thoughts* you experience? (Check all those that apply.)

_____ self-consciousness (I am extremely aware of myself, notice my every action.)

_____ thoughts about the unpleasantness of the situation (This is terrible, I'd like to be out ot it.)

_____ distracting thoughts (I could or should be doing other things.)

_____ negative thoughts about myself (I feel inadequate, insecure, inferior, or stupid.)

_____ thoughts about the evaluations of me that others are making (I wonder what they are thinking of me.)

_____ thoughts about the way I am handling myself (I wonder what kind of impression I am making and how I might control it.)

_____ thoughts about the long-term consequences of this experience

I. Select four or five moderate-threat items (3's) from Worksheet #1. *Select those 3's that are most important to you,* and now *rank-order these moderate-threat items according to the degree of discomfort they cause you.*

#3 item causing me
   most discomfort: _____

   _____

   _____

   _____

#3 item causing me
   least discomfort: _____

You will concentrate your initial efforts on these medium-threat situations (the 3's): there is no point in beginning with a scene so threatening that you are likely to fail (the 5's) or one so trivial that mastering it is no challenge (the 1's). Choose one item from those you listed above where you feel it is *important* to make a change soon, and you have a *reasonable chance* of successfully asserting yourself after some training. From now on, call this moderately threatening situation your "problem scene."

ANALYZE: Describing Your Problem Scene

To complete the ANALYZE phase it is important to come up with a precise description of the problem scene in which you would like to become more assertive. People often are unskilled in describing put-down scenes. Their descriptions tend to be vague and nonspecific, as in the following example.

> I have great difficulty being assertive with my superiors at work. I hold in my opinions when it would be better for me to speak up. I feel that I let them think they can order me around too much.

The trouble with this scene description is that it does not cite a specific superior (who), a specific time or setting (when/where), what the superior does concretely that bothers her (what), what her specific behaviors are in the situation (problem behavior), or what new behavior she wants to learn (assertion goal). A better description for just one of this woman's problems turned out to be the following.

> A supervisor, Mr. Brown (who), often asks me to get his morning coffee (what and when) for him at work (where). I resent his request and feel it is beyond my job duties; but I am afraid that if I tell him so, he will cause

trouble for me at work (problem behavior). So one of my problems is to get Mr. Brown to stop asking me for that favor (assertion goal).

Here is another poor scene-description.

I can't state my position forcefully enough to gain respect from other people. Also, some people around me seem to make a game out of trying to put me down and make me feel inadequate.

The trouble again is that this description does not give any details. The speaker doesn't name who is putting her down, nor exactly when, or what that person does to cause her to feel inadequate. The woman also does not describe her own behavior very concretely; she rather states the desired but vague goal for her assertion ("to gain respect"). Under questioning, this woman identified a number of different problem situations. She isolated and described one situation in more restricted and objective terms:

An acquaintance of mine, Darlene (who), often criticizes my political opinions (what) when we are at parties (when/where). I am afraid I'll lose her friendship if I criticize her ideas (problem behaviors). I want to be able to state my opinions even though they differ from hers when we are at parties. (assertion goal).

These altered descriptions are more objective. This may seem a small matter but it is not. You cannot successfully cope with an unsatisfying situation unless you focus attention on the details of the scene and the specific behaviors (of yourself and the other person) that bother you.

To repeat the rules: in describing a situation, first concentrate on who said or did what, when and where; and second, specify your problem behavior in that situation and state your assertion goal.

Now, analyze your own problem scene, project yourself back to the situation you have chosen, and set down the details in writing.

WORKSHEET #3 (continued)
ANALYZE: DESCRIBING YOUR PROBLEM SCENE

J. Answer these questions about your problem scene.

With whom did it occur?

_____

When?

_____

While talking about what topic?

_____

Where did the situation occur?

_____

What specifically did the other person do or say? (other person's problem behavior)

_____

_____

What specifically did *you* do or say or fail to do? (your problem behavior)

_____

_____

What specifically do you need to do in this scene? (assertion goal)

_____

_____

Now write a concise description of your problem scene, using the above information:

_____

_____

_____

_____

_____

_____

_____

LOOK: Examining Your Feelings

At this point, with a specific problem scene as the focus, it's time to pay closer attention to your emotional reactions. You need to look at your feelings so you can think realistically about the consequences of asserting yourself and decide what you want to do.

Many nonassertive people claim that their emotions prevent them from acting effectively — they get too angry or too scared to act rationally, and they go "all to pieces." Emotions are expressed in physiological signs of arousal and also in the negative self-images you see while in the threatening situation.

To examine these emotional signs, recall your problem scene from Worksheet #3 in vivid detail. Visualize the exact locale, clothes worn, time of day, sounds, and feelings. Now, thinking about your emotional signs, fill out Worksheet #4.

WORKSHEET #4
LOOK: EXAMINING YOUR FEELINGS

A. What *physical signs of arousal or tension* (feelings) do you remember experiencing in your problem scene? (Place a checkmark beside all those that apply.)

__ weakness
__ tremors
__ tingling sensations
__ perspiration
__ blushing
__ fatigue, weariness
__ "butterflies in stomach"
__ hot flashes
__ heart pounding

__ dry mouth
__ shallow breathing
__ increased pulse
__ others (specify below)

_____

_____

_____

B. What *negative thoughts or sentences* did you say to yourself about your behavior during (or after) that threatening scene? Write those negative sentences you said to yourself:

1. _____

_____

2. _____

_____

3. _____

_____

C. During (or after) that scene, did you "see" *negative pictures* of yourself? Describe how you saw yourself behaving:

1. _____

_____

2. _____

_____

3. _____

_____

LOOK: Thinking Rationally About the Consequences of Your Assertion

Having examined your emotional reactions in your problem scene, and assuming you entered the threatening scene again, answer the following (check one for each question).

WORKSHEET #4 (continued)
LOOK: THINKING RATIONALLY ABOUT THE CONSEQUENCES
OF YOUR ASSERTION

1. Would the same *physical feelings* keep you from asserting yourself?

 __ Yes   __ No   __ Maybe

2. Would the *negative sentences* you tell yourself keep you from asserting yourself?

 __ Yes   __ No   __ Maybe

3. Would your *mental pictures* keep you from asserting yourself?

 __ Yes   __ No   __ Maybe

4. How *important* is it to your self-esteem and happiness to improve that problem situation? Rate on a scale from 1 (not important) to 10 (a matter of life and death).

 Importance rating: ____

5. If you assert yourself and ask for change from the other party, how likely are you to succeed in improving the situation in the long run? Rate on a scale from 0 percent (will surely fail) to 100 percent (will surely succeed).

 Success likelihood: ____

6. If you assert yourself in the problem situation, what is your Downer likely to say or do?

 _____

 _____

 _____

7. What negative costs might there be for asserting yourself in the situation?

 _____

 _____

8. What positive benefits are likely to arise from asserting yourself in this situation?

_____

_____

9. You can now decide whether to assert yourself with this particular Downer in this situation: Is it important enough? Are you at least moderately likely to succeed? Do the expected benefits outweigh the expected costs? While assessing your circumstances, remember that nonassertive people tend to overestimate the likelihood of failure and the anticipated punishments; so try to be objective. Weighing all these factors, then, are you willing to risk asserting yourself in this problem situation with this Downer?

__ Yes __ No __ Maybe

If your answer is "no," return to Worksheet #3, Question I (p. 20), find a *less* threatening problem scene, then answer question J (pp. 21—22) and repeat this questionaire for that scene. If your answer is "maybe," think of some more, and change your answer to "yes" or "no." If it is "yes," go to the next step.

10. *Signing a positive action contract with yourself:* You have now identified a situation in which you feel you could successfully assert yourself. How soon would you be willing to SPEAK UP to this person in your problem situation? Check one:

__ Within 2 weeks?
__ Within 4 weeks?
__ Within 6 weeks?
__ Sometime?

Sign this contract and commit yourself to learning how to assert yourself.

Signed: _____

Congratulations! You have taken the first steps toward becoming assertive. A little later in this book we'll return to your problem scene and work out an assertive script that can help you keep the commitment you've just made. Right now, however, you should reward yourself for the good work and move to the next chapter, where you can concentrate on improving your self-esteem.

2

Improving Your Self-Esteem

*No one can make you feel inferior
without your consent.*

ELEANOR ROOSEVELT

People typically place three large obstacles between themselves and the goal of assertiveness — their negative image of themselves, their learned fear of conflict situations, and their poor communication skills. This chapter suggests how you could improve your self-concept; the next chapter gives you information to help you deal with stressful situations. Later chapters in this book concentrate on the skills of effective and expressive communication.

YOUR SELF-CONCEPT: A PRODUCT OF EXPERIENCE

Whether or not you are assertive is determined by your self-concept — by a blueprint or mental picture that you maintain of your strengths, your weaknesses, your personality. You call your self-concept to mind when you predict whether your performance will succeed. It influences your hopes, aspirations, moods, and actions.

We all acquire our self-concept in much the same way — from what other people tell us about ourselves and from our observations of our behavior and its consequences. As we grow up, our parents, teachers, and other adults gradually impart by instruction and example the values, norms, and rules of conduct of their culture. The norms tell us what behaviors are considered appropriate. For example, eating moderately at mealtimes is acceptable; stuffing oneself all day long is unacceptable. Resting at the end of a workday is a reward that is deserved; sleeping all day is laziness. The media also teach us an enormous set of norms about behaviors expected from girls versus boys, from children versus adults, from pupils versus teachers, from husbands versus wives, and from parents versus children.

We tend to be judged in society largely according to how we measure up to the relevant norms. Thus, with respect to her peers, Joyce may be exceptional in athletics, average in reading, and poor in mathematics. Adults constantly make comparisons about all aspects of the behavior of children — their intelligence, beauty, manners, work habits, ability to play with other children, and so on. In addition, adults label children as loving or spiteful, friendly or mean, reasonable or selfish, cooperative or uncooperative, outgoing or shy. As we mature, these comparisons and labels are applied to all of us — first by adults, increasingly by our peers, and eventually by ourselves.

Having internalized the standards and beliefs of those who judge us, we gradually come to describe ourselves in terms of how we deviate from the norm. For instance, we may say to ourselves, "I'm a good bridge player, but I'm pretty stupid at balancing the checkbook." We make such self-judgments not only about our athletic, artistic, and scholastic talents, but also about our social and personal adjustments.

These social comparisons are important because they are hooked directly into the pay-off system of the culture. People who equal or exceed a positive norm are rewarded by gifts, promotions, money, praise, and admiration. Presumably, they are then "successful." Those who fall short of what is expected receive disapproval, loss of privileges, demotions, penalties, and other punishments. Consequently, people become anxious when their performance is being closely evaluated because they fear punishment for possible failure.

THE TOLL OF A NEGATIVE SELF-CONCEPT

Your self-concept is wrapped up in a set of descriptions and images — of good success scenes or bad failure scenes that you've experienced. It is also carried in a set of personality trait labels you use to tell yourself and others what you are really like. Your self-evaluations are important because they influence most areas of your behavior, defining the limits of what you will attempt. You avoid an activity if your self-concept predicts you will perform so badly as to humiliate yourself. For instance, if your self-concept includes the belief that you would be a poor ice skater, you might never try it, and will indeed remain a poor ice skater. Often people excuse themselves with "That's just the way I am." By using this excuse, they deny themselves opportunities for personal growth.

If you could listen in, you would hear nonassertive people saying all kinds of negative sentences to themselves. They selectively remember

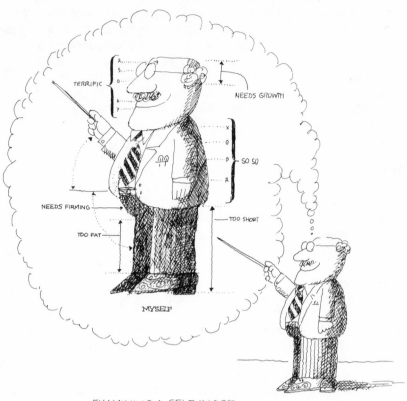

EXAMINING A SELF-IMAGE

some criticism of themselves, exaggerate it to monstrous proportions, and repeat it over and over like a chant. The man battling his bulging waistline might be saying, "I am ugly, fat, and disgusting. No one can stand to look at me. I am a fat worm. I've got no will power." The shy, retiring boy at a dance might be saying, "Those girls are whispering about me. My pimples are horrible. If I talk to that girl, she'll insult and ridicule me. I never know what to say to girls. I'll die if she cuts me down."

The fact is that people are often their own worst Downers. They say to themselves, "I am irrational, emotional, stupid, dull, ugly, shy, cold, submissive, fat, ineffectual, overbearing, bitchy, childish, a bully, a miserable father (mother), a lousy speaker, a failure, and over-the-hill." We all have our own lists. People can be terribly brutal with themselves. Out of the whole animal kingdom, only humans are endowed with this capacity to make themselves miserable. Can you imagine your pet cat or dog moping around, saying such brutal things to himself?

Worse yet, in many cases our negative view of ourselves may be communicated to new acquaintances before they have time to form an independent impression of us. If we tell people we are inadequate, they may do us the disservice of believing us. A woman in one of Sharon's assertiveness classes repeatedly advertised herself poorly by prefacing each remark with, "I doubt if my idea is worth anything, but . . ." Without realizing it, the class did indeed pay less and less attention to her ideas — at least until they stopped to examine the subtle message her remark conveyed.

The toll of a negative self-concept is that it limits what we are willing to try, forestalling opportunities for growth and enjoyment. Doomsday prophesies about our social failures tend to be self-fulfilling. The shy woman who retreats from friendly overtures is indeed judged to be cold, aloof, disdainful, and the man who was turned down for approaching her is even less likely to make another overture to her (or vice versa!) The student with anxiety about taking a test "goes blank" to such an extent that he does indeed fail just as miserably as he had feared.

Many people are plagued by images of failures they have experienced during social encounters. For example, one man experienced difficulty in public speaking because each occasion for a speech reactivated a memory-image of a time when he had lost his voice, blocked and stammered in front of a large audience, and was forced to retreat from the stage in utter humiliation.

Sometimes people imagine bizarre metaphors to symbolize their passivity, inadequacy, or weakness. One timid individual reported that when she thought about the sarcastic replies her Downer might make to her assertion, she visualized herself "melting into a little puddle on the floor!" Images that prevent people from asserting themselves are based on memories of their weaknesses and their prior failures and embarrassment in specific situations. People may also imagine punishments for assertion, such as their spouses hitting them or leaving them, or their friends snubbing or ridiculing them.

To sum up, negative sentences and images continually inhibit nonassertive people. By concentrating on negative evaluations of themselves, these people miss valuable opportunities for growth and enjoyment.

LOOKING AT YOUR RELATIONSHIPS

Our self-concept is often revealed in the way we compare ourselves with the significant other people in our lives. Which people in your life do you feel are most important to you? Which are least important? How do you rate your "power" relative to the other person in each relationship?

The following exercise[1] provides an opportunity for you to explore, think about, and try to clarify the relative positions of power and importance you hold in each of your significant relationships, with spouse, relatives, friends, co-workers. The questions are deliberately somewhat vague because the concern is how you see your relationships. There are no right or wrong answers; you are simply depicting how you perceive and feel about your relations to others right now. Most people find it is an interesting and revealing exercise.

Your first task is to define for yourself what you usually mean by the following terms:

- If you feel someone is of **equal importance** to you, how do you define *"equal importance"?* Also, if you feel someone is of **greater importance** than you, how do you define *"greater importance"?* If you feel someone is of **less importance** than you, how do you define *"less importance"?*

_____

_____

_____

- If you feel someone is of **equal status** with you, what do you mean by *"equal status"?* Also, if you feel someone holds a **dominant** position in your relationship, what does *"dominant"* mean to you? If someone is **subordinate** in your relationship, what does *"subordinate"* mean?

_____

_____

_____

- What makes for a *"close relationship"* with another person?

_____

_____

Now, keeping in mind your definitions, draw and label circles to show how you see yourself in relation to the significant people in your life: *mother, father, brother, sister, colleague, employer, friend, mate, your children* (if any). Observe the following rules in drawing your circles:

Size   Bigger circle = you consider the person *more* important than you.
Smaller circle = you consider the person *less* important than you.
Same size circle = you consider the person of *equal* importance to you.

Position   Circle placed above you = you consider the person holds a position dominant to yours.
Circle placed below you = you consider the person holds a position subordinate to yours.
Circle placed on same plane = you consider the person holds a position equal to yours.

Distance   Circle placed far away from you = you consider the relationship you have with the person as distant (that is, *not* close or intimate but *not necessarily* unfriendly).
Circle placed near you = you consider the relationship friendly.
Circle placed in overlapping position = you consider the relationship warm, close, and intimate.

LOOKING AT YOUR RELATIONSHIPS

Picture your relationships by drawing your circles here:

Now, go back and elaborate on your picture of your social relations. Follow these instructions:

First, for those people toward whom you typically react passively (such as doing too little too late), fill in the circles with this snail-like design:

Second, for those people toward whom you typically react aggressively (such as doing too much too soon), fill in these circles with this warlike design:

Third, for those people toward whom you typically react assertively (such as solving problems easily without bad feelings), fill in the circles with this flowered design:

Are there people with whom you interact in more than one way, say, both passively and aggressively? Draw their circles this way:

What other combinations of behaviors do you observe in yourself when interacting with a friend? The following pictures suggest a combination or alternation of interaction patterns:

Return to your constellation of circles and fill in each circle with whatever mixture of behavior patterns is revealed in your interactions with that person.

Finally, look at this constellation of circles representing your present interpersonal relationships and answer these questions:

- With whom do you feel you enjoy an equal balance of social power? You are able to solve problems to the satisfaction of both of you. You do not feel put down with them. You feel there is mutual trust, admiration, give-and-take. Have you drawn their circles to reflect this?

- What are the assertive behaviors which help you achieve a feeling of balance with these people? If you had had the positive interactions with these people in mind when you answered the Assertiveness Questionnaire (p. 12), what would your score have been?
- Our behavior with others changes over time. If you had drawn this constellation of circles six months ago, would it have looked the same? If not, do you feel the changes "just happened" or did you (and the other) make them happen?
- Which circles would you like to change in size? position? distance? What would a "perfect" picture look like? Draw it on the page below. Picture your perfect constellation!

This is what I would like to have as a "perfect constellation" of relationships. (Draw in significant others at the ideal size, position, and distance for you).

You have now briefly examined how you see your present social relationships and have considered the ideal relationships you would like to aim
for. By working toward assertiveness you will be doing a great deal to bring
your present relationships into closer correspondence to your ideal.

CHANGING YOUR SELF-CONCEPT

To become assertive, you must have a positive self-concept and believe
that you can act effectively. There are two aspects to improving your self-
image: first, you need to increase how often you say good things to yourself
about your attributes; second, you need to decrease how often you say bad
things to yourself about your weaknesses.

The technique of changing your self-concept is one of the most fas-
cinating uses of behavior-change principles. (For a summary of these
principles, see Appendix A.) A remarkable fact is that you can alter your
self-concept by synthesizing a history of successes in the theater of your
imagination. You simply insert into your stream of internal monologues
and images a set of very favorable, self-enhancing statements and images.
With repetition, the new information can alter your self-concept in a dramatic way. The following exercises focus on modifying your self-statements.

Amplifying What's Good About You

First, let's concentrate on what's good about you. Think for a moment, then
list three to five good personal attributes of yourself or of your life —
positive beliefs about your appearance, intelligence, range of interests, life's
achievements, or whatever. These should be truthful and concrete, for
example, "I have a nice smile," "I am well informed about current affairs," "I
have raised four happy children," or "I am a good billiards player." Write
these sentences in the book.

THINGS THAT ARE GOOD ABOUT YOU

1. _____

2. _____

3. _____

4. _____

5. _____

Now, your goal is to increase how often you recall these self-enhancing
thoughts. You can do this by following each positive statement with an
immediate reward. Many everyday activities will qualify as rewards: eating,
drinking, arranging flowers, playing a game, phoning a friend, taking a bath,

resting, reading the newspaper, watching TV, having sexual relations, and so on. Now, to increase how often you think good things about yourself, whenever you are about to carry out one of these rewarding actions, say a few of your positive, self-enhancing sentences to yourself just before the rewarding activity. That way you reward yourself for thinking positive thoughts and so the positive thoughts are strengthened by the pleasurable act that follows!

Simply saying the self-congratulatory sentences whenever you have an idle moment (say, while driving a car or waiting in a line) can increase their frequency even when a reward does not follow. If you find that you are forgetting to practice your positive sentences, you can remind yourself by a periodic "message" which cues you to rehearse. One woman carried her list of positive statements in her change purse, so that she was reminded to rehearse them whenever she opened her purse. An executive wrote "Now" at several specific times on his daily time schedule to cue himself to rehearse his good points for a few minutes.

One client, a middle-aged woman, doubted her drafting ability even though she was appointed head of the entire drafting department of her firm. She wrote a positive statement for herself, "I am good at drafting." After reading and rehearsing the statement for several days, she took the next step and posted it on the bulletin board of the department. Her colleagues were astonished and asked, "Of course, you're terrific at drafting. That's why you're head of the department. But why put up that message?" She replied, "Because I need to see it right up front in order to convince myself." Posting her positive statement brought her many compliments and confidence that the statement was true.

Publicly posting a statement about yourself is neither conceited bragging nor "fishing for compliments." You are simply telling others what you like about yourself. It is up to them to agree or not. Try the following assignment.

Day 1. Write out a positive statement about yourself. Keep it in a place where you can read it several times a day.

Day 2. Post your positive self-statement on the family bulletin board or refrigerator door. At work, you could tape it on your desk or on the office bulletin board.

Day 3. Post a positive statement about one of your family members or a co-worker. Write a positive statement on notepaper and pin it to the person's pillow. In an office, you can write a positive statement about a co-worker in a note.

Here is a homemaker's example.

Day 1. My positive self-statement: I GROW BEAUTIFUL VIOLETS (stuck deep in my violets!).

Day 2. Where posted: I posted that message on a paper flag which I made and stuck in a violet pot near the kitchen faucet (everyone goes there at least once a day).

Day 3. The positive statement I posted about someone else: For a child in the family I posted this on the refrigerator door: I LIKE THE WAY YOU ALWAYS COME TO SAY "HELLO" TO MY FRIENDS.

Now, record your own data.

INCREASE YOUR POSITIVE SELF-STATEMENTS

Day 1. Write your positive self-statement here:

_____

Day 2. Where did you post the positive self-statement?

_____

Record below any comments made about it and how you answered assertively.

*Comments about your positive
self-statement*   *Your assertive reply*

1. _____   _____

   _____   _____

2. _____   _____

   _____   _____

Day 3. What was the positive statement you wrote for someone else?

_____

What was that person's reaction?

_____

Reversing Your Negative Self-Statements

In the preceding exercises you concentrated on your positive attributes. Next, let us concentrate on reversing your negative self-statements, the self-defeating sentences you say to yourself in threatening situations. Look at those you wrote in answer to Question B, Worksheet #4 (page 23).

You can alter your self-concept by exploiting the principle used in advertising and propaganda campaigns: repetition of a message drives it home unconsciously so that it becomes a subjective truth of your belief system. To reverse your negative self-statements, simply repeat and rehearse to yourself the *opposites* of your negative sentences. Instead of thinking "I am easily discouraged," think "I am persistent" (or "I *will be* persistent" or "I *can be* persistent"). That is, change each negative self-statement into a corresponding positive, self-enhancing statement, and then rehearse the positive statements as you repeatedly imagine yourself in the problem scene.

The following are examples of negative-to-positive shifts in self-statements.

Negative self-statements	*Positive self-statements*
I am weak.	I can be strong.
I am too passive.	I can be outgoing.
I am frightened.	I can be bold.
I can't speak up.	I can be assertive.
I am helpless.	I can deal with stress.
I am miserable.	I can be happy.

Now, review your negative sentences from Question B of Worksheet #4 (page 23) and write an opposite for each of them below. The opposite will be a positive, self-enhancing, or encouraging statement aimed at increasing your self-esteem. Aim for two to five positive self-statements.

REVERSE YOUR NEGATIVE SELF-STATEMENTS

1. _____
2. _____
3. _____
4. _____
5. _____

Fine. These are the "propaganda messages" you want to burn into your unconscious belief system. The basic method is to rehearse them repeatedly to yourself, and to follow their rehearsal with some small reward whenever possible. The repetition will automatically inscribe them into your subconscious; your self-concept becomes what you say about yourself.

Remember, it is best if you can reward yourself just after you make a self-enhancing statement. For instance, as you are about to take that first sip of a refreshing drink, quickly call to mind the problem scene and then, instead of rehearsing your negative sentences, say your positive, self-affirming sentences to yourself. With repetition comes belief, and if you keep at it long enough it will be possible for you to believe and think these positive things in actual confrontations. This practice will also help you control yourself in your problem scene, so you can carry through intelligently with your planned assertive script.

Punishing Negative Self-Talk

So far we've stressed the technique of rewarding yourself for positive self-statements. The reverse technique is also very helpful. To eliminate worrying over your inadequacies, arrange to punish yourself whenever you start to dwell on your incompetence. You already know that negative self-talk — thinking or saying "I'm dumb, scared, weak" — is self-defeating. So don't let yourself get away with it! Here's what to do.

1. Make a list of household or professional tasks you need to do, but never get around to doing. Title it: "Boring Tasks to Do to Stop Negative Self-Talk." Estimate the time for each job. Post the list where you can refer to it easily.

2. When you next start having obsessional negative thoughts about yourself, go to your list, choose a chore, and do it. Never make yourself comfortable or reward yourself with food, a good book, or television when you are thinking negatively; instead, punish yourself for negative self-thoughts by forcing yourself to do one of your boring chores. Furthermore, to counter the negative thought, for the final minute or two as you are completing the dull task you should think about several positive, self-enhancing statements (see your earlier list), ones that counteract the negative self-statements that led to the punishing chore. Rehearse these positive thoughts for a few minutes before you stop working on the boring chore. The "Relief Principle" (see Appendix A) implies that thoughts occurring just *before* relief from an unpleasant situation will be rewarded and strengthened. See to it that negative self-statements bring on a punishing chore, whereas positive, countervailing self-statements come just before relief from the chore.

Here is an example of how one person used this technique.

1. Boring tasks to do to stop negative self-talk:

- Clean my closets (2, 1-hour jobs)
- Clean each kitchen drawer (15 minutes per drawer; 10 drawers = 150 min.)
- Write checks for monthly bills (1 hour)
- Make out grocery list (15 min.)
- Clean silverware (1 hour total)
- Answer weekly correspondence (1 hour).

2. Record of my negative self-talk:

Date	What I said to myself	Chore I did and positive sentence I said at the end
1/1	"I can never remember items for shopping."	Made out my grocery list and finally said, "I know I'll be able to remember these few items."
1/2	"I can't get myself organized to do anything."	Answered weekly correspondence and said, "Wow, I'm really efficient and well organized."
1/4	"I can't sleep." (Insomnia can be caused by negative thoughts.)	Cleaned silverware for 30 minutes and said, "Now I can sleep like a bear!"

Try this punishment technique for a week or so. Observe and record how often you fall into obsessional worrying about your negative self-evaluations. See if the punishment procedure reduces the frequency of your worrying. Answer the following as you do the exercises over the week.

STOPPING YOUR NEGATIVE SELF-TALK

1. Boring tasks to do to stop negative self-talk:

Job	Estimated time to do job
_____	_____
_____	_____
_____	_____
_____	_____
_____	_____

2. Record of your negative self-talk:

Your negative self talk	Chore you did and positive sentence you said at the end
_____	_____
_____	_____
_____	_____
_____	_____
_____	_____

Hopefully, your negative self-talk will decrease as you punish yourself by doing these jobs. Not only will you learn to keep your negative thoughts in check, you will also probably get a lot of necessary chores done with this method!

Another way to punish yourself for self-deprecating worrying is to put yourself in "solitary confinement." Although you won't get any work done by this method, you may find it a very effective form of punishment. You arrange for a "worry chair" or "cell" in the house (one woman used a corner in her garage!) where you go when you catch yourself worrying about your inadequacies. The worry chair must be a distinctly unpleasant place to sit: the chair is hard, it faces a blank wall, you are isolated from music, reading material, and conversation. It is Dullsville. When you catch yourself fretting about how terrible or miserable you are, force yourself to your worry chair and stay there until you become thoroughly bored. This is your punishment. Of course, as in the preceding exercise, you should think countervailing positive self-statements just before you release yourself from this unpleasant situation.

Revising Your Mental Picture Show

In the past, you may have seen your Downer as a supremely powerful personage who dominates a meek, sniveling you. This kind of mental picture will inhibit your attempts to assert yourself with your Downer. Therefore, you must rework your mental images so they encourage assertive expressions. There are two types of exercises: first, you recast your Downer in a more playful, less threatening role, so you'll be less frightened by him or her; second, you picture yourself as a stronger, more outspoken assertor, so you can express your assertive message forcefully when the chips are down.

Making Your Downer Less Frightening

As a first exercise, think of some nice, friendly favor done for you or special tenderness shown to you by your Downer. Picture how your Downer looked, acted, and sounded at the time — in a calmer, more positive mood than the one that is associated with your problem scene. If you can't recollect a good deed, then just picture your Downer at peace, with his or her characteristic appearance which you find lovable or admirable (or at least acceptable!). In your imagination, blot out your Downer's threatening influence; soften that harsh image which prevents your assertions.

What affectionate characteristics or admirable concrete acts can you associate with your Downer?

_____

_____

Having found this anti-fear image, practice seeing your Downer in this way.

Picture the "beneficent Downer" image for 20 seconds, then stop; then picture it again. Do this picturing several times a day for five days.

As a second exercise, imagine your Downer looking and acting in a meek and timid manner. If he or she speaks loudly with great force, picture a puppy, yelping and playful, or a nervous, skitterish mouse. Experiment! Change your Downer's picture in the theater of your mind, as though you were switching the TV channel from a scary movie to a light comedy.

What playful animal will your Downer become in your imagination?

Now, picture this image for 10 – 20 seconds several times a day for a week. This can help reduce your fear of the Downer.

You can also attack your fears by the desensitization techniques described in Chapter 3. For now, let's turn to changes you can make in your pictures of yourself.

Picturing Yourself as a Strong Assertor

The next two exercises aim at improving your positive self-image, so you see yourself as strong and effective in stressful scenes. Look back at Question C of Worksheet #4 (page 23) where you described your negative self-images in the problem scene. You can change these by repeatedly creating in your mind the "opposite" picture from the one you had before. That is, you convert your negative self-image into a positive, self-enhancing image. Then you rehearse by repicturing it several times during each day and rewarding yourself.

In the "opposite" of an image, the emotions, achievements, and roles of the actors are reversed. For example, if you pictured yourself as a tiny chihuahua cowering before a Great Dane (the Downer), just reverse the roles, and see yourself now as the Great Dane in that scene. If you pictured your Downer screaming criticisms at you, now imagine him or her whispering tender encouragement in your ear. If you pictured yourself as a trembling weakling, see yourself now as a strong, courageous person, unafraid and able to stand up to a dictating Downer.

Write below the opposites of the negative self-images you want to alter. Refer to Question C of Worksheet #4 (page 23) and describe in detail your new, strong image.

YOUR POSITIVE SELF-IMAGE

_____

_____

_____

_____

_____

These are the self-affirming mental images you can rehearse, reward yourself for, and use when the old put-down scene recurs. So, rehearse these images several times a day for a week or more. This can help you control your emotions in that actual confrontation so you can deliver your assertive script without going to pieces.

As the last imagery exercise, picture yourself acting in new, assertive ways just as an actor might see himself in a new role. Here is what to do.

1. Write a few sentences describing a very assertive person you know or have seen on television or in movies. Picture that person and notice how he or she walks, sits, stands, and gestures. What facial expressions make that person appear assertive?
2. Close your eyes and see your assertive model do something you are afraid to do or you feel you do awkwardly and poorly.
3. Now see yourself doing what your assertive model does. Feel yourself acting and speaking as though you were that assertive model.

One woman wrote up this exercise as follows:

1. My assertive model has excellent, upright posture. She moves with ease, without excess movement. She has no fidgety hand gestures; her hands remain relaxed at her sides. She can move smoothly and easily in any direction she chooses. She also looks composed when just sitting still. She looks pleasant, eager, and happy. She looks intently at people, she asks questions and expresses her own feelings openly. She most closely resembles my grandmother and Katherine Hepburn.
2. I can vividly imagine this person entering a room full of strangers and walking over to meet the hostess. She is not disturbed by the stares of strangers, hardly noticing them except to smile quickly at two or three people.
3. I've continued seeing my assertive model act in this way. After several clear "run-throughs" imagining her, I substituted seeing myself in this role. After visualizing the scene several times, I could almost hear myself greeting my friend, the hostess of a party I'm to attend next week.

PICTURING YOUR NEW SELF

Now, select an assertive model and picture yourself acting as assertively as your model would in your problem scene.

1. Write a description of an assertive "model" — one who you have observed carefully. Describe your assertive model in detail.

_____

_____

_____

_____

2. Visualize your assertive model doing something you are afraid to do or you feel you do badly. Describe how he or she carries off the action.

_____

_____

_____

3. Now see yourself performing as your assertive model does. Feel yourself acting and speaking like your assertive model. What do you do and say? In what manner?

_____

_____

_____

The point of this exercise is for you to imitate in imagination the assertive actions of an exemplary model. You change your self-image in this scene by then visualizing yourself acting in this assertive manner. Practice visualizing your assertive self several times a day for a week or more. Copy the actions of your assertive model as you visualize how that person would act in diverse threatening situations that would upset you. These exercises can enhance your assertive picture of yourself.

EXTENDING YOUR PLEASURES

A frequent outcome of nonassertiveness is frustration and depression. The shy recluse is often depressed and morose while getting very little pleasure out of life. The last exercise introduces you to a method for amplifying and extending the occasional pleasures of your life.[2] Plan out and practice visualizing yourself in some pleasurable activity. By frequently experiencing these pleasures in your imagination, you manage to spread small pleasures around and throughout your daily routine. You stretch out your good times by rehearsing them mentally in anticipation of the activity. The steps are as follows:

1. Choose one small activity you have enjoyed or believe you would enjoy, but which you have postponed. The activity should be one which you can enjoy alone for its sheer pleasure and which fits your time schedule and pocketbook. Record what you will do and when.

2. Write three sentences describing the experience for yourself. For instance, you might write a sentence describing the enjoyment you feel before the activity, a sentence about enjoying the activity as it happens, and a sentence about the pleasure felt at the end of the activity.

3. Choose three times during the day when you can practice visualizing these three pictures in your imagination. Find a quiet time when you are alone for about two minutes. Practice visualizing and enjoying the scenes with all your senses — seeing, touching, hearing, and smelling. Make the scenes vivid in your imagination. Try to experience the pleasure you will feel from the activities.

4. Tell other people what activity you have planned. Let them know you will not postpone your planned pleasure to do their chores, meet their needs, or respond to last-minute appeals.

5. Perform the activity as planned. And after you experience one pleasurable activity, plan for and practice another one. Choose one or more new pleasures to image, rehearse, and perform every week.

Here is an example:

1. An activity to be done on the weekend. *I will go swimming on Saturday.*

2. Three sentences describing the experience and attendant feelings.
   I will enjoy standing at the edge of the pool before diving in.
   I will enjoy swimming through the cool water.
   I will enjoy lying on my towel and feeling warm as I dry off in the sun.

3. When will I rehearse these images?
   I will practice in the morning when I wake up.
   I will practice in the afternoon when I am through with lunch.
   I will practice in the evening when I am ready to fall asleep.

4. When will I tell others? *A week in advance.*

5. A second activity after this one: *I'll spend two hours browsing in the library.*

EXTENDING YOUR PLEASURES

Now, record how *you* will picture a forthcoming pleasure:

1. Choose an activity you can do by yourself at the end of this week. Make a contract with yourself:

   I will

   _____

2. Write three sentences which describe the experience before, during, and after the activity.

   I will enjoy

   _____

   I will enjoy

   _____

   I will enjoy

   _____

3. Choose three times during the day you can mentally rehearse these pictures:

I will practice in the morning when

_____

I will practice in the afternoon when

_____

I will practice in the evening when

_____

4. When will you tell others what activity you are planning?

_____

5. Plan another activity as soon as you have enjoyed this one. What will it be?

_____

Use whatever variations on the exercises suit your style and interests, but it is important that you practice them as you would practice the piano or some other skill. These "assignments" can help bring more pleasure in your life, and lighten the depression caused by nonassertiveness. Taken together, the techniques introduced in this chapter can help lift your spirits and put you in a mood in which personal goals become important and worth defending. Above all, by using the techniques you are affirming your basic right to control yourself and to experience some enjoyment in your life.

3

Coping with Stress

*Courage is resistance to fear, mastery of fear,
not absence of fear.*

MARK TWAIN

A frequent complaint of nonassertive people is that they feel they are "too emotional," or they "can't control" their emotions. In distressing social situations their emotions take control. But at one time or another, all of us must deal with stress. To become a person who can act assertively when you want to, you must learn how to cope successfully with conflicts. In this chapter, we will explain some specific techniques for learning to relax and for desensitizing yourself to anxiety. With this information and some practice, most readers can improve their ability to handle tense situations.

HOW EMOTIONS CAN KEEP YOU
FROM BECOMING ASSERTIVE

A learned emotional reaction (such as social anxiety) has four aspects: the environmental situation, your bodily reactions, your overt (observable) behavior, and your covert (silent) behavior. For example, suppose the *situation* is your Downer insulting you; your *physical reactions* may be shallow breathing and heart palpitations, your *overt behavior* may be withdrawn shyness, and your *covert behavior* may be saying sentences to yourself such as "I can't stand it" or "I'm too weak to talk back" or "I'm a coward," or seeing yourself as a helpless victim submitting to an all-powerful Downer. The relations among these factors are diagramed in the accompanying chart.

The important thing to keep in mind is that your emotional reaction is a learned reaction — the current situation provokes this reaction because it

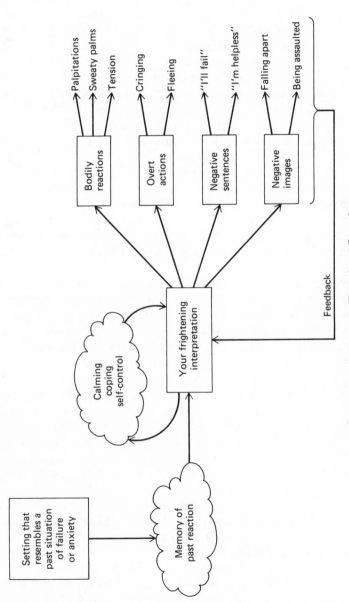

Dynamics of a Learned Emotional Reaction

resembles a past situation where you felt anxiety or humiliation. Old emotional reactions, partly revived from memory, cause mild physiological reactions along with an "interpretation" of what is happening, what you predict will happen, and how you feel about it. This interpretation — which depends largely upon your emotional training and emotional habits — shapes the behavior you then display. You may feel physical signs of tension. You may adopt a cringing posture. You may say negative sentences to yourself ("I'm weak, helpless, exhausted, stupid"). You may be assailed by negative images — of some metaphor to the current scene ("I see myself as a sniveling puppy trying to stand up to an enormous bulldog"), or of a feared outcome or consequence of the current scene ("I see the person screaming at me, then leaving for good"), or of yourself ("I'm a weakling") and your Downer ("He has nerves of cold steel"). Note that there is a feedback loop from these emotional behaviors to the interpretation. For example, in some cases noticing signs of slight tension can cause even further anxiety in an accelerating spiral.

How, then, can you change your emotional reactions? You do it by practicing certain coping skills. You learn to say calming, tranquilizing things to yourself when you begin to feel afraid; also, you learn to reinterpret the situation so that it's not nearly so frightening. In this way you can change how you feel and how you behave in threatening scenes. The exercises in this chapter, like those in Chapter 2, are designed to help you do these things.

Before describing a technique for controlling tension let's look more closely at what happens to you when you experience an emotion. Earlier, in Question A of Worksheet #4 (page 23), we asked you to examine your physical signs of arousal as you pictured your problem scene. There, you noted those physical signs you remember experiencing, such as blushing, pounding heart, tremors, and feelings of weakness.

Since you were remembering yourself in a moderately threatening scene, you probably checked off a few signs, indicating the mild tension and other reactions that most people feel when anxious. The important point is not to overreact and interpret any of these signs as an emotional attack. A blush does not mean you are hopelessly shy, nor a dry mouth that you can't speak up forcefully. Emotions are not debilitating *per se* — the same physical signs are associated with joy or delight, yet ecstatic people have no trouble speaking out.

We are familiar with occasions when people blow things up out of proportion. It happens when your physical reactions and your negative self-statements get into a feedback loop so that each system fuels the fire of the other one. Consider an example.

George is waiting to address a small audience. While being introduced, he notices that he is breathing fast and shallow, feeling a trifle light-headed. He says to himself, "I think I'm scared. I wonder if I can do it. What would

happen if I faint or forget my speech!" As he reflects upon these sentences, his heart starts pounding, his pulse increases, and he hears a buzzing in his ears. He interprets, "I'm freaking out. I'm too scared to concentrate. I'm clutching up. I won't be able to stand up or talk; I'll stammer and forget my lines. My God, I've got to get out of this. I'll pretend I'm sick and leave quickly."

George overreacts to the symptoms of mild tension anyone feels before a public performance. Effective people attribute the tension to the slightly stressful situation and carry on, knowing they will be all right once underway. But George tells horror stories to himself, about his disabilities and likely failure. These increase his tension and exaggerate the physical signs of arousal. Seeing these increased physical signs sets off another cycle of increasingly frightening self-evaluations, ending with the strong urge to flee from the situation. If he does, George will look back upon this disaster as evidence that he "could never give a public speech." Clearly, he

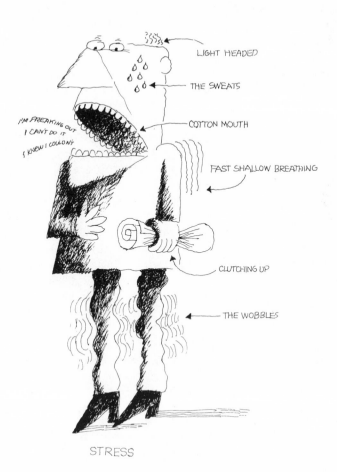

STRESS

is the victim of his own flim-flam, having conned himself into a self-defeating belief on no evidence except that provided by his mistaken and overblown interpretation of normal tension. He defeated himself before getting on stage.

LEARNING TO RELAX

One good way to keep your emotions from getting the best of you and to relieve the tensions of a stressful life style is a process known as progressive relaxation.[1]

We would all like to be able to turn off our inner tensions at the end of the day. The search for a method to overcome nervous tension has been pursued by doctors, scientists, and common folk. If you ask people how they control tension, you will hear a smorgasbord of home recipes: hot baths, massage, diets, hot milk, exercise, reading, transcendental meditation, television, hypnotic suggestion, and drugs.

From 1908 to 1960 Dr. Edmund Jacobson[2] studied nervous tension and its relation to muscle relaxation. He found that muscle tension is always present in people who are anxious. Worry, anxiety, irritability, impatience, and restlessness are supported by tense muscles. Jacobson concluded that tension could be reduced by learning the simple skill of progressively relaxing these muscles. He then developed a technique for relaxing. He found that muscle relaxation controlled emotions to a great degree. Through his technique, thousands of people have learned to control formerly "uncontrollable" tension by learning to relax muscles that are controllable. By relaxing muscles which tense up during their negative thinking, they are able to turn off the worrying brain that prevents them from enjoying life.

Learning to relax takes practice. But after devoting 30 minutes a day for at least a month to practicing, most people do learn to progressively relax their muscles. And the practice really pays off. One woman who practiced relaxation for three months before an important piano recital (which she anticipated with terror) reported, "It was the best recital I've ever played and the most I've ever enjoyed it." Another individual put it this way: "Learning to control my tensions by relaxing has helped me enjoy the moment I'm living now, instead of dreading the moment I think I have to live tomorrow."

How To Practice Relaxation

Muscle tension is specific and physical. Experience it so you can learn to control it. Try this experiment: make a tight fist and notice the feelings from the fist muscles as you tense them. That is the sensation of tension. Now, let your fist become limp; the feeling as your hand loosens is relaxation. Now try to produce the same experiences with other parts of your body. For instance, make as big a smile as you can, squinching up your face — feel the tension in the jaw, lips, and throat. Now, let it go and feel the sensations of relaxation.

Appendix B of this book has detailed instructions for relaxing your entire body. It tells you how to practice tensing one muscle group, then relaxing it, then tensing and relaxing another muscle group, until most muscles in the body have been tensed and relaxed. You can learn to identify the different sensations of tension and relaxation in various muscle groups. With repeated practice sessions, you can learn to monitor, identify, and control even small tensions such as those in the neck, eye muscles, or forehead. As you monitor, you can catch yourself at almost any moment during your workday with some excess tension; once you detect a tense muscle, you can deliberately let it go and experience relaxation. For example, many people have unnoticed tension in their eyes (squinting), or in their forehead (wrinkling of forehead when concentrating), in their shoulder muscles while they are writing or reading, or in their neck muscles when walking or sitting. Your goal is to detect and eliminate such muscle knots.

We strongly recommend that you practice the progressive relaxation instructions in Appendix B. Record these on a tape recorder, then play the tape whenever you want to practice. If you do not own a tape recorder, try to rent or borrow one temporarily. If hearing yourself on the tape is bothersome, ask a friend to record the exercise. When you are ready to practice, prepare the setting. Select a quiet room, darken it, take the telephone off the hook, and lie down on a sofa, bed, or floor. If you feel cold, put a light blanket over you. Lie down, turn on the tape recorder, close your eyes, and follow the instructions.

Relaxation is pleasurable, so try to practice it once or twice a day for 30 minutes. Continue the exercises for as many weeks as you like. Think of the relaxation exercises as you would think of jogging or physical exercise: it is generally worth working at it whenever you can — even for a period less than 30 minutes. The instructions can be abbreviated for a 10 or 15 minute relaxation session.

A good way to help bring instant relaxation in your daily life is to associate a verbal command with the reaction of going into the relaxed state. As you listen to the tape and feel yourself becoming more relaxed, take a big breath, then exhale and silently say the magic words, "Relax. Let go and relax!" Your calming words will become associated with the physical state of deep relaxation. Then you can start to practice relaxing your muscles throughout your whole working day. As you sit at work, at lectures, in your car, at the movies, as you walk or stand, attend periodically to your physical state. If you do detect some tense muscles, take a deep breath, exhale and say to yourself, "Relax! Let go and relax!" and repeat it over several times. Try in those moments of attention to place yourself into your accustomed state of deep relaxation while keeping your eyes open. Be on the lookout for areas of subtle muscle tension; these are focal points for emotional tension. You can feel a lot freer, happier, and less high-strung and nervous if you can detect and eliminate these pockets of muscle tension.

DESENSITIZING YOURSELF TO ANXIETY

Some individuals learn to develop excellent assertive scripts and yet may be frightened to use the new assertive lines with their Downers. They are sure they will blank out, forget their lines, and become so scared in the actual confrontation that they can't deliver their lines without help. Such people simply won't assert themselves. They ask, "How can I stop my shaking, my dry mouth, and the butterflies in my stomach?" Their situation is much like that of an inexperienced actress who has her lines memorized but still has the opening-night jitters. What can be done to control the anxiety you might expect as you assert yourself with a Downer?

Systematic desensitization[3] is a technique that can be used to relieve anxiety in a stressful situation, whether it is giving a speech or speaking up for your rights. This technique, which is based on the Fear Reduction Principle (Appendix A), has proven very beneficial for practically all types of people.

You can understand the desensitization concept by comparing it to the way you get used to hot water in a shower or bathtub. Few people can tolerate jumping into an extremely hot shower. Rather, they enter a warm shower, then make it progressively hotter. To understand the desensitization procedure, just think of an intensely stressful situation as though it were analogous to extremely hot water. To learn to tolerate intense stress, you begin by exposing yourself to a very mild stress; then once you are accustomed to that, you move up to a slightly greater stress much as you would increase the hotness of your shower.

In using systematic desensitization, you carry out this exposure to stress through *imagining* a series of stressful scenes while trying to stay relaxed. First, you make up an "anxiety hierarchy," a series of scenes which progressively resemble or which come progressively closer to a frightening event. To make an anxiety hierarchy for your problem scene (the one in which you are to assert yourself), consider that situation as defining the highest point on a "fear thermometer." Label the anxiety it arouses as 100 degrees. Then, starting from that 100-degree fear situation, alter or remove various elements from the total situation to create scenes that produce progressively less fear — one scene that registers 90 on your fear thermometer, one that registers 80, 70, and so on down the scale to zero. The low-scoring scenes should be ones that either *resemble* the problem scene to lesser degrees, or ones that are more remote in time to events leading up to the problem encounter.

The desensitization procedure is this: Let yourself become thoroughly relaxed. Now imagine the *lowest-threat* scene in your hierarchy for $10-20$

seconds. Stop imagining, relax for a minute, then move up to the next scene in your hierarchy, imagining that for 10-20 seconds. Stay relaxed while picturing these scenes to yourself in vivid detail. As you move progressively upward through your hierarchy, monitor your tension. If you experience much tension with any image, then practice it several more times and advance to the next scene only after you have eliminated any anxiety provoked by the current scene. Work on the hierarchy each day, repeating steps and trying to move up the complete hierarchy while remaining relaxed. Eventually, you should be able to imagine yourself in what was formerly your most terrifying scene while remaining relaxed, without fear. By that time, your fear in thinking of those scenes will have been counterconditioned and replaced by deep relaxation. That is what systematic desensitization is all about.

To illustrate a fear hierarchy, the following scenes are used in a course Sharon developed on control of speaking anxiety. This is used by students in desensitizing themselves for their first two-minute speech, which was videotaped in class. The fear thermometer rating is in parentheses after each scene to be imagined.

Least
threatening → 0. Sitting at home reading a book (0°)
scene   1. Reading about the course in the catalog (10°)
                2. Going to the Speaking Anxiety class for the first time (20°)
                3. Learning that I will give a two-minute taped talk with a replay (30°)
                4. Wondering about a topic for the speech at the breakfast table (40°)
                5. Sitting at my desk working on the speech (50°)
                6. Practicing the speech aloud at home in front of a mirror (60°)
                7. Thinking about the speech on the day when I have to speak (70°)
                8. Arriving in the classroom on the night of the speech and wondering if I should go first (80°)
                9. Getting up from my chair, walking to the lectern, and facing
Most   the people (90°)
threatening → 10. Giving the speech (100°)
scene

These steps represent events that cause a speech-anxious person to become progressively more nervous just in thinking about them. After students have mastered the hierarchy and enacted all the events, they are encouraged to develop a hierarchy for a specific speech at a specific location which they are to deliver outside of class.

Keep in mind these criteria for generating items for an anxiety hierarchy.

- Make the scenes realistic; that is, they should be similar to or, better yet, represent actual experiences you have had, or threatening situations you can imagine you might have to face in the future.
- Insert some concrete detail so you can easily picture the scenes. For instance, it is important to be able to picture yourself "wondering about your speech" in a particular place such as "at the breakfast table." This makes it easier for you to see yourself doing those tasks in your imagination.
- Try to include a broad sample from the array of situations in which the fear might operate. Usually 8 – 15 items are adequate for most people who are nervous about their performance.
- Use scenes that are about equally spaced along the fear scale (say, 10 scenes at 10-point intervals). Then there will be no unusually large or small jumps in the desensitization process.

Developing a Fear Hierarchy for Approaching Your Downer

You can use desensitization to control the anxiety you might feel for the few hours (or days) preceding the confrontation you plan to have with your Downer. For example, Judy wrote a script for confronting her husband, who always criticized her housekeeping. She decided to speak out as soon as he produced his usual criticism, "This house looks like a tornado. What have you been doing all day?" Two weeks before "Target Day," Judy listed events that would happen just before she confronted her husband. She regularly got "uptight just knowing he'd be coming home and starting his criticism of me." Here's her list.

1. I notice the clock says 4 o'clock. (0°)
2. I prepare an easy casserole. (10°)
3. I set the table attractively. (20°)
4. I take a shower. (30°)
5. I wear my most "assertive" clothes. (40°)
6. I lie down on the couch, close my eyes, and relax. It's 4:50. (50°)
7. I hear my husband close the door and yell, "This house looks like a tornado. What have you been doing all day?" (60°)
8. I rise from the couch, walk to him as I say, "I had a terrific day! Sit down. I'll fix you a drink and tell you about it!" (70°)
9. I fix him a drink and relax my shoulders and forehead. (80°)
10. I give the glass to him and start counting the stripes in his shirt so I won't attend to his hostile body language. (90°)
11. I look at him and begin my script: "When you came into the house, you yelled, 'This house looks like a tornado.'" (Her assertive script proceeds from this point.) (100°)

Judy felt that once she started saying her well-rehearsed script she could proceed without losing control.

Now, record your personal hierarchy of scenes that either resemble or lead up to the problem scene where you'll be asserting yourself. Below are spaces for 10 items (scenes). Describe briefly the problem scene involving high threat with your Downer in space #10, and assign it a fear thermometer rating of 100. Construct nine scenes of lesser fear that either resemble the problem scene or lead up to it over time. After you write the problem scene at 10, record next the 9, then 8, 7, 6, and so on until you describe briefly a neutral scene for 0. If desirable, increase the number of scenes to as many as 15.

THREATENING SCENE HIERARCHY

Scene number	Scene description	Fear thermometer rating
Least threatening→ 0	_____	(0°)
1	_____	( )
2	_____	( )
3	_____	( )
4	_____	( )
5	_____	( )
6	_____	( )
7	_____	( )
8	_____	( )
9	_____	( )
Most threatening→ 10	_____	(100°)

After you've constructed your hierarchy, memorize the scenes and their order, and then check out their vividness in your imagination. Close your eyes and visualize each specific scene in as vivid detail as possible. If you have difficulty visualizing details, check out the real scene. For instance, if you wanted to improve in "remembering" your kitchen, go there and examine it carefully, see the clock on the wall, the stove, the cupboards, the kitchen counter, and so forth. Notice the lights, the smells, the temperature, the sounds around you. Now, close your eyes and "see and sense" the details of the scene in memory. Open your eyes and check your memory for what you missed. Close your eyes again and include the missed items in your altered image. The more detail you can see, the more vivid will be your memory of the scene and the more easily you can experience and "feel" the scene in your imagination.

Your memory for detail can be improved. Practice noticing and re-membering the shapes and colors of things, the weight, texture, sound, taste, and smell of things. Sharpen your senses by observing a scene, closing your eyes, recalling details, checking out missing parts, closing your eyes a second time for a retest at remembering the details. Such exercises teach you to concentrate and to discriminate features of your world. These abilities are useful in desensitization.

Desensitizing Yourself to Problem Scenes

Begin each desensitization session by listening to a progressive relaxation tape. If you've already had much practice at relaxation you can dispense with the full 30-minute tape and begin imagining your first scene after only a few minutes of relaxing. But beginners should do the relaxation exercise in its entirety before the desensitization part of the session begins. That way they are thoroughly relaxed as they picture the first scene in their anxiety hierarchy.

The objective during the desensitization process is to remain relaxed while visualizing one by one the increasingly threatening scenes. After you are relaxed, with your eyes closed, proceed as follows.

1. Picture Scene #1 for 10–20 seconds while remaining relaxed. Pour yourself into the picture; see it vividly and transport yourself into the scene by respond-ing to the sights, sounds, odors, and touches of a scene. Don't worry if you can't feel yourself into the part the first few times you try it. The more you try to visualize the detail, the more likely you will achieve this feeling of actually being there and living the scene directly. Keep deeply relaxed as you visualize the scene for about 10–20 seconds.

2. Now, stop visualizing Scene #1 and see yourself in a familiar, relaxing, and comfortable place that means security and peace for you. This is your "com-fort zone"; for you it may be a beach, a quiet forest, your easy chair, or a flower garden. Return to this pleasantly relaxing scene after each visualization of a scene in your hierarchy. The objective at this step is for your muscles to relax after you imagine the previously uncomfortable scene.

3. Then, picture Scene #2 for 10–20 seconds while remaining relaxed.

4. Now, turn off Scene #2 and see nothing (or see a beach or other calming image which represents your comfort zone).

5. If you felt any tension at Scene #2, stop the scene. Return to your comfort zone for 20 seconds and then repeat seeing Scene #2. Only if you felt no tension should you proceed to the next scene.

Continue the procedure with successive scenes, always relaxing as much as you can during the visualization and afterward when you are picturing your comfort zone. The first day, practice seeing only three to five scenes,

IMAGINING A COMFORT ZONE

and work for no more than about ten minutes. Always stop before you are tired, bored, or feel mounting tension.

Desensitization requires that you be more than a spectator of your pictures, rather you must remain relaxed while you "pour" yourself into the picture and feel yourself moving and speaking in your imagination.

People occasionally have difficulty visualizing a scene which is merely named on their tape recorder. Their minds may wander and fill with intruding thoughts. To focus attention on a scene and increase its vividness, force yourself to describe aloud and tape record the scene as it unfolds in all its concrete particulars.[4]

Identify which muscles become tense and learn to relax them as you imagine a stressful scene. You will know you have achieved success when you can think about a formerly terrifying scene without feeling anxious and upset. Because you cannot be nervous and relaxed at the same time, you will be replacing nervousness with relaxation. The remarkable fact is that desensitizing yourself to a threatening scene in your imagination carries over and allows you to remain calmer when you enter the real-life scene. If you can go through your imaginal hierarchy several times while remaining relaxed and fearless, you will be ready to confront your Downer with greater confidence.

Using Desensitization for Other Put-Down Scenes

You can also use desensitization to reduce upsets from a variety of every-day put-downs. Instead of building toward a single problem scene, you can list a number of things people say or do which threaten or diminish you, and rank these items by the degree of discomfort they cause you. For example:

- *Wife to husband:* "You don't care if these children live or die. You treat them like they're dirt. They'd be better off in an orphanage."
- *Father to daughter:* "When are you going to listen to me? Don't you know you always screw things up. You can't do anything right!"
- *Sister to sister:* "You just did that to satisfy yourself. You're always on an ego trip."
- *Husband to wife:* "Why can't you look sexy like other women?"
- *Father to son:* "Why are you so clumsy? You look like you're falling apart all the time."
- *Relative to relative:* "Maybe you shouldn't have gotten married in the first place."
- *Teacher to student:* "Stop asking so many questions. If you don't know what you are doing, you shouldn't be in this class."
- *Employer to employee:* "What do you think you're getting paid for anyhow?"
- *Co-worker to co-worker:* "Well, hurry up, let's hear your bright ideas. You're the expert, aren't you?"

After listing the different put-down sentences which recall a range of scenes for you, assign a fear rating to each one, and arrange them in order. Then carry out the desensitization procedure with your hierarchy, starting with the low-fear scenes. Start easy — with one toe in the tub, so to speak — and work your way in relaxed fashion to progressively greater threat scenes, until you are in up to your neck! The idea is to use the powerful desensitization technique for general purposes, to reduce the fear you might experience in a variety of social settings.

Keep in mind the following five points about the desensitization process:

1. Maintain deep relaxation as you imagine progressively more frightening scenes.
2. Imagine each scene for approximately 10 – 20 seconds before you shut it off (unless you grow tense visualizing the scene, in which case stop imagining the scene immediately.)

3. Advance to the next scene in the hierarchy only if you can handle the current one without tension.

4. If a given scene arouses persistent anxiety, create several scenes of lower threat leading up to that difficult scene.

5. Work each session only so long as you can put full mental effort into the process.

ADDITIONAL STRATEGIES FOR COPING WITH STRESS

Desensitization is future oriented, aimed at reducing fear in a specific future situation: you imagine yourself acting and reacting positively in successive events which lead up to your problem scenes so you will have less fear when you actually enter those scenes later. But how do you keep your fear in check at the time you actually go through a confrontation scene? Essentially you must learn to have thoughts that cope with stress, that hold your fear in check so you can perform successfully.

But how can you control your thoughts? Let's again equate your "thoughts" with the sentences you silently say to yourself. Recall from the preceding chapter that emotions are partly controlled by a conscious "interpretation" of the scene. You can feed new "information" into the interpretive process by the sentences you say to yourself. Thus you control your fearful thoughts when you are confronting another person by silently saying to yourself a stream of fear-reducing statements. Some silent statements might be: "Relax; take several deep breaths; keep calm; this is really a minor matter in the grand design of the universe; this will pass; keep cool; this person can't hurt you; relax, it'll be over soon." The method requires that you make up your own stress-coping remarks, memorize them, and recite them feelingly as an internal monolog whenever you enter any stressful situation. You don't have to give 100 percent of your attention to your Downer in the encounter. Rather, you can make it a 60−40 split: the Downer gets 60 percent of your attention, while you devote 40 percent to silently saying and listening to your internal, stress-coping monolog. Time spent tuning in to your coping thoughts will pay off with less fear and better performance.

Research has shown the effectiveness of coping self-statements in reducing people's fears. Meichenbaum and Cameron used relaxation plus the stress-coping statements in Table 1 to "inoculate" their clients against certain kinds of threats. Clients who used only coping self-statements were as successful as clients who used only systematic desensitization in overcoming a phobia about handling a live snake. Significantly, clients who used the coping self-statements were better able to manage other fears (for instance, they were able to pick up and handle a formerly terrifying rat). In contrast, clients receiving only desensitization of their snake fear were still afraid of picking up a rat.

Table 1   Example of Coping Self-Statements[5]

Category 1. **Preparing for a stressful situation**

What is it I have to do?
I can develop a plan to deal with it.
Just think about what I can do about it. That's better than
    getting anxious.
No negative self-statements, just think rationally.
Don't worry. Worry won't help anything.
Maybe what I think is anxiety is eagerness to confront it.

Category 2. **Confronting and handling a stressful situation**

I can meet this challenge.
One step at a time; I can handle the situation.
Don't think about fear — just about what I have to do. Stay relevant.
This anxiety is what they said I would feel. It's a reminder to use my
    coping exercises.
This tenseness can be an ally, a cue to cope.
Relax; I'm in control. Take a slow, deep breath. Ah, good.

Category 3. **Coping with the feeling of being overwhelmed**

When fear comes, just pause.
Keep focus on the present; what is it I have to do?
Let me label my fear from 0 to 10 and watch it change.
I was supposed to expect my fear to rise.
Don't try to eliminate fear totally; just keep it manageable.
I can convince myself to do it. I can reason my fear away.
It will be over shortly.
It's not the worst thing that can happen.
Just think about something else.
Do some thing that will prevent me from thinking about fear.
Just describe what is around me. That way I won't think about
    worrying.

Category 4. **Reinforcing self-statements**

It worked; I was able to do it.
Wait until I tell my buddy about this.
It wasn't as bad as I expected.
I made more out of the fear than it was worth.
My damn ideas — that's the problem. When I control them,
    I control my fear.
It's getting better each time I use the procedures.
I'm really pleased with the progress I'm making.
I did it!

Several such experiments show that coping self-statements like those in Table 1 can be used as a general anti-stress inoculation. Thus one advantage of self-control statements over desensitization is their generality. Whereas you might use desensitization only as preparation for a specific problem situation, you can use your coping statements for any number of stressful situations. In particular, you can use self-calming remarks in unexpected or novel stresses.

Examine the four classes of self-statements in Table 1. The first class, preparing for a stressful situation, contains statements said to yourself (with meaningful emphasis and genuine feeling) as you anticipate a stressful confrontation. (Of course, some stresses such as accidents, fires, or attacks arise unexpectedly and you don't have time to prepare.) The second class, confronting and handling the stressful situation, contains statements to be used when the situation actually arises. These keep you oriented to the task at hand, concentrating on the problem to be solved rather than on your inadequacies. The third class contains self-statements to help you cope with the feeling of being overwhelmed. Saying these statements silently helps you control anxiety during the confrontation. Reinforcing statements, the fourth class, are used to reward yourself for coping successfully just *after* a stressful confrontation. It is important that you deliberately reward yourself for coping with situations where formerly you went to pieces. Chances are you will be less likely to fall apart in the future if you reward yourself for present successes.

The self-statements in Table 1 are simply suggestions for how you can make up your own self-statements. We suggest that you try this as an exercise right now. You know better than anyone else what calming self-statements will keep you focused on a job. Change the self-statements in Table 1 to suit your circumstances and reword them in meaningful personal phrases. As you write your self-statements, group them into the four categories shown below. Aim for at least four statements in each category.

MY COPING SENTENCES TO
REDUCE STRESS

Category 1. Preparing for a stressful situation

_____

_____

_____

_____

_____

_____

_____

Category 2. Confronting and handling a stressful situation

_____

_____

_____

_____

_____

_____

Category 3. Coping with the feeling of being overwhelmed

_____

_____

_____

_____

_____

_____

Category 4. Reinforcing self-statements

_____

_____

_____

_____

_____

_____

Fine. Now study this list until you can smoothly recite each category of self-statement. During the week, return repeatedly to study and recite these statements. Try to feel the emotional significance of the statements. Your aim is to become so proficient at reciting these that, at a later encounter, you can silently and swiftly run over them with only 40 percent of your attention.

Once you memorize and rehearse these self-statements you can more easily use them automatically in any stressful confrontation. If you plan to assert yourself with a Downer, get ready for the confrontation by rehearsing your Category 1 self-statements (preparing). As you approach the actual scene with your Downer, say the silent monolog using the self-statements in Category 2 (confronting). Use Category 3 statements (coping) immediately before and during delivery of your message. When the assertive scene is over, use the self-reward statements from Category 4 (reinforcing).

It is a good idea to refresh your self-statement list periodically, deleting old or adding new statements. You could keep them available by copying them on small cards to carry in your purse or billfold for frequent practicing. Use your list flexibly, dropping out whatever statements don't fit the occasion. And remember, as you say your silent statements, to invest them with emotional significance; don't let the monolog become a superficial recital without emphasis or meaning. Like a good actor or actress, try to maintain a deep emotional impact in your monolog, despite reciting the lines hundreds of times.

Giving yourself positive information with coping statements is one of the most valuable ways to control yourself. It can be used in many different contexts — in studying, in thinking creatively, in giving a speech or musical performance, in interviewing for a job, in carrying out some complex procedure (learning to drive), and so on. Your silent sentences can instruct you what to do and how to feel in any of these situations. They represent a simple and inexpensive way to deal more effectively with stress.

4

Small Steps: Beginning Assertive Exercises

A great part of courage is having done the thing before.

EMERSON

A saying in the theater is that there are no small parts, only small actors. Even small parts have possibilities for greatness. Performers, whether musicians, acrobats, or actors, know the importance of practicing their drills, warm-ups, and improvisational exercises, to ready their performance. Important assertive behaviors also need the same careful preparation and practice. By practicing small assertions you can prepare yourself for speaking up assertively when a bigger role is demanded.

In this chapter, you practice some small parts and experience success with them. These short exercises are interesting, fun, and teach elementary assertions that encourage personal growth. After each exercise, there is space to record your observations. We have included illustrations to show you how others have handled the exercises. Try to do one exercise a day. You'll soon notice how these new, positive behaviors affect the way you feel about yourself. And you will be preparing yourself for more demanding assertive behaviors.

KEEPING A RECORD OF YOUR ASSERTIVE BEHAVIOR

To see your progress day by day, it is useful to keep a logbook or diary. In it you can keep track of the times you practice your exercises and the times you asserted yourself in real-life situations. You can also record the times you should have asserted yourself but didn't and note what actions you should have taken. The best time to write in your logbook is at the end of the day.

You can organize your logbook in daily or weekly sheets that look something like this:

ASSERTIVENESS LOGBOOK

Date (or Week) _____

Setting (time and place)	Put-down situation (who said what to whom?)	My response (words and actions)	What happened? (how I felt about my behavior)

Any other format will do as well; just be sure to provide space to record the setting, a brief description of the situation, what response you tried, and its consequences — what the other person did, and how you felt about the situation. If you failed to assert yourself, decide what assertive response you think would have been most effective, and note this beneath your actual response.

Your logbook will serve several functions: first, it will remind you to practice your exercises each day (remember to record your practices); it will help you to mentally rehearse those actions, and to praise yourself for being assertive and doing the exercises. Second, writing out assertive behaviors for situations where you failed can prepare you for an appropriate and forthright assertion the next time. Finally, your logbook will reveal the historical development of your assertive behaviors.

BEGINNING ASSERTIVE EXERCISES

The following exercises vary from easy to more difficult, with early ones generally causing little discomfort for most people. Each exercise suggests that you perform some small assertive action. If you already perform such an action routinely without becoming upset, then just skip that exercise. Treat these exercises like a physical conditioning program; do any of the exercises whenever you can. You can start working on them today, alone or with a friend or buddy. Working with another person can help motivate you to keep on the road to a more assertive lifestyle.

The sequence of exercises is as follows:

EXERCISE 1. LISTING YOUR PUT-DOWN SENTENCES

The English language provides us with a versatile weapon for putting down a person by direct assault, implication, and innuendo. When someone tries to pressure you unfairly, to invade your privacy, to belittle or patronize you, the attempt is often heralded by some pat phrase, cliché, or idiom. In becoming assertive, you can learn to recognize such put-down signals and to reply assertively in your defense. Remember that an assertive answer is not an angry, aggressive one, but rather a calm response by which you show that you won't allow the put-down to succeed.

Suggestions. The following list includes a number of common put-downs, though there are infinitely more. In the right-hand column write your best-considered assertive replies — what you could say the next time someone uses those put-down lines on you. Possible assertive answers appear on the following page, with comments in parentheses to sum up the general approach we are suggesting. Compare each of your answers with ours and judge which is more assertive. You can extend this exercise by adding some put-downs from your own experience, together with your assertive replies.

Examples

Downer behavior	*Put-down sentence*	*Your assertive reply*
Nagging about details	"Haven't you done this yet?"	
Prying	"I know I maybe shouldn't ask, but. . ."	
Lecturing, Pollyana style	"We should be more cooperative, so there won't be so much tension."	
Putting you on the spot socially	"Are you busy Tuesday?"	
Questioning the value of your choices	"Are you sure this course really relates to your job?"	
Giving unwanted advice	"If I were you. . ."	
Pigeonholing you	"That's a woman for you!"	
Using insulting labels for your behavior	"That's a dumb way to. . ."	
Basing predictions on an amateur personality analysis	"You'll have a hard time. You're too shy."	

Downer behavior	Put-down sentence	Suggested assertive reply
Nagging about details	"Haven't you done this yet?"	"No, when did you want it done?" (Answer without hedging, and follow up with a question.)
Prying	"I know I maybe shouldn't ask, but. . ."	"If I don't want to answer, I'll let you know." (Indicate that you won't make yourself uncomfortable just to please this person.)
Lecturing, Pollyanna style	"We should be more cooperative, so there won't be so much tension."	"How can we be more cooperative?" (Ask for concrete examples of the behavior being urged.)
Putting you on the spot socially	"Are you busy Tuesday?"	"What do you have in mind?" (Answer the question with a question.)
Questioning the value of your choices	"Are you sure this course really relates to your job?"	"I think it relates to me and therefore to my job." (Emphasize your right to make personal judgments.)
Giving unwanted advice	"If I were you. . ."	"But you aren't!" (Cut off the advice by denying the "if.")
Pigeonholing you	"That's a woman for you!"	"That's *one* woman, not *all* women." (Disagree — assert your individuality.)
Using insulting labels for your behavior	"That's a dumb way to. . ."	"I'll decide what to call my behavior." (Refuse to accept the label.)
Basing predictions on an amateur personality analysis	"You'll have a hard time. You're too shy."	"In what ways do you think I'm 'too shy'?" (Ask for clarification of of the analysis.)
		"You're entitled to your opinion — but I think I can do it." (Indicate that you feel capable of judging your own strengths.)

RECORDING YOUR PUT-DOWN SENTENCES

Put-down sentence   *What you could say next time*

_____   _____

_____   _____

_____   _____

_____   _____

_____   _____

You may want to record put-down sentences said to you (and others) by using a pack of 3 × 5 cards which you carry in a pocket or purse. During a week you may encounter several put-down sentences. If you can't write an assertive (not aggressive) reply, ask others to help you. Parents find this an easy way to teach their children to assert themselves appropriately and positively.

EXERCISE 2. ACTIVE LOOKING

It's instructive to try observing what another person really looks like and how he or she reacts to you. Most people think they look directly at other people, but usually they don't. For example, on entering a public place they glance quickly toward a person ("Is this someone I know? Will we need to speak?") and thereafter they do not focus directly on that person unless there is a clear desire to initiate conversation. Of course, you do not want to stare fixedly at others; this makes most people uncomfortable. But there is a middle ground. In active looking, which you try in this exercise, you maintain a pleasant expression while you take a series of three- to five-second "snapshots" with your eyes, focusing on different spots on the other person's face.

Suggestions. Try going to a restaurant with a friend who would like to do the exercise with you and share the results. As you wait to be seated or as you walk to your table, deliberately look pleasantly at one or two people and note what you see and how you feel while you are looking. Exchange your observations with your friend. If you prefer, you could choose another setting (say, a zoo or park) or you could try it by yourself.

As an instructive variation, try smiling and looking cheerful, as though you want to convey some great delight to others. This exercise will make you aware of your facial expression and how it affects others. Don't worry now about the unnaturalness of trying to look pleasant. This is only an

PRACTICING ACTIVE LOOKING

experiment for you to observe how your looking and smiling behavior affects the way *you* feel and the way *others* react. People who try it usually get a happy lift from this simple exercise.

Example. Here's what Hattie recorded after actively looking at someone on her lunch break:

1. What were the physical characteristics of this person? *He had wavy, brown hair, well-kept. He was about 30, about 6 feet tall, 185 lbs.*

2. What was this person wearing? *He wore a plaid sports coat of muted browns, a yellow sports shirt without tie, dark brown slacks, unpolished shoes.*

3. What physical reactions were associated with your feelings when you looked at him or he looked at you? Check your reactions:

    __ "butterflies in the stomach"   ✓ tingling sensations
    ✓ blushing   __ tremors
    __ dizziness   __ weak knees
    __ dry mouth   __ others (specify below):
    __ fatigue
    __ heart pounding   _____
    __ perspiration
                                  _____

4. What did he do when he noticed you were looking at him? *He looked away momentarily but he looked at me again — and smiled!*

5. What did you do when he looked at you? *I kept on looking and smiled, too. Then I turned to leave. I felt good, and I think he did, too.*

RECORDING YOUR ACTIVE LOOKING

1. What were the physical characteristics of this person?

_____

2. What was the person wearing?

_____

3. What physical reactions were associated with your feelings when you looked at him or when he looked at you? Check your reactions:

___ "butterflies in the stomach"   ___ tingling sensations
___ blushing   ___ tremors
___ dizziness   ___ weak knees
___ dry mouth   ___ others (specify below):
___ fatigue
___ heart pounding   _____
___ perspiration   _____

4. What did he do when he noticed you were looking at him?

_____

5. What did you do when he looked at you?

_____

6. Did you catch yourself looking down or away from people? Notice whether you avoid eye contact with others.

_____

7. Did looking pleasant change your feelings and attitude? If so, how?

_____

EXERCISE 3. INITIATING GREETING-TALK

Although most of us would like to be friendly, we often avoid public socializing because we fear we'll be rebuffed as "prying" or "nosey." See what happens if you try greeting strangers in safe but public places. Smile, too, as you open the conversation.

Suggestions. You could strike up a conversation with the person standing near you in a line waiting at the bus, supermarket, or movie. You can use any of the following conversational openers.

- Notice an item you can ask a question about. "I have never tried that product. Do you recommend it?" or "I see you're buying artichokes. How do you cook them?"
- Refer to a common experience. "This item cost 10 cents last month. Do you think inflation will ever stop?" or "This line makes a long wait. Next time I'll bring my sleeping bag!"
- Express a positive feeling about the efficiency, cleanliness, or originality of the people or the setting. "What a beautiful store!" or "I like to shop here! The salespeople are so helpful." or "I think it's a glorious day! This is the kind of day that makes me want to climb mountains."

Example. Peter tried the Greeting-Talk Exercise at a grocery where he often shopped.

1. Where did you practice greeting-talk? *At a fresh fruit and vegetable stand.*
2. With whom? *Woman behind me.*
3. What did you say? *"I noticed endive in your basket. I've often wondered how to prepare them. Do you have a special way to use them?"*
4. What did the other person say? *She seemed pleased to tell me she used them as "boats" to hold cold shrimp hors d'oeuvres.*
5. What were your reactions to performing the greeting? How did you feel about yourself? *I was slightly embarrassed but then got genuinely curious. I felt slightly tense at first, but was very relieved when the woman reacted warmly to my question.*

RECORDING YOUR GREETING-TALK

1. Where did you practice greeting-talk?

_____

2. With whom?

_____

3. What did you say?

_____

_____

_____

4. What did the other person say?

_____

_____

_____

5. What were your reactions to performing the greeting? How did you feel about yourself?

_____

_____

EXERCISE 4. GIVING AND ACCEPTING
GENUINE COMPLIMENTS

Rewarding other people is a way to say you value their friendship, enjoy their company, and want to make them happy. One way people reward each other is with compliments. Unfortunately, people often fail to reinforce someone who gives them a genuine compliment. False modesty may impel us to disagree with the compliment, so we unthinkingly punish our complimenter and belittle his or her judgment. This exercise can help you accept genuine compliments and reward your complimenter. If you agree, tell your complimenter "Thank you for noticing and telling me." If you disagree, you could qualify your answer but still thank your complimenter.

You may also need to learn how to *give* compliments. People often unwittingly give "double-edged compliments" that nullify each other. Examples: "This cake tastes good. Is it a box cake?" or "Your eyelashes are beautiful! Are they false?" or "Your hair looks nice. Is it a wig?" In each case the tag question ruins the opening compliment. Avoid such double-edged compliments. Learning to give and accept genuine compliments is a way to show others that we care about them.

Suggestions. You can make a point of complimenting someone you see often. Remember to give an open, honest compliment, with sincere enthusiasm. Don't put a "double edge" on it.

Example. Al wanted to learn how to express positive feelings, so he looked for opportunities to practice.

Compliments I made	*Other person's reply*
"Carol, those warm earth colors suit you beautifully."	"Thank you. I feel very much at home in these colors."
To a short-order cook: "This has got to be the best taco in town!"	"We try harder." (I replied: "It shows")
Compliments paid to me:	*My reply:*
"You are looking very well."	"Thank you. I feel great, too."
"You get a lot done."	I avoided my usual remark which is "Not enough though," and said, "Thanks! And I enjoy it!"

RECORDING HOW YOU GIVE AND ACCEPT COMPLIMENTS

Compliments you made   *The person's reply*

_____   _____

_____   _____

_____   _____

_____   _____

_____   _____

_____   _____

Compliments paid to you   *Your reply*

_____   _____

_____   _____

_____   _____

_____   _____

_____   _____

EXERCISE 5. ASKING FOR CLARIFICATION

Often we are uncertain how to interpret someone's remarks about us. We're not exactly sure of what was said, but we do know that the remarks made us feel uneasy. In this exercise, you can learn to ask others to clarify their puzzling statements. Amazingly, many Downers will hint at an aggressive message but become embarrassed if they are asked to "put their cards on the table" and say exactly what they mean. Although feedback from a reliable critic can be important for your growth, often critics are uninformed and unable to support their opinions of you. Asking clarifying questions is one way to decide what the person meant and whether this is a valid observation. Assertive people can take and use criticism to change themselves when it is appropriate.

Suggestions. Make a list of negative, enigmatic statements that have made you feel uneasy, and write a clarifying question you could have asked the person. Practice your clarifying questions aloud. Hear yourself asking the clarifying question; simply thinking it over won't convince you that you can speak it.

Example. Helen felt she "swallowed" too many accusations, not knowing what others meant. She set out to learn the skill of asking clarifying questions to reduce her anxiety and gain important information.

Negative statements said to me	*Question I asked to get clarification*
"You sure are defensive."	"I'm not clear what you mean by 'defensive.' In what ways is my behavior 'defensive'?"
"You sure get 'cold feet.'"	"What do you mean 'cold feet'?"
"You make mountains out of molehills."	"That may be easy to say but it does not tell me what you mean. How am I 'making a mountain out of a molehill'?"

RECORDING YOUR CLARIFYING QUESTIONS

Negative statements said to you	*Clarifying question you asked (or could have asked)*
_____	_____
_____	_____
_____	_____
_____	_____
_____	_____
_____	_____

EXERCISE 6. REQUESTING HELP

Do you feel overworked and want others to help you? Can you request help without feeling guilty, fearful, or angry? An important assertive behavior concerns requesting help when you feel overworked. To get results from your request, know what kind of help the other person can reasonably give.

Suggestions. Decide which jobs have been picked up incidentally by you. They could just as well be done by another family member or fellow employee. Why do you have to do them? Make a chart indicating the time each job requires and how you could use that time for some activity you like. Then write a simple sentence asking for help with one small job the other person can easily and reasonably do. Rehearse the request aloud first. Finally, ask the person for help when he is most likely to say yes.

Example. Emily, a working mother, felt rushed to death. She decided to ask for help in an assertive way.

SCHEDULE FOR REQUESTING HELP

Jobs I can ask my family to do	Time saved	How I can use this time
Set the dinner table, fill water glasses and bread basket.	10 minutes	I'll turn on my relaxation tape after supper for 35 minutes and rest an extra 15 minutes every night: Total 50 minutes
Clean up after supper.	20 minutes	
Empty the dishwasher.	10 minutes	
Set the table for breakfast.	<u>10 minutes</u>	
	50 minutes	

What sentence did you write requesting help with a job? *"Jane, there are too many jobs at supper time and I need everyone's help. Here are the jobs I feel I need help with. Could I count on you to do one of them every night?" (I practiced this request aloud several times, pretending I was saying it to Jane.)*

When will the person be most agreeable? *Jane is a teenager whose most agreeable time is Saturday afternoon, so I'll ask her then, instead of when I'm so angry I can't think.*

RECORDING HOW YOU WILL REQUEST HELP

Jobs you can request help with	Time saved	How you'll use this time
_____		_____
_____	_____	_____
_____		_____
_____	_____	_____
_____		_____
_____	_____	_____

Whom will you ask? *To do which job?*   *What will you say?*

_____ _____ _____

_____

_____

When will be the best time to ask? _____

_____

EXERCISE 7. SPEAKING UP FOR YOUR REASONABLE RIGHTS

Do you endure discomforts because you are afraid to assert yourself in public? Are you afraid you will be called a complainer or troublemaker? Do you worry that people will stare at you with disapproval? This exercise can help you overcome excessive inhibitions in public situations requiring assertiveness.

Suggestions. Record instances when you felt some public discomfort. Perhaps someone pushed you, stepped on your toe, made you wait, or asked you to do an onerous task which you thought was unreasonable. Remember those bad scenes and write an assertive response to them. Rehearse your assertive answer aloud several times. Use a mirror to monitor yourself as you practice.

Example. Julie felt guilty because she thought her irritation over small matters was unreasonable. Writing them down and sharing with others helped her realize she was not petty but had a right to express herself on these matters.

Public discomforts I have known:	*What I said (or will say next time):*
Someone pushed in line ahead of me.	"I was first and deserve to be served first."
Someone turned up his radio to hear another ballgame at the local baseball park.	"Please turn down your radio. It is interfering with my enjoyment of this game."
A local bike repairman refused to serve me for a while because he was "too busy" unloading bikes: "Go out and shop, lady, and come back in an hour." (He had 3 helpers unloading bikes.)	"I have no shopping to do in the next 30 minutes, and I need to pick up my repaired bike now. Please help me."

I had a small growth removed from my skin. After the minor surgery, I was asked to carry the tissue in a plastic cup to the receptionist's desk, and stand in line to turn it in for lab tests. I felt strongly that this embarrassing task should not be done by me while I was still upset from the surgery.

"I'm upset by the surgery. I don't think a distraught patient should have to do this, and so I'm leaving the tissue cup here."

RECORDING YOUR PUBLIC DISCOMFORTS AND YOUR ASSERTIVE ANSWERS

Public discomforts you have experienced

What you could have said assertively

_____   _____

_____   _____

_____   _____

_____   _____

_____   _____

_____   _____

_____   _____

EXERCISE 8. PARTICIPATING IN CONVERSATIONS

Do you have trouble conversing? Do you sit in uncomfortable silence as others carry the conversation with ease? The following exercises can make your interactions easier.

Suggestions. Find appropriate ways of turning the conversation to your subject; prepare to relate an experience or deliver an opinion.

Activity 1. Telling about an experience. Decide what has been your funniest (or saddest, or most meaningful) experience in the past week, month, or ever. Tell the story to yourself aloud. Do this in the privacy of your bedroom or car as you drive. Relive the hilarity (or other emotion) of the story by exaggerating the events with your voice, facial expressions, and gestures. If you wish, use a tape recorder to record your story; use a mirror to evaluate your facial expressions and gestures. Try to improve your delivery. When you can readily tell the story to yourself, tell the story to a friend you feel comfortable with. At first limit your audience to one person. Some people tell their story to a stranger on a bus or plane. With strangers, you may feel less inhibited, able to let go and adopt a new identity. Next, decide how you will introduce your story in a familiar group, how you will get in your first word during a conversational lull. You can begin by saying something like, "Last night I thought about something I hadn't remembered for years. It happened . . ." and go on with your story.

Example. Ted wanted to dwell on happier times. He decided this exercise would help him accomplish his goal.

1. What experience do you want to tell someone about? *My first success story.*
2. When will you practice saying the story to yourself? *While shaving in the morning.*
3. Will you tell this story to a friend or stranger? *My car pool partner.*
4. What words will you use to introduce the story? *"I often think folks think only of their failures. I've decided to remember some of my successes. Last night I thought of one I'd nearly forgotten . . ."*
5. What happened when you told your story? How did you feel? How did the person react to your story? *He started telling me about his own success story! We decided to share at least one success a week — either past or present.*

RECORDING THE PERSONAL EXPERIENCE
YOU COULD TELL ABOUT

1. What experience do you want to tell someone about?

   _____

2. When will you practice saying the story to yourself?

   _____

3. Will you tell this story to a friend or stranger?

   _____

4. What words will you use to introduce the story?

   _____

5. What happened when you told your story? How did you feel? How did the person react to your story?

   _____

   _____

   _____

Activity 2. Developing an opinion. To contribute to conversations, you need to prepare informed opinions. Get in the habit of reading newspapers or weekly news magazines to inform yourself about current events. More important, as you read or listen, pose questions and draw conclusions about what you learn. When friends or co-workers are expressing their opinions about the events of the week, decide what you believe and encourage yourself to speak up.

Example. Jimmy felt left out during mealtimes at his dorm. He determined to form some opinions of his own.

Personally interesting facts I have gathered	*Conclusions I'm willing to make*
X has won in the same crucial primaries as Y did in 1972.	I think X will win the nomination because Y did.
On the average only 38% of the students vote.	I bet only 30% will turn out for this election.

RECORDING THE OPINIONS YOU COULD CONTRIBUTE

Personally interesting facts you have gathered	*Personal conclusions you are willing to make*
_____	_____
_____	_____
_____	_____
_____	_____
_____	_____

Rehearse these several times aloud in preparation for using them at the next opportunity. Extend this list and update your topics list periodically.

EXERCISE 9. USING BODY LANGUAGE THAT SAYS YES OR NO WHEN NECESSARY

To become assertive, you must be aware of what messages your body is in the habit of sending. We often convey fear, worry, sadness, elation, surprise, and suspicion by facial expressions and body movements. Body language has an impact on others, and the activities described in this exercise can help you become more aware of that impact.

Suggestions. To study your body language, observe what your body is doing and what effect your posture, movements, gestures, and facial expressions have on people you talk to. Read both exercises before practicing and recording your experiences. The experiments can be done with the same person or different ones.

Activity 1. Body language that says yes. To see how your body language influences another person's behavior, first agree with someone actively. Look at the person directly and smile, lean forward, and make positive remarks like, "Yes, I see," "Hey, that's interesting," "Right," or "Um-hmm." Record what you do and what reactions you provoke. It is important to choose a conversation which is not heated or crucial to your relationship with another. Also, choose someone who would be receptive to discussing body language.

Example

1. Describe briefly the setting (with whom? when? where?) *My boyfriend was telling me about his weekend river raft trip.*

2. Describe your body language: What did the other person do?
   I looked at him.   *He hardly took his eyes off me.*
   I nodded.   *He became more animated.*
   I smiled.   *He smiled the whole time.*
   I leaned forward.   *He leaned forward and took my hand.*

3. How did you feel about deliberately sending positive signals? *"I felt a little deceptive at first, but I began to get really interested in his story. I really got caught up in it because I had to listen so I would nod and exclaim Wow! at the right times. When I've listened to his stories before, I've never become so interested as I was this time when I actively listened!"*

RECORDING YOUR EXPERIENCE WITH "YES" BODY LANGUAGE

1. Describe briefly the setting (with whom? where? when?):

   _____

2. Describe your body language: What did the other person do?

   _____   _____

   _____   _____

   _____   _____

3. How did you feel about deliberately sending positive signals?

   _____

   _____

Activity 2. Body language that says no.

Example

1. Describe briefly the setting (with whom? when? where?) *My boyfriend was trying to convince me to ride the rapids of a local river with him the next weekend. Usually, I would go along with his adventures because I didn't want him to think I am a coward. This time I wanted to say no so I tried to show him my feelings with an expressive face and body.*

2. Describe your body language:

Describe your body language:	What did the other person do?
I looked away often, distracted, fidgeting.	*He talked louder to me.*
I kept myself from smiling.	*He didn't smile and he seemed to be getting angrier.*
I shook my head sideways.	*He came back with another reason why I should go.*
I shuffled my feet (restless activity) and slouched.	*He noticed and said, "You aren't interested."*

3. How did you feel about deliberately sending these negative signals? *I felt more uncomfortable than I did during the first experiment where I showed positive body language. I believe I could use more effective ways of saying no to another person's request, but negative body language sure turns people off. I also learned that sometimes when I say no the message is confused because my body language isn't saying no, too. I need to make sure my words and body language say the same thing, both yes or both no. When my words and body language were out of step, my boyfriend didn't know what to think.*

4. What happened when you explained the purpose of these body language exercises to the other person? *We discussed how our body language could show what our words meant. We also discussed how body language, without words, conveys our opinion of a person. To improve our communication, we agreed to question one another when unclear about the meaning of a particular gesture, facial expression, or posture.*

RECORDING YOUR EXPERIENCE WITH "NO" BODY LANGUAGE

1. Describe briefly the setting (with whom? where? when?):

_____

_____

2. Describe your body language: What did the other person do?

_____   _____

_____   _____

_____   _____

3. How did you feel about deliberately sending negative signals?

_____

_____

4. What happened when you shared the purpose of these body language exercises?

_____

_____

_____

EXERCISE 10. STOPPING SELF-JUSTIFICATION

Passive people often feel they have to justify with rational arguments every opinion and statement they make. When someone questions or criticizes them, they either shrink away or feel compelled to defend themselves with lengthy reasons. Although reason giving is a valuable educational practice, it has limited value in interpersonal relations. In interpersonal relations, feelings and rights are every bit as important as are reasons. We think you have a right to say, "Because I just feel that way" as your ultimate reason. You can use such final "feeling statements" to discourage debate, to stop a Downer who is making you feel defenseless with "why-why-why" questions. To answer a charge against you, you could defend yourself with a simple denial — for example, to the accusation that you are too sensitive, you could simply reply, "I don't think so," or "That's your feeling, not mine." To the demand that you justify your feelings, you could answer, "That is the way I feel about the matter, and I don't have to keep supplying you with reasons."

Suggestions. Identify the stock words which upset you, which set off your anger or defensiveness. Next, develop some one-line statements which show you will not argue the opinion or feeling which is being attacked or challenged. Then rehearse these one-liners aloud several times until they become part of your verbal habits.

Example

Sentences that seem to require justifying an opinion or feeling	Assertive answer
"You sure are bossy!"	"That may be, but the problem we are facing now is how we will share the work around here. Let's talk about that."
Someone challenges every point I'm trying to make by repeatedly asking, "But why is that idea important? I don't understand the significance of that idea."	"I really haven't thought of all the reasons I think this idea is important. But I think it's interesting and for that reason, worth pursuing."

RECORDING SITUATIONS WHERE YOU FELT COMPELLED
TO JUSTIFY YOUR OPINIONS OR FEELINGS

*Sentences that seemed to require
justifying an opinion or feeling*

Assertive answers

_____   _____

_____   _____

_____   _____

_____   _____

_____   _____

Are there any situations in which you might reasonably ask people to justify their opinions or feelings about you? If so, when? What would you say?

_____

_____

_____

EXERCISE 11. USING EXPRESSIVE TALK
TO SHOW FEELINGS

Shy people rarely speak with much expression regarding their feelings. Because of this, they appear to be dull and uninteresting. Consequently, they have difficulty making friends. Friendship tends to develop by mutual self-disclosures — by accepting and rewarding self-disclosing information given by the other person and by giving similar information about yourself. This self-information consists largely of statements about your life history and goals as well as your opinions, thoughts, and feelings. Because shy people often do not know how to express feelings, they are sometimes misidentified as "aloof," "stuck-up," or "cold." To become assertive (less shy) you can practice expressing your feelings openly more often. This is important in developing an interesting personality. This exercise can help your expressiveness.

Suggestions. Make a list of feelings or emotional experiences you have had in the past few days but have not expressed to anyone. Think in terms of your reactions to events: How did you feel when you got up this morning? How did you feel while driving to work? While reading the paper? While watching that movie or television program? Then write sentences you could have said to express those feelings, and rehearse your sentences aloud. Try for an expressive tone in your voice quality. Vary the pitch, pace, and loudness of your voice. Try to sound "lively." Use a tape recorder to check out the expressiveness of your voice. Do you sound interesting to *you*? . . . When you are ready, decide that tomorrow you can tell an acquaintance how you feel at least two times during the day. On the next day encourage yourself to make three "feeling expressions." Continue to speak up, gradually increasing your expressions over the next week or so. Talk to those people who would be most interested in hearing about your feelings. Talk to them at a time and place which are appropriate for expressing feelings. Record how you felt, what you said about it, and what response the other person made to you.

Example. Howard was feeling squelched. He had grown up with the idea that he was a man of few words but many thoughts. He decided he would practice saying a few of those thoughts and express his feelings.

Feelings I have experienced in the last few days	*How I could express my feelings*
Relief	"I am relieved to have my income tax completed!" (to my car pool)
Hunger	"I smell something delicious. I'm starving for those stuffed pork chops." (to my spouse)
Depression	"I'm really feeling lousy tonight." (to my son)
Disappointment	"I'm really disappointed I missed your school program." (to daughter)
Excitement and anticipation	"I enjoy our lunches together." (to a friend)

When you rehearsed the expressive sentences aloud, what did you notice about your voice or actions? *I actually sighed with relief as I said, "I am relieved to . . ." I sniffed the air as I smelled the porkchops! I sounded tired when I told about my depression.*

RECORDING YOUR FEELINGS AND DECIDING HOW YOU WOULD EXPRESS THEM

Feelings you have experienced in the past few days	*How you could express those feelings and to whom*

Rehearse these expressive sentences aloud. Tape record yourself if possible. Does your voice convey different feelings? Try out some "feeling expressions" in conversation and record the results.

What were your feelings today?	*What did you say to express those feelings? How did your listener respond?*

This is an exercise that can be carried out every day so long as it interests you. It is one of the best exercises to share with a buddy.

CONCLUSION

In this chapter, you have taken some small steps along the road to assertiveness. Hopefully, you have carried out most of these exercises successfully and thus acquired some assertive skills. Continue to practice these skills whenever you can, using whatever variations and elaborations help you develop your assertive personality. When practicing in public, keep in mind what is socially appropriate: you don't want to overdo acts like complimenting someone, smiling, looking someone in the eye. But — since nonassertive people usually don't do enough of these things — you could probably do them more often than you have usually done in the past.

Remember, record your assertive behaviors and your rehearsals in your logbook. Reward yourself in some way for practicing your assertive skills. Do something you enjoy after you finish an exercise. Also, bask in the glory of your improved self-esteem as you notice how you can better control yourself and your life by your assertiveness.

5

DESC Scripting:
A New Approach for
Dealing with Conflicts

*Speaking without thinking
is like shooting without aiming.*

OLD PROVERB

In this chapter, we will introduce a new approach for dealing with interpersonal conflicts. Using this approach, called DESC scripting, you can learn to analyze conflicts, determine your needs and rights, propose a resolution to the conflict, and, if necessary, negotiate a contract for change with your Downer. In other words, you'll be preparing to SPEAK UP, to do something about the commitment you made at the end of Chapter 1.

NEGOTIATING FOR POSITIVE CHANGES

In conflicts with other people, you basically have three options: you can knuckle under, you can fight, or you can negotiate a satisfactory resolution. Since you're reading this book, you're probably tired of knuckling under, of subordinating your rights and interests to those of your Downers. On the other hand, if you're like most people, you don't enjoy fighting. Fighting is almost always fruitless because it usually upsets relationships and creates more problems. So the best alternative is negotiation. We recommend that you try negotiating solutions to interpersonal conflicts in more areas of your life, not only with overbearing mates, relatives, and friends, but also with children, bosses, co-workers, neighbors, and even businesses.

Negotiation is a process by which conflicting parties (people, companies, or governments) arrive at an agreement stipulating what specific "actions" each will perform in return for what specific "goods and services." A familiar example of negotiation is the haggling between a buyer and seller over the price of an item such as a used car, a house, or jewelry at a craft fair.

Consider Sam's selling his old truck to Joe. In negotiation, the parties have partly complementary and partly conflicting goals. The complementary goals for Joe and Sam are that Joe wants to buy a used pickup truck and Sam wants to get rid of one. But Joe and Sam also have conflicting goals: Sam wants as much money as possible for his old truck whereas Joe wants to pay as little as possible. In negotiating over the price, each makes offers and counteroffers, but both are kept going by the desire to reach an agreement. In the process, both Joe and Sam give up a little so that a mutually satisfactory exchange can be made.

The outcome of a successful negotiation is an agreement or contract. (See "Rules of Contracting" in Appendix C.) You agree to give the other person some reward in return for performing the action specified in the contract. Thus, Joe agrees to pay Sam $400 for his truck. Contracts have the general form: "If you do X (or stop doing Y), I will give you Z." For example, "If you study more, I'll buy you a radio," or "If you clean the aquarium, I'll iron your shirts," or "If you give me your truck, I'll give you $400."

A form of negotiation can be used in adjusting interpersonal relations and resolving conflicts. If a friend consistently takes advantage of you, we think you have a right to negotiate with him to change his behavior. As things stand, he is getting more "goods and services" from you than you are getting from him. You negotiate by asking him either to do more for you (for example, to pay for gas when he borrows your car) or to reduce his demands on your time, energy, and possessions (for example, to stop borrowing things from you).

Negotiating is not deceitful, manipulative, or artificial. Many problems arise because a person's immediate, natural reaction to a stressful situation can lead to unhappy consequences. With negotiating skills, you can plan to equalize your balance of social power. This, in turn, makes you a more assertive and effective person. Also, negotiating helps you be more open about what you want from other people and what you see happening in a given conflict. This open communication builds a mutuality of concern among friends and often serves to avoid conflicts altogether.

WHY WRITE SCRIPTS?

The first step in learning how to negotiate effectively is to analyze and "rewrite" your recurring bad scenes. This process will lead you to writing your own scripts for approaching interpersonal conflicts effectively.

Consider your bad scenes for a few minutes — concentrate especially on the ones that occur over and over, leaving you feeling inadequate and dissatisfied. Analyze each put-down situation as though you were watching a scene from a play. Your scene has each of the following.

Characters You and at least one other person, your Downer.

Plot You want certain goals, as does your Downer. Some conflict arises, leading to actions that frustrate, humiliate, or frighten you. Threats, insults, may be exchanged. The scene ends in your "defeat," with you feeling angry, upset, and ineffectual.

Setting The time and place where the scene typically occurs.

Script (message) The lines your Downer speaks and to which you would like to reply assertively. The script also includes the "body language" of the actors — the forcefulness of the voice, facial expression, shoulder shrugs, hand gestures, carriage of the body.

Most of us have little difficulty remembering our really bad scenes in these terms. We go over them repeatedly in memory, replaying the dialog, the insults, the threats, and the bad feelings. We scold ourselves for our bungled replies, and make up devastating comebacks as we nurse our bruised egos.

We recommend that you think through and rewrite the scripts of your bad scenes, much as a playwright would write and revise a scene to achieve the goal he intended in his overall dramatic plan. By writing a script, you devise an action plan for the future and a way to negotiate a change in your Downer's behavior (and possibly yours too!) in that put-down scene or a similar one. The script props you up and promotes self-assurance.

Planning is the key; members of a labor negotiating team would never enter a bargaining session without a detailed plan — an imaginary "script" — spelling out their objectives, what proposals they intended to make in what order, what they expected the opposition to do, what counteroffers they expected to make in response, and so on. Although asserting yourself is not as formal as labor negotiations, it needs just as much preparation if you want it to work.

There are additional reasons for writing an assertive script:

- Writing out your script gives you some small concrete task as a starting point toward assertion.

- Writing out your script forces you to clarify the situation and define your needs; you stop and think objectively about your actions.

- A script gives you confidence in handling the next confrontation assertively because you know what your "considered proposals" are going to be. You avoid stupid, thoughtless outbursts you will later regret.

- Because you might often say things in a self-defeating way, it is important that you plan out the right words which will express exactly what you want. By reading and revising your lines you can hit upon the intended message with just the right balance. You have a written record of your planned message which you can review for its effectiveness instead of relying on your memory.

- For maximum effect an assertive message must be delivered in a forceful voice and with affirmative body language. A well-planned and well-rehearsed assertive message is a major antidote to "stage fright" in the put-down situation. The best way to practice voice tone, phrasing, and gestures is by repeatedly going over a known set of lines you will say to your Downer.

Scripting a scene is itself a new kind of behavior. It is a concrete way to take responsibility for the quality of your relations with others. Nonassertive people function as passive or aggressive reactors to situations that others develop around them. By working on an assertive script you can become an actor, not just a reactor, and can gain some self-determination and control over the outcomes of your interactions with others.

DESC SCRIPTS

Sharon has developed a four-step program called DESC which enables people to write successful assertive scripts. It has been field-tested successfully with many hundreds of individuals. In this method, you can organize a script around specific questions about your conflict. Take a minute now and think about your problem situation from Worksheet #3, page 21. Ask yourself these questions about that conflict:

- What unwanted behavior has my Downer been displaying? (DESCRIBE)
- How can I tell my Downer the way I feel about this behavior? (EXPRESS)
- What behavioral changes might I contract for? Also, what might I need to change in my behavior (SPECIFY)
- What rewarding consequences can I provide to my Downer for sticking to the contract? (CONSEQUENCES)

The acronym DESC (pronounced desk) abbreviates the four key phrases — DESCRIBE, EXPRESS, SPECIFY, CONSEQUENCES. You describe the offensive behavior objectively to your Downer, express how you feel about that behavior, specify how you would like to see that behavior changed, and spell out the consequences of such a change.

The DESC components provide the main lines of an assertive script for your problem scene. It is not always necessary to say the entire DESC script. In Chapter 7, we discuss abbreviated scripts for those occasions when a short assertive message will do the job.

Let's look more closely now at each phase of the DESC script.

Your DESCRIBE Lines

You begin your script by describing to your Downer the exact behavior you find bothersome. Be as objective and specific as possible. People generally are not in the habit of describing another's behavior objectively. They tend only to label its emotional impact on themselves or to infer possible motives behind the act. Avoid this "psychoanalyzing" because it provokes

people. Instead, use simple, concrete terms to describe your Downer's behavior so the person will have little basis for quarreling with you at this point. Don't accuse him or her of bad faith; avoid guessing at motives. You can't know another person's motives, and such accusations only open you to denials and counterarguments. Avoid vague terms such as "You're *ignoring* me"; use specific terms such as "You *don't look at me* when I talk to you." Avoid "all time" generalizations such as "You're *always nagging* me"; rather, cite specific times and actions, for example, *"The last four times* we discussed balancing the checkbook, you *criticized the way I keep records."*

Before saying your DESCRIBE line, you should ease your way into the script with "slide-ins" such as "I would like to discuss a matter with you now" or "Are you aware that . . .?" or "I've noticed that . . ." You can develop your own slide-ins which will prepare your Downer for the directness of your DESCRIBE lines. The slide-in should help you get the attention of your Downer and set the tone of your assertive message.

Your EXPRESS Lines

Express what you feel and think about your Downer's offensive behavior (just described) in the specific situation. Select the exact words to tell your Downer what your reactions are when the behavior occurs, and make sure you acknowledge squarely that these are *your* feelings. You can signal emotional expressions by words like "I feel . . ." or "I have the feeling that . . .," and statements about your personal beliefs or values by "I believe that . . ." or "I think that . . ." When you hope to negotiate a problem, aim for objective clarity and moderation rather than an emotional outburst or crushing sarcasm. Avoid hurting your Downer or provoking feelings of guilt.

Whenever possible, express your feelings about offensive behavior from a positive rather than a negative perspective. Negative expressions state your dislike, as in "I hate you when you do that," "You make me angry," "You make me feel insecure and unloved," or You're insensitive and overbearing." Though you may have such negative reactions to your Downer's put-down behaviors, you can be more effective if you focus on the common goals and the shortcomings of the interaction, rather than your hatreds. Goal oriented statements might be, "I think that your behavior and my reaction to it are preventing us from having a pleasant relationship," or "I feel insignificant and diminished when you criticize me so often." A discussion leader might cut off digressions from group members by saying, "I feel uneasy when we stray off the subject, particularly when I feel responsible for moving through our agenda," or "I think those remarks lead us away from the problem immediately before us." A shy man being "lectured" by a friend might express his feelings by saying, "I feel stifled when I can't get my two cents in and I think our meetings would be more fun if we had more two-way exchanges, where we each contributed equally." A teenager might express his feelings toward an overbearing parent by saying, "I feel frustrated and think I would mature faster if I were allowed to make more of my own decisions."

Such feeling-statements appear not as a hostile attack but as a suggestion that the combination of the Downer's behavior and your reaction to it is preventing your relationship from achieving mutual goals. Positive feeling-expressions thus stand a chance of being heard sympathetically instead of being denied and or inviting counterattack.

Long-standing friends tend to settle into a small set of shopworn "feeling" words like *hate, resent, miserable, embarrassed, angry,* or *frustrated.* By overuse, these become hackneyed, lifeless. You might try new ways to express your feelings, using metaphors or describing the concrete aspects of your emotional reactions. Thus you might express embarrassment by the metaphor "I feel naked and exposed," or express conflict by "I feel my head spinning in two directions at once." Striking metaphors may produce a greater impact than the accustomed "emotional words" that have been worn out in your interchanges with others.

Your SPECIFY Lines

After describing your Downer's offensive behavior and expressing your feelings and/or thoughts about it, the third step is to ask explicitly for a different, specified behavior. Essentially, you ask, "Please stop doing X and start doing Y instead." Research shows that such requests are most likely to be accepted and adhered to if there are only a few of them at any one time. Best results happen with only one request. The request should be concrete and specific, and the language should refer to objective responses rather than personality traits or attitudes. Say "Please stop playing your electric guitar at 7 a.m. Sunday mornings," instead of "Stop being so inconsiderate." "Please take back this defective radio," instead of "Why don't you stop ripping off consumers?"

The request must be reasonable and within the power of the other person to meet. The wife of a pauper cannot demand a new fur coat; a child cannot demand total freedom from parental authority and responsibility. Because your appeal relies partly upon a charge of injustice and unfairness in your Downer's dealings with you, you lose that advantage if you make unrealistic and unfair demands. Even if your request is not unjust it may be unreasonable because it is too large a job or too much behavior change to ask for initially. If you wish large changes in your Downer's behavior, approach it by a series of smaller agreements over time.

Remember also that contracts often specify new behaviors for *both* parties. There may be aspects of your behavior in the problem situation that your Downer wants you to change. Successful negotiations involve some give and take; you come to agree "If you do *this* for me, then I'll do *that* for you." So analyze your behavior in the problem situation to see whether there is something your Downer might ask you to change. How difficult would it be for you to modify that behavior? The better prepared you are for such counterrequests, the better able you will be to negotiate effectively.

If your Downer asks you to change something which you like very much ("stop smoking cigars"), then you have to talk over the relative costs and benefits of the exchange. Is getting her to go to movies more often worth giving up that after-dinner cigar? Is his help with the dishes worth letting him watch the TV football game of the week without your criticism? There are no hard and fast rules for assigning "value." That is why the two parties talk honestly about their needs, the magnitude of the "bothers" versus the "pleasures" of particular activities mentioned in the exchange. Hopefully, you can work out an equitable contract or exchange. Some specific rules for contracting are summarized in Appendix C.

Your CONSEQUENCES Lines

Contractual agreements spell out the consequences (payoffs and penalties) to both parties if they do or do not live up to the terms of the contract. The agreement spells out concretely and simply the reward your Downer gets for abiding by the contract and/or the penalty for breaking it.

Rewards. Rewards are not just material things like money, candy, mink coats, or trips to Disneyland. Such material rewards are small in number compared to the vast array of "social rewards" we give to others. There are hundreds of small ways we give affection or approval or show our appreciation for another — touching, hugging, kissing, making complimentary remarks about that person's appearance, intelligence, or personality. Many social rewards consist of allowing someone to engage in an enjoyable activity — letting a child watch a television program, a teenager practice his electric guitar at full amplification, a spouse go out to a movie alone, or an elderly person talk to an attentive listener about her earlier life. Although we do not think of such small acts as rewards, they are very powerful motivators to bring about behavior changes in those around us.

Often the only reward in a contract is simply "I will feel better" if the Downer stops some annoying behavior. We do this all the time with such statements as, "I'd be pleased if you would stop doing X (or start doing Y)." This promise of a mild social reward derives its sole power from the Downer's wanting to please you. A man will stop smoking a cigar at the dinner table if it annoys his honored guests; a woman will stop wearing false eyelashes if it annoys her cherished mate. Such small favors are exchanged all the time.

Punishments. Social punishments exist in great supply and we all use them frequently. We punish by ignoring or criticizing someone, by showing indifference or boredom, by going against someone's wishes, by devaluing something or someone the other person likes, by making insulting remarks about the person's appearance, and by attacking, ridiculing, or humiliating the person. A common form of punishment is withholding privileges or denying permission to do something. For instance, parents punish children by sending them to their rooms, by reducing their TV viewing time, or by not letting them play with their friends.

Emphasize the Positive Consequences. In contracting, you are more likely to succeed by emphasizing the positive, rewarding consequences for the desired behavior than by dwelling on the negative consequences for undesirable behavior. The punishment for breaking a contract need not always be spelled out. Implicit in the statement "If you help me, I will bake you a cake" is the implication that "If you don't help me, then I won't bake it for you." Loss of a hoped-for reward is a frustrating penalty.

Try to avoid use of frequent punishments for "bad behavior." Use punishment sparingly, and make it relatively mild and brief. The sample scripts below often spell out a "negative consequence" for not changing, but you should understand that these lines are to be used only if the contract with positive consequences seems to have failed.

If your contract employs punishments, spell them out, and be sure to make them realistic and believable. The punishment should be small but nonetheless significant at the personal level. Examples would be: "For each scheduled homework hour you miss, I will deduct 50¢ from your weekly allowance," or "If you don't give me more job responsibility, then I will start taking more of my accumulated sickleave at unannounced times."

Exaggerated threats are ineffective and counterproductive. You lose credibility when you threaten that if the opposite party fails you will "stop loving him," or "leave her," or "go to pieces," or "give the children up to an orphanage!" Such dire threats only postpone the necessary business of specifying the *actual* consequences. Stipulate only punishments of a magnitude that "fit the crime" of breaking the contract. And confine yourself to actions you can really imagine yourself carrying out against the other party should the contract be broken. Evaluate these against your own needs. For example, if you enjoy eating out at restaurants frequently, you would not use "no dining out" as a punishment for your partner since it punishes you too.

Always be aware, however, that punishment can produce undesirable side effects. When you punish someone, that person is likely to feel anger and deep resentment toward you. Although you merely intended to change an annoying behavior pattern, by punishment you may produce a hateful rebel who wants to strike back or just stay out of your way. For such reasons the best contracts emphasize and deliver positive, rewarding consequences.

SCRIPTS FOR TROUBLED TIMES

WORKING OUT A DESC SCRIPT

One way to learn assertive script writing is to read examples of scripts that others have developed. To illustrate the evolutionary process that results in the final written script, let's consider a counseling session between Sharon and Joan.

Joan, a 45-year-old woman, was separated from her husband and living with her three children and elderly mother. After 25 years as a housewife, Joan was returning to a full-time job. To acquire work skills, she was attending college classes part-time. She came to the counseling center for help in reentering the work world. The transition was not easy for Joan. She felt depressed and anxious because her academic knowledge and skills were very rusty; moreover, she believed the cultural myth that her long years as a housewife had made her passively ineffectual, brain-rotted, and incompetent. She felt depressed and incapable of dealing with "worldly" matters. She couldn't speak up for her rights; she needed to be more assertive in struggling for self-fulfillment against people who insisted she stay in her place. Although one of her initial complaints concerned her mother, who was very critical and domineering, Joan did not formulate her problems as ones requiring assertiveness. She was upset by her mother's domineering ways, but felt she could not risk offending her because she needed her mother's help with finances, housekeeping, and babysitting when Joan was working. She also expressed concern for her mother and wanted to improve their relationship. It seemed clear Joan needed to learn how to stand up for her rights with a domineering mother.

First, Sharon and Joan isolated one scene which was causing her trouble. It was important to know *when* the mother dominated Joan, regarding *what* subjects, under what *circumstances,* and *when* and *where* the scenes occurred. Many questions were needed to pinpoint the setting of the problem, to clarify and reformulate the factors in a given scene.

Joan's initial complaint was that her mother "nags me all the time." Asked to focus on a particular topic (DESCRIBE), Joan mentioned she was particularly upset by her mother's nagging about where Joan went to church. Every Sunday morning her mother would say that Joan's preferred church was too far away, too costly in gasoline and time to get there, so why didn't Joan just go to this nearby church her mother liked. Joan said the nagging made her feel like a child unable to make her own decisions (EXPRESS). She wanted her mother to stop telling her where to go to church (SPECIFY). It took a lot of questioning before Sharon could get from Joan what reasonable consequences she could provide her mother. Finally it was decided that, as a reward, Joan would take her mother and the kids on a picnic (a delight of the mother) after church if the mother did not criticize Joan about her church-going (positive CONSEQUENCES). On the other hand, if she nagged, Joan would calmly walk out of the room and refuse to listen (negative CONSEQUENCES).

After testing the appropriateness of the language, Joan wrote the final assertive script for her Sunday kitchen scene of confrontation with her mother:

DESCRIBE You are telling me not to go to my church and giving your own reasons for why I shouldn't go there.

EXPRESS When you do this, I feel like a child. I believe I am an adult, and adults make their own decisions about where to go to church.

SPECIFY Stop commenting now on where you feel I should go to church.

CONSEQUENCES *Positive:* If you stop commenting now on where to go to church, we can all enjoy a Sunday picnic after church this Sunday.
[*Negative* (to be said only if necessary): If you continue to talk about church to me. I'll simply walk out of the room. I refuse to listen to you on this subject anymore.]

Joan practiced delivering this message with assertive gestures and learned how to continue steadfastly through her script despite attempts by

OLD BAD SCENE

NEW POSITIVE SCRIPT

the mother (role-played by Sharon) to deflect or impede her. After perfecting the scene in the counseling situation, Joan performed it "on stage" the next Sunday morning before her mother. She was a brilliant success. She not only was pleased with her courage, but also got her mother to agree not to continue with the church topic. That small success motivated Joan to draw up DESC messages for other put-down scenes of her life and to translate them into action. Later she told Sharon,

> I had misgivings, I confess, especially when I visualized actually saying the words to mother. But when the time came, I used the words in the script almost verbatim. I felt a "safety" using the script. Eventually, I became more sure of myself as I saw the effect of my assertiveness and was able to stop using a script and simply be myself (my *new* self).[1]

There are some standard difficulties people have in writing good scripts. For example, Joan had difficulty describing her mother's offensive behavior in concrete terms. Instead, she used vague generalities. If we were to record Joan's initial formulation of her script, it would have sounded about like this:

> **DESCRIBE** Mother, you're a nag!
> **EXPRESS** I hate you!
> **SPECIFY** If you don't stop nagging, . . .
> **CONSEQUENCES** I'll scream and leave you.

This script is a caricature of errors; it commits about every mistake possible in four short lines. Compare it with the final script Joan and Sharon developed to note the contrasting language. In the less effective script the DESCRIBE consists of a vague, name-calling label; the EXPRESS is a very negative attack on the whole person rather than an expression of Joan's feelings about her mother's constant commenting; the SPECIFY asks for wholesale change of a nebulous trait; and the CONSEQUENCE is only negative, is too severe, and will punish Joan as much as the mother. Joan's two scripts highlight the features of better and less effective scripts.

SUMMARY OF RULES FOR WRITING DESC SCRIPTS

Table 1 summarizes the dos and don'ts of writing a good assertive DESC script. The rules are numbered for later reference. Often, the don'ts are more relevant or pointed than the corresponding dos.

You will find it helpful to read over, study, and test your learning of these rules, not only now but at several later times. They are one of the more important parts of this book, and you will be called upon to use them again and again.

Table 1 Rules for Assertive DESC Scripts

	Number	Do	Don't
DESCRIBE	D1	Describe the other person's behavior objectively.	Describe your emotional reaction to it.
	D2	Use concrete terms.	Use abstract, vague terms.
	D3	Describe a specified time, place, and frequency of the action.	Generalize for "all time."
	D4	Describe the action, not the "motive."	Guess at your Downer's motives or goals.
EXPRESS	E1	Express your feelings.	Deny your feelings.
	E2	Express them calmly.	Unleash emotional outbursts.
	E3	State feelings in a positive manner, as relating to a goal to be achieved.	State feelings negatively, making put-down or attack.
	E4	Direct yourself to the specific offending behavior, not to the whole person.	Attack the entire character of the person.
SPECIFY	S1	Ask explicitly for change in your Downer's behavior.	Merely imply that you'd like a change.
	S2	Request a small change.	Ask for too large a change.
	S3	Request only one or two changes at one time.	Ask for too many changes.
	S4	Specify the concrete actions you want to see stopped, and those you want to see performed.	Ask for changes in nebulous traits or qualities.
	S5	Take account of whether your Downer can meet your request without suffering large losses.	Ignore your Downer's needs or ask only for your satisfaction.
	S6	Specify (if appropriate) what behavior you are willing to change to make the agreement.	Consider that only your Downer has to change.
CONSEQUENCES	C1	Make the consequences explicit.	Be ashamed to talk about rewards and penalties.
	C2	Give a positive reward for change in the desired direction.	Give only punishments for lack of change.
	C3	Select something that is desirable and reinforcing to your Downer.	Select something that only you might find rewarding.
	C4	Select a reward that is big enough to maintain the behavior change.	Offer a reward you can't or won't deliver.
	C5	Select a punishment of a magnitude that "fits the crime" of refusing to change behavior.	Make exaggerated threats.
	C6	Select a punishment that you are actually willing to carry out.	Use unrealistic threats or self-defeating punishment.

Learn to identify violations of the rules in Table 1. To illustrate violations, consider again Joan's situation. You have seen a good script for her
along with one ineffective script. In Table 2 we have added a few alternative bad lines under each step to illustrate the kinds of mistakes people
commonly make. The name and number of the violated rule is given to the
right of each line.

Table 2 Poor Versions of Joan's Script

	Version	*Rule violated*	*Rule number*
DESCRIBE	1. You're always nagging.	Generalizes ("always"). Vague label.	D3 D2
	2. You're always out to dominate me.	Generalizes ("always"). Infers motives.	D3 D4
	3. You make me uptight.	Describes self, not other.	D1
EXPRESS	1. I hate you.	Extreme emotional outburst. Negative. Attacks whole person.	E2 E3 E4
	2. I don't feel anything about you anymore.	Denies feelings. Attacks whole person.	E1 E4
	3. That makes me angry.	Negative.	E3
SPECIFY	1. Stop nagging me!	Nebulous trait. Too large. Satisfies only you.	S4 S2 S5
	2. Just shut up!	Too large a request. Loss to other. Satisfies only you.	S2 S4 S5
	3. You should know how to better our relationship.	Ask explicitly. Nebulous request. Satisfies only you.	S1 S4 S5
CONSEQUENCES	1. I'll throw you out of the house.	No reward. Unreasonable punishment. Willing to carry out?	C2 C5 C6
	2. I'd smile more if you'd leave me alone.	Desirable enough? Big enough reward?	C3 C4
	3. We'll get along better.	Not explicit. Big enough reward?	C1 C4

FIND THE ERROR: SOME POOR
AND BETTER SCRIPTS

The best way to learn the rules for writing an effective assertive script is to work with some examples. For each of the following three situations the left-hand column presents a poor initial script aimed at dealing with a situation, while the right-hand side contains a better version. Write in the blank space the numbers of the rules in Table 1 which the poor script violates. (A single line in a poor script may violate several rules simultaneously.) Take a pencil now and go through the poor scripts, always comparing them with the better scripts. Refer to Table 1 to see which rules (if any) you think are being violated by the lines in the poor scripts. (You'll find the correct answers on page 105.) Following each situation and script, answer the questions to help you focus on important points.

Situation 1. Saying No to An Unwanted Job

For years you have been unable to say no to unreasonable demands on your time from charitable organizations. You are constantly being enlisted into collecting money for every worthy cause, even though you dislike door-to-door collecting. You now want to devote your energies elsewhere and want to be relieved of any further collection duties. When a campaign chairperson calls upon you to work this year, you say the better script you have written. Analyze the poor script for errors.

Poor script	*Better script*
D I've always worked for your organization.	I've collected for the XYZ fund for five years in a row.
(Rules violated? _____)	
E I'm too tired to keep on going with this business. You should be more considerate.	I'm feeling pushed on this request. I have already committed myself elsewhere, so I'll say no to your request this year.
(Rules violated? _____)	
S So please count me out and stop bothering me.	I want you to take my name off your list of possible volunteers. Will you do that?
(Rules violated? _____)	
C If you let me off this year, I might be able to help again next year.	*Positive:* Thanks, I appreciate that. [*Negative:* If you call me again next year, I'll still say no.]
(Rules violated? _____)	

When you have finished listing the rules violated, answer these questions about Situation 1.

1. If you were the campaign chairperson, how might you argue in replying to the specific lines of the poor script?
2. How could a persistent campaign chairperson try to shame you into taking the job?
3. How might you reply assertively to an attempt to make you feel guilty for not volunteering on this occasion?

Situation 2. Requesting Participation

A joint faculty-student committee at the college is trying to come up with a proposal for curriculum reform. As a student you feel left out of the discussion and you feel ignored. You want to be listened to. Compare the poor and better scripts. Find the errors and read aloud the better script.

	Poor script	*Better script*
D	You people are doing all the talking and I'm doing all the listening.	I've heard your suggestions for our proposal.
	(Rules violated? _____)	
E	Do you have to dominate these discussions?	I'd like to make a suggestion.
	(Rules violated? _____)	
S	If you'll be quiet, maybe I can put in my two cents' worth.	I'd like to have the floor to make my suggestion now. Is that possible?
	(Rules violated? _____)	
C	That way you'll get something important to students into the final proposal.	*Positive:* I'll work more optimistically and efficiently if I feel everyone has a chance to contribute ideas. [*Negative:* I'll have to say I'm unfairly treated if I'm not equally included.]
	(Rules violated? _____)	

Now answer these questions about Situation 2.

1. If you were a faculty member, what might you say in reply to the *poor* script lines?

2. If you were the student, what assertive reply would you make to that faculty member?

3. This situation involves a younger person trying to deal with older authority figures. Do you think the script would need to be changed if the committee were composed of all students? How would you change the wording for that situation?

Situation 3. Stopping an Annoying Habit

You are a company supervisor. One of your subordinates is making decisions that are not his responsibility, and should have been referred higher up. What errors would you be making if you delivered the poor script? Read the better one aloud!

Poor script	*Better script*
D You're making too many decisions that are not your responsibility and most of them are poor decisions anyway. (Rules violated? _____)	Last Thursday when you told Mr. Jones that our company would grant a 20% discount to him, you did something that was not within your authority.
E I am mad at having to correct your mistakes in judgment. You're just out of line. (Rules violated? _____)	I feel irritated and want you to realize it is important that everyone does only the job assigned to him.
S Your job is simply to decide which of our warehouses get particular orders for merchandise, right? (Rules violated? _____)	I have drawn up a list of guidelines on what you can authorize and what you should refer to me. Here is a copy for you to read. Let's go over them, answer any questions you may have, and come to some agreement about them.
C Things will go better for you if you do your own work and leave mine to me. (Rules violated? _____)	*Positive:* With this agreement, I'm hoping we can avoid such problems in the future. [*Negative:* I'll call all such errors in judgment to your attention immediately.]

Now answer these questions about Situation 3.

1. If you were the employee, what might you say in reply to the *poor* script?

2. If you were the supervisor, what assertive reply would you make to that employee?
3. If you were a supervisor asking an employee to "shape up," what would be the major aim of your assertive script?

Some Poor and Better Scripts:
An Analysis

The poor scripts on pages 102–104 violate these rules.

Situation	DESCRIBE	EXPRESS	SPECIFY	CONSEQUENCES
1. Saying No to an Unwanted Job	D1 D2 D3	E2 E3 E4	S2 S4	C4
2. Requesting Participation	D3	E3	S2 S6	C3
3. Stopping an Annoying Habit	D1 D2 D3	E2 E3 E4	S4 S6	C1 C4

6

Sample Scripts for Standard Situations

How forcible are right words!

OLD TESTAMENT: JOB

Before you try your hand at writing a DESC script, it may be helpful to study some more DESC scripts that others have worked out and delivered successfully. This chapter presents sample scripts which cover a variety of situations requiring assertiveness. In each case we first make some general comments and suggestions. We then describe a specific problem, present the sample script, and give a report of the results.

The scripts that we have chosen cover the following situations.

Requesting a Billing Adjustment
Requesting Information
Requesting Help
Clarifying Your Instructions
Requesting a Raise
Requesting Reconciliation
Requesting Participation
Saying No to Unreasonable Demands
Protesting Annoying Habits
Protesting Unjust Criticism
Protesting Physical Violence
Protesting Emotional Outbursts
Protesting a Rip-Off
Dealing with Another's Drug Problem
Establishing Independence
Dealing with the Silent Treatment

"Aha!" you may say, "My problems are all right here and I won't have to write a thing myself!" Well — not so fast. Though nearly everyone has to confront a number of these situations at one time or another, there is no "standard" script that will solve your own problem without any input from you. We definitely do not recommend that you regard these scripts as easy recipes for success. You will still have to write your own scripts in your own words. But seeing what others have done should make it easier for you to do that.

REQUESTING A BILLING ADJUSTMENT

To foresee and forestall overcharges for household repairs, when you first call a repair shop, ask: "How much is your labor charge per hour? Is there a minimum charge? Do you charge driving time to my home?" If you know what is wrong with your appliance, you can eliminate costly trips back to the shop by telling the repair service the model number of your appliance and asking them to bring the necessary parts to do the job. Note the arrival and departure times of the repairman and ask him to verify these times. In this example, when the repairman came, Jane Doe said, "I notice it is 9:15" and when he left, she remarked, "It's now 10:00. You have been here 45 minutes."

Situation. A dishwasher repair company overcharged me. I decided to use DESC to write an assertive letter of complaint.

Dear Sirs:

[**DESCRIBE**] I deliberately took note of the time your repairman spent fixing my dishwasher. Your repairman arrived at 9:15 and worked until 10:00.

[**EXPRESS**] I am surprised by your billing and I am seriously questioning the bill for $24.

[**SPECIFY**] I expect the bill to be adjusted to the correct charge of $20 which, as I understand it, includes travel time ($8) plus three-quarters of an hour labor at $16 per hour.

[**CONSEQUENCES**] I am counting on continued satisfaction with your service.

Yours truly,
Jane Doe

Results. I received a courteous letter saying that my bill had been reduced to $20. The billing department had made a mistake.

REQUESTING INFORMATION

Are you embarrassed if you must ask someone to show you how to do something? Some people feel it is an imposition or a sign of weakness to ask for help with a task. However, sometimes we really want to be shown and we feel slighted when we are ignored, as the following story reveals.

Situation. At the bank where I work, I was irritated with my boss because he had not explained how to make and register loans. I decided to assert myself. I wrote out and practiced this script for two days before I went to see him.

DESCRIBE I have asked you several times to teach me loans. You have replied, "Yes," but you haven't taken any action.

EXPRESS I feel I'm not learning an important part of the job. This is frustrating and undermines my performance.

SPECIFY I want to arrange with you a specific date when you will teach me loans.

CONSEQUENCES *Positive:* If I learn loans now, I will be able to save time later and do a better job.
[*Negative:* If I don't learn soon, I will simply not know my job when I need to, and time will be wasted later.]

Results. We made an appointment for Wednesday when he would teach me about loans. I learned about loans then (it's easy), and feel more competent in my job.

REQUESTING HELP

Household chores should be shared if everyone in the house is to have some leisure. Frequently, parents allow themselves to become slaves responsible for everything, and feel annoyed when their children ignore household jobs which cry out to be done. Overworked parents can assert themselves by stating the problem and asking for help in doing a list of specific jobs. If the consequences for doing (or not doing) the jobs are made clear, children will pitch in and help.

Situation. Our children were home on vacation eating, lounging about, and watching TV, but not offering to help with necessary gardening chores. Although my husband had been extra busy with a demanding experiment, he and the kids were hoping to squeeze in a few days of skiing. But chores had to be done before they left. Looking forward to some quiet time while they were away, I realized I would have to take the initiative if they were to go on that vacation. I delivered this script to my children during a TV commercial.

DESCRIBE You are looking at TV even though we have asked for your help with the gardening.

EXPRESS I am annoyed that you relax so much under these circumstances and then complain about not going skiing. If Dad found the garden weeded and spaded he would feel less pressured and would take you skiing.

SPECIFY The garden must be weeded and spaded before you can go skiing. Will you help do that today?

CONSEQUENCES *Positive:* There will be time for a ski trip tomorrow only if this job is done today.
[*Negative:* If this is not done today, there's no skiing tomorrow.]

Results. They agreed they would turn off the TV as soon as the show was over, then go out and spade the garden plot. They all went skiing and I enjoyed a quiet weekend.

CLARIFYING YOUR INSTRUCTIONS

If someone fails to understand your message or instructions, don't say, "Well, everyone else understands me, why can't you?" Such statements create defensiveness and communication blocks. That person is even less likely to understand you after your accusation! Rather than blaming the other person, think of what you can do to give instructions more clearly.

Situation. As a supervisor in a governmental agency, I had reached the end of my patience with an employee. I explained and reexplained his job. Nothing helped. Up to the point of script-writing, I had simply dismissed the employee as stupid and uncooperative.

DESCRIBE When I ask you to do a project, I explain the procedure and even repeat it if I don't feel you understand. Yet, sometimes when you try to apply what you've heard, you still have questions and say that you worry about making mistakes.

EXPRESS When this happens I get frustrated and irritated with you.

SPECIFY I want us to solve our communication problem. So, instead of my repeating an explanation, I would like you to paraphrase what you've heard so I can correct any misunderstanding you have. Could we try this way?

CONSEQUENCES *Positive:* I'll be able to work more efficiently if I can get this immediate feedback from you and it will take less wear and tear to complete the project.
[*Negative:* I'll continue feeling frustrated and irritated unless I get some fast feedback.]

Results. It was tough going. He took a long time to understand the procedure, but the time we spent working out the misunderstandings saved time on the total project for him and me. I'm no longer interrupted with having to answer his questions and give explanations. Next time should be easier.

REQUESTING A RAISE

Money matters require special planning and assertiveness. Although most of us would like higher wages, we are reluctant to make such a bold request. Get the facts to answer relevant questions: What do comparable people make in this job? What are their benefits? Why do I merit a raise? What am I willing to do if I don't get what I want?

Situation. I am underpaid and have tried to hint this several times to my boss (a dentist). For instance, I'd casually say, "Well, I've been here two years, time for promotion (ha-ha)." Only it wasn't funny because he never responded. To take action, I wrote this script and delivered it.

DESCRIBE I have been working for two years without a raise. My salary is $25 less than the average monthly salary for dental hygienists in this area.

EXPRESS I feel unfairly treated. I have worked conscientiously to build your practice. When I started there were barely enough patients to fill one day. Within a year we had more than 40 hours filled each week and we have maintained that work load for more than a year now. I think I contributed to that success.

SPECIFY I want to discuss a 15% pay raise and employee benefits. Will you discuss these with me Wednesday after work?

CONSEQUENCES *Positive:* I want to continue working here because I enjoy this office.
[*Negative:* But I cannot continue unless my salary and benefits are raised to reasonable figures.]

Results. I set up a special time to talk to the dentist, and delivered this script. I didn't want to give it hurriedly or when he could dismiss it quickly. I knew he would not be prepared to talk about my requests at that time, so I asked for another meeting for this purpose in two days. He took my request seriously because I had gathered specific information documented in my DESCRIBE step. We met in two days and negotiated a favorable agreement regarding salary and health insurance plan.

REQUESTING RECONCILIATION

Suppose that an angry argument results in the termination of a close friendship. Although you think the argument wasn't your fault and you don't want to take the blame, you do want to reconcile matters, and you think your friend feels the same way. What can you do? Here is what one person did.

Situation. I discontinued a close and valued friendship because of a particular misunderstanding. I greatly missed the friendship, but I was reticent to approach my friend and talk things out. I had reason to believe she might also be unhappy about the situation but probably would never approach me; therefore, I had to initiate the contact.

REQUESTING RECONCILIATION

DESCRIBE We don't see each other any more and we haven't even talked on the phone together.

EXPRESS I feel saddened by these unfortunate silences because I have enjoyed a lot of good times with you and I feel our friendship had a lot of positive things going for it. How do you feel about it?

SPECIFY Could we get together for lunch this week and talk about what causes these uncomfortable silences?

CONSEQUENCES *Positive:* It would be really nice to see you again.
[*Negative:* If we can't get together to talk I feel we'll grow further apart.]

Results. Planning this script helped me go through with it. She was glad I broke the ice. We talked for about half an hour and made a date for lunch the next day.

REQUESTING PARTICIPATION

Many people are afraid to speak up in group discussions. They sit back passively and let others steamroller the discussion, while inwardly they resent the misuse of their time. One young woman joined an assertiveness class to learn to speak up in committees where she was the only woman.

Situation. In a newly established administrative position, I felt I was often bypassed at meetings, and generally felt as if I were a recording clerk. I wanted more recognition and participation. I delivered the following script.

DESCRIBE I have been listening to this discussion carefully and have noted that in the past 20 minutes only three people have spoken and they have spoken mainly to each other.

EXPRESS I would like to contribute but I have a difficult time doing this because there seems to be no appropriate time to interrupt. It is a very unnerving situation for me.

SPECIFY It would help me if whoever is speaking would speak to everyone by looking at each of us and by pausing several seconds after making a point. This way we can ask a question or help to clarify a point without interrupting. Do you agree?

CONSEQUENCES *Positive:* I plan to ask questions for clarification from now on, and I hope others will, too, so we can all participate equally.
[*Negative:* If I don't participate, I won't feel as if I'm a member of the committee.]

Results. Everyone began participating on a more equal basis. One man slipped me a note saying, "Thanks. I've been sitting here trying to get up the courage to tell those three monopolizers where to go." I don't need to sit and get angry anymore and I feel as if I'm a useful committee member.

SAYING NO TO UNREASONABLE DEMANDS

Many people feel resentful that they haven't enough time to enjoy their leisure interests. They have accumulated too many jobs by letting people take advantage of them. While we enjoy helping others, we dislike excessive demands on our time, talents, and money. We may feel too guilty or embarrassed to say, "No, I'd rather not spend my time or money that way." Here are two scripts, one written by a harassed mother, another by an overworked store clerk. By saying no to excessive requests they reduced that uptight feeling.

Situation. I knew I would be asked again to drive for my son's Cub Scout activities. The solicitor who called each year was persuasive, using arguments like "We need dependable, reliable drivers like you, who can take charge of this important function. Without your help, we would fall apart." I had a script ready when she called this autumn.

>   DESCRIBE   As I understand it, you are asking me to drive for six Cub
>   Scout functions.
>
>   EXPRESS   I feel put upon because this is very costly — both in gas-
>   oline and my time.
>
>   SPECIFY   I'll drive for three excursions only this year — once in
>   November, again in January, and in March. Please mark me
>   down as a parent to call for those months and no others.
>
> CONSEQUENCES   *Positive:* That way I'll be happy to help you in future years.
>   [*Negative:* But if you ask me to do more, I'll simply refuse.]

Results. I had this script ready by the phone. The solicitor was taken aback by my assertive voice, especially when I cut off her guilt lines about how much she needed me for the job. From the tone of her voice, I think she was glad I agreed to drive three times!

Situation. As a clerk in a big department store, I was being asked to take on progressively more jobs, such as taking inventory, ordering, stocking of shelves, etc. Since I was also busy with customers, these extra responsibilities were getting to be too much. I prepared and delivered this script to my floor supervisor.

DESCRIBE   We have been very busy almost every day this past month, yet you have asked me to do several extra things almost every day.

EXPRESS   I feel overworked and I'm getting exhausted.

SPECIFY   I usually have about 30 minutes free right before lunch. If you would tell me in the morning the extra job with the highest priority, I will do it right before lunch or at another time when I have a few free minutes.

CONSEQUENCES   *Positive:* I can do a better job with the customers and with the extra work if you will tell me which job has the highest priority.
[*Negative:* If I don't know which job is most important, I may not finish work you think is urgent.]

Results. The manager rank-ordered the jobs she wanted done so I knew which were more important. After my script she knew how much time I could give to her extra jobs. Our relations were much improved, and I felt much less harried since I knew which extra jobs had what priorities for my time.

PROTESTING ANNOYING HABITS

Most of us would not hesitate to complain to a person who consistently stepped on our toes or belched in our faces, but we shrink from pointing out less blatantly annoying behaviors. We think it may be rude and embarrassing to point out someone's irritating mannerisms. (Except with children — with them we are probably overzealous in pointing out faults!) But small irritations, repeated often enough, can wreck an adult relationship; often, the longer you put off asking the person to change, the more irritating the annoying habit becomes. The following script shows how one person handled a minor irritation without sounding like a nag.

Situation. I had been quiet about my brother's annoying habit of interrupting my speaking because we shared an apartment and I wanted to keep the peace. I prepared this script, practiced it, and used it the next time he interrupted me.

DESCRIBE   Did you know that you stopped me before I could finish stating my main point?

EXPRESS   When you do that, I feel foolish, as though my ideas are insignificant, and I feel like giving up.

SPECIFY   Let's try this: when one of us finishes speaking, the other one will count silently "one-two-three" before jumping into the conversation. That way each of us can finish what he has to say without being interrupted. If either of us slips, we can remind each other — like I'm doing with you now. Okay?

CONSEQUENCES *Positive:* That way, we'll both be able to have enjoyable conversations.
[*Negative:* If this agreement doesn't work, I'll have to start interrupting you frequently, just to get my point across!]

Results. It worked. He became more aware of his bad habit, and tried to eliminate it. He also told me about a few of my annoying habits! That's good. Life is better. We even had some humorous moments trying to catch each other in the annoying habit of interrupting.

PROTESTING UNJUST CRITICISM

While some constructive criticism can be valuable, if you think someone's criticism is excessive or unfair, you can call a halt to it. Protesting excess or unjust criticism is a problem practically everyone has.

Situation. I was a newly appointed supervisor, replacing a Mr. Cannon, who retired. I inherited Mr. Cannon's secretary, who had been in her position for 15 years with an excellent work record, but had never worked for a woman. During the first two weeks, she constantly said, "But that's not the way Mr. Cannon did things," or "Mr. Cannon was more organized," etc. Though I needed help from this woman, I realized that her frequent reference to Mr. Cannon was her way of criticizing me. I felt this indirect criticism was unfair and was interfering with my functioning in my new job. I planned and delivered this script.

DESCRIBE Just this morning and on several occasions in the past days, you have mentioned Mr. Cannon and his procedures.

EXPRESS I find it very annoying to be continually reminded by you that Mr. Cannon did things differently. I realize Mr. Cannon had his way of doing things, but I have some of my own ideas that I want to try out.

SPECIFY Please stop telling me how Mr. Cannon did things.

CONSEQUENCES *Positive:* Actually, if you did stop mentioning Mr. Cannon I could institute some of my plans faster. Of course, in order to do that I'd like to know some of your ideas.
[*Negative:* However, if you continue to compare me with Mr. Cannon we will have a very hard time working together.]

Results. She mentioned Mr. Cannon a couple more times; when she did, I reminded her of our agreement. I feel better about our relationship because I can see she has really tried to stop using "Mr. Cannon" to criticize me.

Situation. My mother-in-law visits us once a year. She disapproves of the fact that I have a full-time job and therefore do not indulge every whim of her son (my husband). On several occasions, she made subtly critical remarks, such as, "Oh, you don't iron his handkerchiefs?" or "Do you mean to say that he did your laundry this week?" I decided I'd had enough of her attempts to make me feel guilty. I prepared the following script which I delivered the next time she made this kind of remark.

> DESCRIBE You just said "He shops for you?" That is but one of several remarks you have made about the way we live.
>
> EXPRESS I find this kind of remark very irritating. It suggests to me that you disapprove of the marriage arrangement Jim and I have, and that you feel I am failing as a wife.
>
> SPECIFY Please stop making critical remarks about the way Jim and I have arranged our lives.
>
> CONSEQUENCES *Positive:* If you can hold off such remarks, I'll drive you to the city Sunday so you can visit your good friend, Mrs. Bedlow.
> [*Negative:* If you make any further such remarks, I will remind you of what you've done by simply walking away.]

Results. When I delivered the script, she glared at me, said "Harumph," and muttered that her son deserved a better wife. The next day, she criticized me twice, and I simply walked out on her (the second time in a cafe!). After that, she seemed to hold herself in check pretty well, so I drove her over to Mrs. Bedlow for a visit, reminding her why I was able to do so.

PROTESTING PHYSICAL VIOLENCE

Some people react to frustration with violence: they hit, slap, scream, slam doors, kick, break plates, and yell. Passive people discover they need to learn how to speak up to such aggressive Downers. If you contract for change with an aggressor, propose an alternative response the person can make to negate frustration, and try to cite effective positive consequences that will encourage him to alter the behavior. Many times the best way to assert with an aggressive person is by letter or phone.

Situation. A high school boy got into heated arguments with his father about curfew hours, school, work, household chores, car availability, allowance, smoking, and beer drinking. These invariably escalated until the father slapped the son. The son was on the verge of leaving home when he came to an assertiveness class. He developed the following script in a letter and delivered it an hour *after* the father's next bout of violence. The consequence about "fishing" was realistic — that was the activity the father most enjoyed with the son.

Dear Dad,

[**DESCRIBE**] We've just been through a debate that escalated into shouting and your slapping me. This has happened frequently.

(**EXPRESS**) I am really upset by your slapping me. I don't think we can solve our problems this way.

[**SPECIFY**] I want you to stop yelling and hitting me when we get in an argument. Let's do this: after each of us makes a remark in an argument, we have to wait seven seconds before the next statement can be made, either by you or me. During that time, we think of how to defuse and cool off the situation. Will you try counting the seven seconds as a "time out" plan?

[**CONSEQUENCES**] If you do this seven-count when we argue next time, then I'll go fishing with you next Sunday. If you don't, I'll remind you to count to seven. If we continue to argue with physical violence, I am going to see a school counselor.

Your son,
Bill

Results. I delivered the letter an hour after a fight over my smoking. Because he was feeling guilty, he accepted readily. However, he went back to his old habits in the heat of our next argument. I had to remind him four times to count to seven, and he reminded me twice. That argument seemed to go so incredibly slowly that we quit because it was boring. We have had only minor arguments for the past week, and we enjoyed fishing last Sunday.

PROTESTING EMOTIONAL OUTBURSTS

Popular dogma misleads us into thinking emotions are like steam backed up in a pressure cooker: if we "let off steam" with a hostile outburst, the pressure to be angry will go down. But scientific research has shown just the reverse:[1] Acting aggressively when you're angry simply makes it more likely that you will escalate your current aggression and act aggressively again the next time a similar frustration occurs. You can learn to keep calm in emotionally arousing circumstances, first, by talking calmly to yourself about your interpretation of the situation, and second, by carrying out alternative actions that control anger. In the situation below, a woman contracted with her son to help him control his emotional outbursts.

Situation. Our 11-year-old son started a paper route, his first job. Several unfortunate circumstances arose with the route manager, causing our son to feel he had been treated unfairly. He reacted with violent temper tantrums. I wanted him to stop his temper tantrums and deal directly with the problem. I wrote and delivered the following script.

> DESCRIBE Son, you are displaying a big emotional scene, screaming and stomping around.

> EXPRESS I find your emotional outbursts very unpleasant and disturbing, and I do not think they solve your problem. I begin to feel angry with you when you scream and stomp around.

> SPECIFY I want you to stop that behavior and begin planning how to handle these situations constructively. Will you do that?

> CONSEQUENCES *Positive:* If you stop yelling and stomping, I'll be glad to talk over a reasonable approach with you.
> [*Negative:* If you continue this yelling, I will deduct 50¢ from your allowance and will deduct 50¢ each time you act like this in the future.]

Results. Our son stopped yelling, asked for some suggestions, and together we worked out an assertive script that he might use with his paper route manager. Happily, he confronted the manager assertively, got his money, and decided to continue his job.

PROTESTING A RIP-OFF

Rare indeed is the person who has never experienced a rip-off. Sharon's files are full of scripts protesting poor service, haphazard repairs, shoddy merchandise, or false advertising. The person who delivered this script had some property literally "ripped off" by some neighborhood boys.

Situation. I came to class very distraught because my house had been burgled and my son's bike, which had been locked to his bed, had been dismantled and stolen! I had definite proof that three neighborhood boys were selling the parts from my son's stolen bike. I wanted to protest, but to whom and how? After some brainstorming with the class, I decided the script should be directed to the errant boys, rather than their parents or the police. I asked the three boys to my home, and delivered this script with deliberate forcefulness.

> DESCRIBE Hank tells me one of you admitted that you boys took Hank's bike. I have proof you boys took Hank's bike. I have proof you boys have been selling parts from Hank's bicycle.

EXPRESS I'm angry that you took the bike and stripped it. It's unfair that you should get away with it.

SPECIFY I want each of you to go home tonight and tell your parents what you did. Within 48 hours I expect to hear from each of your parents about what will be done to restore that bike to its original shape. And finally, I want a promise from each of you that this won't happen again. Will you do this?

CONSEQUENCES *Positive:* If you and your family cooperate, I'm willing to think more kindly of you.
[*Negative:* If I don't hear within 48 hours, I'll go to your parents myself. If we can't reach an agreement, I'll take the matter straight to the police.]

Results. I was amazed how I could carry through. I had my script on my lap but they didn't know I had my words written out. The meeting lasted about five minutes. I heard from all three sets of parents within 48 hours. The stolen parts were paid for by the boys.

DEALING WITH ANOTHER'S DRUG PROBLEM

Serious situations involving the misuse of a drug are often not effectively dealt with by well-meaning and sympathetic relatives, friends, supervisors, or employers. Most of us feel that if we love enough or understand enough, the problem will be solved; in fact, we may only be perpetuating the problem with our sympathetic behavior. A supervisor had the following experience with an alcoholic worker.

Situation. An employee frequently showed signs of heavy drinking when she returned from lunch; at these times she was irritable and fell behind with her work in the afternoon. In the past weeks, she had not typed or filed accurately, and her defective work had to be retyped and lost files had to be recovered. I realized her increased irritability was intimidating all of us, and her poor work was requiring time from others. Previously, I had offered to be her friend and comforted her (she was having troubles at home), but now I realized her lunch hours were longer and her work hours shorter. Most of her problems were too big for me to help her with; however, as a supervisor I needed to call her attention to her lessening productivity and I wanted to suggest counseling. I was advised by the Counseling Department not to play buddy anymore, so I wrote this businesslike script. (It is important to know what actions your agency or company takes in these matters. Research first!)

DESCRIBE Your work performance has not been up to par in the last two months.

> EXPRESS I feel unskilled in helping you with this problem. Or: I feel I can't help you with solving this problem.

> SPECIFY I want you to see Mr. Brown at our Counseling Center. Here is his phone number. Will you call him? (A specific referral and commitment is necessary.)

> CONSEQUENCES *Positive:* If you do this I feel certain you can improve your work standards in the next two months.
> [*Negative:* If you don't talk to the counselor I will have no alternative but to let you go.]

Results. She phoned the counselor. I was relieved of the inappropriate role of therapist or counselor, and she received the professional help she needed. Her work performance improved when she received help with her problem and no longer drank during the lunch hours.

ESTABLISHING INDEPENDENCE

When people feel they can make their own decisions wisely, they want the chance to take effective control of their own lives. In establishing their independence they say, "I am old enough to make reasonable decisions about myself and to take responsibility for my actions." Establishing independence from loved ones is difficult because we want to move out of their shadow while remaining within their warmth. To become independent, we must be assertive, be able to say, "This is who I am, what I like, and what I believe in." The search for independence is the search for oneself. A young college man wrote the following script.

Situation. I had a domineering father who tried to control my every move — telling me what courses to take, what friends to make, what clothes to buy, where to shop, etc. I decided to reduce his unsolicited advice-giving.

> DESCRIBE You are giving me detailed instructions on everyday things — like what to do with my clothes, my car, and how to plan my time.

> EXPRESS When you give these kinds of detailed instructions, I feel really helpless, as if I'm a small child. I am an adult now!

> SPECIFY Stop planning everything for me and do not give me suggestions unless I specifically ask for suggestions. Allow me to learn to take care of my own plans.

> CONSEQUENCES *Positive:* If you do this I will learn to make my own decisions and be responsible for myself. Then you can be proud of me and we will get along much better.

[*Negative:* However, if I think you're instructing me on things I should decide myself I will remind you once. If you continue, I will simply turn away from you and walk out of the room.]

Results. I delivered the script to Dad the next day when he started telling me where to buy clothes. He apologized, said he didn't mean to be overbearing. But the next day he did it again, telling me which college friends I should cultivate. I reminded him of the agreement, and walked out of the room. After that, his annoying habit occurred less and less.

DEALING WITH THE SILENT TREATMENT

Some Downers seldom say what's on their minds, but instead relay their feelings — hostility, disapproval, and resentment — by negative body language. You feel manipulated and upset that they won't discuss what's bothering them. The best way to counter the silent treatment is to assert your rights and ask for a speaking partner. Here is one woman's account.

SILENT TREATMENT

Situation. My apartment-mate is a master of negative body and facial language. Frequently, I will say something to which he will not reply except to throw me a look that could cut steel. I have become increasingly irritated with his angry looks, so I told him what I needed to continue living with him.

DESCRIBE   You frequently throw hostile glances at me when I've said or done something. I ask what's the matter but then you shrug your shoulders and look away from me.

EXPRESS   I feel really unhappy when you are silent. Yet, I feel I may be stepping on your "space" inadvertently. This, too, is very upsetting because I want to consider your feelings and wants.

SPECIFY   I want you to tell me directly when I have said or done or not done something which angers or hurts you. Perhaps we could begin by setting aside 30 minutes a day to talk over such things. Would you agree to that? What time would be best for you?

CONSEQUENCES   *Positive:* If we do this I will make every attempt to fulfill your wants or work out a mutually satisfying compromise.
[*Negative:* If you don't express your feelings and wants to me directly in words, I will no longer concern myself with improving our relationship and I'll cancel this living arrangement.]

Results. This problem was very difficult and it took several more specific requests to work out our communications. It turned out that I had developed several irritating behaviors, such as looking down and doing "busy work," which annoyed him. With both of us working to help each other improve, we began to feel closer and happier about our relationship.

CONCLUSION

The scripts we have presented in this chapter show how DESC was used to work through a variety of problems requiring assertivensss. You probably recognize one or more of your problems among the examples. But, as we said in the beginning the scripts are not intended as rigid blueprints. When you develop your script, use your own style while following the rules for assertive messages. Hopefully, you are well on your way to learning assertive skills for solving interpersonal problems. Learning how to negotiate, to solve problems so everyone wins something, is a humane way to equalize the balance of power. Hopefully you are acquiring the courage and skills needed to speak up positively when your situation requires assertive action.

7

Writing Your Own DESC Scripts

Nothing will ever be attempted if all possible objections must be first overcome.

SAMUEL JOHNSON

In this chapter, you'll analyze your situation from Worksheet #3, page 21, and write a DESC script to fit that situation. But first, you'll get some writing practice in the following exercise.

Situation. Last week you bought a blouse (if you are a woman) or shirt (if you are a man) in a high quality store, and it shrank beyond use during its first washing. You want a new blouse (shirt) to replace it, or credit at the store. You are a little nervous about returning merchandise, so you work out a script to say to the salesclerk.

Write something down as a first approximation. You can always edit and revise it. Take a pen or pencil and write out the best lines you could say to the salesperson. Make your DESCRIBE step a statement of the problem as you see it rather than a description of the clerk's behavior (which is not at issue here). Then plan the other steps.

DESCRIBE _____

_____

_____

EXPRESS _____

_____

_____

SPECIFY _____

_____

CONSEQUENCES *Positive:* _____

_____

[*Negative:* _____

_____]

Now check whether you have followed the rules for good scripts (Chapter 5, page 100). Compare your script with the model script below.

DESCRIBE   I bought this blouse (shirt) here last week. It shrank so much when I first washed it that I can't wear it.

EXPRESS   I think that a blouse this expensive should be preshrunk.

SPECIFY   I want this store to give me full credit on this blouse. Will you do that?

CONSEQUENCES   *Positive:* If so, I will apply that to buying another blouse here to match my outfit.
[*Negative:* If not, then I will not patronize this store again.]

WRITING A SCRIPT FOR YOUR PROBLEM SCENE

The way to begin writing a script is to force yourself to start, and then reward yourself for small accomplishments. Although you can refer to the rules in Chapter 5, don't get bogged down trying to apply them before you even put pencil to paper; that will just inhibit your first efforts. You can always revise and reshape your lines later for a better effect.

To begin, turn back to Worksheet #3 in Chapter 1 (page 21) and review the moderately threatening scene for which you want to work out a script. On that worksheet, you summarized the who, what, and when of your problem scene. As a preliminary step, review that information quickly and objectively.

1. Who are the people in this scene? You and who else?

_____

2. What was the place and time of the old scene?

_____

_____

3. What happened in that old, bad scene? Describe your Downer's behavior and
    your behavior.

    _____

    _____

    _____

    _____

4. Roughly speaking, how do you feel about this situation?

    _____

    _____

    _____

    _____

Now, using the guidelines on page 126, begin writing your lines. Using
pencil (so you can erase later if necessary), write out the words you could
imagine yourself saying when you play the role of the assertor. Keep each
step in your script brief — only one or two sentences. When you have
finished, return to this page and continue reading below.

Editing Your Script

Once you have put on paper some ideas of what you want to say, you can
review your script and refine your wording. Your objective now is to replace
those first hurried phrases with the exact words you will say. To do this, first
look over your lines and check them against the rules on page 100. Correct
any glaring violations of the rules. Now, try reading your lines and "listening" for exaggerated or emotionally loaded overtones. Again, where necessary, rewrite your lines, this time aiming for restraint. Remember that your
script should be short and to the point; a sentence or two at each step is
enough.

As a final check, read the questions on page 127 and make further
changes if they are needed. Then continue reading on page 128.

Step 1. DESCRIBE the other person's offensive behavior in objective terms. Look, observe, examine exactly what he or she has been saying and doing. Describe the behavior concretely here. (If it is an impersonal problem with a company, describe the problem.)

_____

_____

_____

_____

Step 2. EXPRESS your feelings or thoughts about this behavior or problem in a positive, new way.

_____

_____

_____

_____

_____

_____

Step 3. SPECIFY one behavior change you want the other person to make. Ask for agreement.

_____

_____

_____

_____

Step 4. Stipulate the CONSEQUENCES you will deliver (or what will happen) if the other person keeps the agreement to change.

Positive: _____

If necessary, tell your Downer what negative consequences you will provide if there is no change. Write them here, but understand that you do not _say_ them unless it becomes necessary:

[_Negative:_ _____

_____]

[_Return to page 125._]

Your DESCRIBE Lines

- Does your description clarify the situation, or does it just complicate it? Replace all terms that do not objectively describe the behavior or problem that bothers you. Be specific.
- Have you described a single specific behavior or problem, or a long list of grievances? Focus on one well-defined behavior or problem you want to deal with now. One grievance per script is generally the best approach.
- Have you made the mistake of describing the other person's attitudes, motives, intentions? Avoid mind-reading and psychoanalyzing.

← Revise your DESCRIBE lines now, if necessary.

Your EXPRESS Lines

- Have you acknowledged your feelings and opinions as your own, without blaming the other person? Avoid words that ridicule or shame the other person. Swear words and insulting labels (*dumb, cruel, selfish, racist, idiotic, boring*) very likely will provoke defensiveness and arguments.
- Have you expressed your feelings and thoughts in a positive, new way? Avoid your "old phonograph record" lines that your Downer is tired of hearing and automatically turns off.
- Have you kept the wording low-key? Aim for emotional restraint, not dramatic impact.

← Revise your EXPRESS lines now, if necessary.

Your SPECIFY Lines*

- Have you proposed only one small change in behavior at this time?
- Can you reasonably expect the other person to agree to your request?
- Are you prepared to alter your own behavior if your Downer asks you to change? What are you prepared to change about your behavior?
- What counterproposals do you anticipate and how will you answer them?

← Revise your SPECIFY lines now, if necessary.

Your CONSEQUENCES Lines*

- Have you stressed positive, rewarding consequences?
- Is the reward you selected really appropriate for the other person? Perhaps you should ask what you might do for the other person?
- Can you realistically carry through with these consequences?

← Revise your CONSEQUENCES lines now, if necessary.

---

*The rules of contracting (Appendix C) very often apply directly to the SPECIFY and CONSE-QUENCES steps, and you may wish to read through these rules now as an additional check.

Anticipating Reactions

You have now completed the basic substance of your script. But there are a few additional elements to consider. After all, you won't be delivering this script in a vacuum. Some one — your Downer — will be responding to you as you go along. So it makes sense to anticipate as far as possible what objections and replies this person might make at each step along the way. You can then either try to think of an assertive reply to each anticipated reaction, or rewrite your script lines so as to forestall the most likely rejoinders.

Usually a sentence or two can be used to prevent some one from getting you confused, upset, and lost in the middle of your assertion. A phrase like "That may be, but . . ." allows you to return to the next line of your script. So does "Please don't interrupt me until I've finished what I want to say." Or an argument given by the Downer midway in your script may be answered with "You may have a point there; I'll think about it. But right now I want to get back to my point, . . ." Such sentences permit you to shift the conversation back to the problem you wish to talk about.

Let's work on this now. In the spaces below, copy your lines, as edited, from page 126. Then imagine yourself in your Downer's shoes, and write a plausible reply which that person might make to each of your lines. Write the reply in his or her characteristic words and phrases. Then write a counterreply you could make in each case to deflect or avert the rejoinder and to bring the conversation back to the next step of your script.

DESCRIBE _____

_____

_____

_____

Downer replies: _____

_____

You reply: _____

_____

EXPRESS _____

_____

_____

_____

Downer replies: _____

_____

_____

You reply: _____

_____

SPECIFY _____

_____

_____

_____

Downer replies: _____

_____

_____

You reply: _____

_____

CONSEQUENCES *Positive* _____

_____

Downer replies: _____

_____

You reply: _____

_____

[Negative _____

_____]

Downer replies: _____

_____

You reply: _____

_____

These rejoinders will come in handy when you deliver your script. Chapter 8 tells you more about how to speak up without allowing counterarguments to confuse you and sidetrack you from your assertive script.

Bargaining for Agreement

As you may have foreseen in working through the preceding section, a Downer may listen to a script but then want to negotiate the details of the contract, the SPECIFY and CONSEQUENCES parts. For instance, he or she might want to dicker over the appropriate reward for the behavior change you have requested, or to propose that you modify your behavior in return. Such negotiation is desirable insofar as it is task-oriented. You might haggle a little like a bargain hunter at a flea market, but the process is innocent. You are bargaining over what a specific change in your Downer's behavior is worth to both of you.

At this stage you are to some degree ad-libbing. Your script has brought you to a desirable stage if you and your Downer are indeed able to focus on "what it's worth" — and since you've already given careful thought to what it's worth to *you*, the need for a precise set of lines to speak is not so pressing. Just try to keep in mind your own and your Downer's needs, and you should be able to stay on the right track.

A word of caution — beware of ending a negotiation too hurriedly. Do not be in such a rush that you forget or are unclear about what contract terms you finally agreed to. Discussion of emotionally sensitive problems is often embarrassing and discomforting, so there is an understandable pressure to "hurry up and get it over with," a desire to escape to more comfortable conversation. But in the confusion of contract offers, counteroffers, fast bargaining back and forth, if you do rush to get it over, you may forget the terms finally agreed upon. Sometimes it is advisable, therefore, that you and the other person record in writing (even sign!) the final agreement. A signed agreement provides a touchstone for reference weeks later. You can post it in a prominent place if necessary. It keeps each of you from "remembering" terms of the agreement in ways that are slanted in your own favor. A signed contract resolves most later disputes about who is to do what for what consequences. Its presence, say on the household refrigerator, also serves to remind each other what you have agreed to do.

Ending the Scene

Suppose you have given your assertive message to your Downer, and have negotiated a contract. What post-negotiation remarks could you make?

First, it's important to thank the other person for agreeing to change. Express sincere appreciation, perhaps have a little celebration if appropriate. Second, while the post-negotiation relief is upon you both, you might suggest that your future conflicts or discomforting situations be handled in a similar manner — by describing the problem, by expressing feelings, and by stipulating desired behavior changes. But do *not* bring up at this time some other annoying behavior which you want changed. Just rejoice in the agreement already concluded. Third, say that since you want to have a more pleasant relationship with this person, you sincerely intend to keep your end of the bargain.

Consider now the closing comments you could use if your Downer agrees to your contract. Imagine the scene, including reactions to your script, and then write two closing comments you can plausibly hear yourself delivering to this person. Be sure they do not raise new problems! Practice saying these closers aloud several times.

Closer 1: _____

_____

Closer 2: _____

_____

Remember to say these closing remarks if appropriate after actually negotiating a contract.

The script you have just written is not a hypothetical exercise. Keep it, because you may wish to revise it further after reading Chapter 8, and you will be practicing it along with the "assertive body language" exercises and other work in Chapter 9. For now, let's turn to some related topics.

ABBREVIATED SCRIPTS

The full four steps of the DESC procedure are not always needed. People will often do something for you as soon as you speak up and say what you want. Consider these examples, in which a brief DESCRIBE line may bring about the desired change immediately:

- To an overweight visitor: "You are sitting on a chair with a broken leg!"
- To people who are dominating the conversation: "I have been waiting ten minutes to get into this conversation."
- When returning defective goods to a store: "This radio has a defective speaker."

In abbreviated scripts, the DESC steps are squeezed together by ellipsis, cutting, and compacting. Thus, for example, a simple EXPRESS statement may take the place of a needlessly long DESC script. Consider, for example, "I don't like your eating with your elbows on the dinner table." This means:

DESCRIBE You are eating with your elbows on the dinner table. You do this frequently.

EXPRESS I get irritated when you have your elbows on the table while we're eating.

SPECIFY Please eat with your elbows off the table. Keep them at your sides.

CONSEQUENCES *Positive:* If you do that, I will approve of your table manners, and you will make me happy.
[*Negative:* If you continue to eat with your elbows on the table, I will continue to disapprove.]

It sounds farcical to draw out the four steps of the "elbows" ellipsis. But the unpacking illustrates how the four DESC steps are often contained in a single "negotiating" sentence requesting behavior change. Using shared assumptions about social norms and *why* people say things to one another, we figure out the conveyed meaning and implications of the compacted statements.

To gain some practice, write abbreviated assertive scripts for the following situations.

Situation 1. You are waiting in line to buy tickets and a stranger cuts in ahead of you in the line. You say:

_____

_____

Situation 2. You have finished all the business you want to discuss with a salesman in your office, but he hangs on, talking endlessly. You want to get him out of your office. You say:

_____

_____

Situation 3. You insulted a friend yesterday. You feel contrite today and want to apologize effectively. You say:

_____

_____

Such abbreviated scripts are useful for dealing with the casual problems of everyday living. However, their effectiveness depends upon mutual assumptions and goals of the people involved. The change that can be accomplished merely by saying "I feel unhappy when you do X" depends on whether your happiness means more to the other person than doing X, and sometimes on whether he or she thinks you really mean what you've said. Persistent problems usually aren't solved with one-line scripts. Often, another person's assumptions differ from yours, so the full assertive message should be spelled out. You must decide for each problem whether to use a full DESC script. We recommend writing full scripts for first attempts even if you decide it is unnecessary to say all four steps.

SCRIPTS FOR MAILING OR TELEPHONING

We have treated your assertive scene as involving face-to-face confrontation with a Downer. That is indeed the most threatening situation in which to speak up effectively. But you can also deliver an assertive script over the telephone or in a letter. One assertive individual wrote this letter to her doctor.

Dear Doctor Jones:

[**DESCRIBE**] I have been trying to reach you by telephone for three days. Your receptionist has taken my messages and told me you would call back, but so far I have not heard from you.

[**EXPRESS**] I feel put off at a time when I have a matter of urgent concern to me.

[**SPECIFY**] Please call me immediately.

[**CONSEQUENCES**] If you don't call me by Friday, I will be forced to call you at your home on your personal time.

Sincerely yours,
Jane Doe
Phone 841-7921

She registered the letter. The doctor took her letter seriously enough to call her the minute he received it.

A letter can also be an effective way to communicate with someone you see every day but have difficulty talking to. A teenage boy could not get his father to listen to him. Though they lived together, the boy nonetheless wrote a scriptlike letter he mailed to his father. The letter also explained briefly why the boy was communicating in this unusual way with his father. For once, the busy father attended fully to what the teenager had to say.

For shy people, the attractive feature of a letter is that it is a monolog; it is not interruptible. You say what you want and avoid exposure to counterattacks and "body language" messages your Downer uses to set you off (in anger) or put you down (in fear). Therefore, the writing of scripts that become mailed letters can be recommended as a preliminary stage in becoming assertive. The letter can be sent to an individual about a personal problem or to a company about a consumer problem. A letter about a personal problem may have to be followed up by live conversation with your Downer, so that you seal an agreement, but at least the letter has established the basis for the conversation. On the other hand, a consumer letter to an impersonal company, say to a utility company complaining about an increase in rates, rarely leads to face-to-face contacts.

The telephone is another medium for communicating your script to a Downer. Have your script in front of you as you talk. The advantage of the

TIME OUT FOR SCRIPT-WRITING

phone is it isolates you from your Downer's threatening body language and from physical attack (if you anticipate that). A disadvantage is that the Downer can terminate the conversation whenever he or she pleases. One Downer may reply, "Don't bring up that stuff now! Goodbye!" and hang up on you. Another, sensing his powerless position, may say, "We can't solve that over the phone. We'll go into it when I get home tonight." Despite this disadvantage, telephoning a script is an easy way for shy people to begin delivering their assertive scripts.

Remember the desensitization procedure, which starts you on the easy, low-threat situations and, with success, moves you on to more difficult, high-threat situations. For a frightened nonassertor, delivering a script by letter is a relatively low-threat event, whereas telephoning a script to a Downer is a somewhat greater threat. Of course, eventually the goal is to speak up effectively in face-to-face confrontations of high threat. So start at the "easy end" of the scale, and assert yourself by letter or phone whenever convenient. Don't pass up any opportunity to practice!

PRACTICING YOUR SCRIPT-WRITING

The best way to improve your script-writing ability is to work on scripts whenever you can. Think of the bad scenes from your past and write new assertive scripts for them. Try writing script-letters to people or to companies. Remember to start with conflicts and situations that are moderately threatening. This is not yet the time to tackle the Big Downers in your life. Rather, use this time to improve your skill and build your self-assurance.

When Is the Best Time to Write a Script?

Practically any time is a good time to write a DESC script. Once you get the habit, you can write a script anywhere, any time, and as you become more skilled you can think one up on the spur of the moment. Whenever you find yourself fretting over some personal problem, write a script to solve it assertively. Even if you never expect to deliver the lines, write them down since they may help you solve a similar problem in the future. Also, many people report that script-writing helps them control their anxiety about a current problem.

Ideally, a DESC script should be written when you are quiet, relaxed, and reflective. If you get into a battle where you could use a good script, consider leaving the squabble to compose a rational script. Excuse yourself, take "time out," and compose a quick script before you act irrationally. To protest a car repair bill, one student controlled his anger enough to say, "Excuse me, I want to think about this problem." He sat in his car for five minutes, prepared a DESC script, then returned and delivered it to the garage manager. By planning his complaint, he convinced the manager to adjust the bill.

Practicing with a Buddy

Working with a buddy makes it easier and more enjoyable to learn assertive script-writing. Friends, relatives, mates, and co-workers who learn DESC script-writing can work together to edit and practice their assertive messages. Getting someone else's suggestions for improving your skills can help you build confidence. Buddies usually work together as follows.

WORKSHEET #5
PRACTICING WITH A BUDDY

1. **Prepare ahead:** Buddies prepare DESC scripts before they meet.

2. **Focus on the problem:** Take up one script at a time. When it's your turn, briefly tell who did what to you, when and where. Then tell what is preventing you from asserting yourself in this situation, and spell out what you would like to say and do in this situation.

3. **Edit the script step by step:** First read your entire script aloud to your buddy, then analyze, criticize, and edit each line of your script with your buddy's suggestions for changes in the wording.

4. **Role-play your Downer:** Have your buddy read your edited script and deliver the assertive message while you play the Downer, replying to the lines read by your friend.

5. **Brainstorm replies:** Think together of any other replies the Downer might make to each step of your script. Write them on the script. Also jot down your assertive counterreplies.

6. **Practice the revised script:** Switch back to speaking your own part, and read your lines while your buddy plays the Downer. Go through the scene three or four times this way, using the script less and less during repeated run-throughs.

7. **Get feedback about your delivery:** Ask these questions and write down your buddy's comments.

   About your voice: Is it loud enough? too loud?

   _____

   Is it forceful enough? too forceful? too emotional?

   _____

   Are you speaking at a good rate? too fast? too slow?

   _____

About eye contact: Do you look directly at the person or do you look away too often?

Do you glance away appropriately from time to time or do you stare at your Downer buddy?

Do your eyes help express your feelings? How?

About your body language: What are your hands doing? What do your hands express to your Downer?

Do you fidget with "props"? What can you do to relieve nervous movement of your hands?

Would you sit or stand in this scene? What is your posture?

Do you have any giveaway movements that your buddy reads as aggressive or passive?

About your facial expressions: Do you look as if you really stand behind what you're saying?

Are you overplaying your firmness by looking too severe and imposing?

8. **Ask your buddy what seem to be your most assertive behaviors, and make notes about these positive behaviors below.**

Think about your positive behaviors from time to time as you go about other matters. Visualize yourself acting positively and realize what good things you already have going for you. Use these behaviors to assert yourself positively in the many interactions you experience daily. Enjoy expressing yourself!

WHEN IS A SCRIPT A SUCCESS?

A script is a success if it runs off smoothly *and* if it achieves the goals you planned it for. In other words, the successful script not only helps you get agreement from your Downer but does *in fact* lead to behavior changes that are mutually agreeable, so that both of you are more satisfied with your relationship. Our discussion of your DESC script is therefore not complete unless we pay some attention to the results you get.

Consider first the possibility that your script may "fail" because it produces no agreement. In Chapter 8 we discuss some of the tactics Downers use to avoid coming to an agreement during your assertive scene, and we make suggestions that can help you deal with those Downer "detours." But there will be times when you can't seem to reach an agreement. If your problem situation requires some kind of accommodation, reanalyze the terms of the contract. Perhaps you can ask for a less drastic change, give a greater reward or punishment, give greater weight to your Downer's needs, or reevaluate the importance to you of the requested behavior change.

Even if no agreement results from your script, you will have gained a great deal by using it. You will feel better about yourself for having expressed your feelings and for trying to eliminate an offensive situation. You will have gained more self-respect and can live with yourself a little more easily now. Also, even if the Downer doesn't change, you will probably feel freer to express how you feel about the issue. For example, your script may fail to get an old uncle to stop making bigoted remarks about racial groups, but you need no longer pretend you approve.

Suppose, on the other hand, that you have delivered your assertive script, the Downer has agreed to it, and you're feeling wonderful and all aglow. Great! But as we've already seen, an agreement is only as good as the change that comes out of it — it's worthless unless it's carried out.

Making the Contract Work

The first thing to look to in making the agreement work is your own contractual responsibilities. It's essential that you make any changes that you have agreed to on your part, and that you deliver the promised rewards at the promised time to a Downer who performs as agreed. If you promised a dollar for mowing the lawn, don't give half a dollar. If you promised that you would go out dancing together tonight, don't try to make a last-minute switch to the bowling alley instead.

Second, you have to help your Downer live up to his or her end of the contract. Unfortunately, some Downers are perfectly agreeable to making promises — they fill the air with their resolutions and good intentions — but then they don't change at all. They "forget," or "can't help it," or "don't have time" to do what they promised. In the beginning, it's probably wiser to take such excuses at face value (from the Downer's point of view, they are perfectly valid). But that doesn't mean giving up. Instead, consider yourself a sympathetic teacher helping a struggling student to learn something. If you think your Downer has made well-intentioned tries, reward responses that are at least headed in the right direction. Hopefully, as you reward more adequate responses your Downer's behaviors will become more satisfactory. This is especially likely to be true if the behavior is of the kind that is learned very slowly. For example, a partner who promises to dance more at parties may have a hard time developing this new behavior. Don't expect 100% improvement at the first party. Rejoice at (and reward) a 10% improvement!

But what about the Downer who continually produces nothing but excuses? Obviously the contract is not working at all. To help get it back on the track, think about some of the possible reasons for your Downer's broken promises.

- The rewards may be inadequate — too infrequent or too small in relation to the change you want. For example, suppose a husband has agreed to get home from work at 5:00 on Tuesdays to babysit while his wife goes to a class. And suppose he has accepted the idea that his wife will say thank you as a reward. Nevertheless, he may find when Tuesday arrives that this reward isn't enough to encourage him to rearrange his whole work schedule. He may make some other excuse (not wanting to hurt his wife's feelings) — but if she really wants the change in his behavior, she ought to consider the possibility that the reward isn't big enough and cast around for a better one.

- When someone has promised to *start doing* something you want, the cues to remind the person of the desired behavior may not be present in the situation when the action must be performed. The agreement is temporarily "out of sight, out of mind." The late-arriving husband may simply get caught up in details at work and genuinely forget his promise to his wife. In this case, it may be helpful to find ways of supplying the necessary reminder cues. We'll discuss this subject in detail below.

- In the case of a person who has promised to *stop doing* something that bothers you, the annoying habit may be so automatic that the person is not conscious of it and therefore can't control it without help. Again, reminder cues may be helpful.

- You may have overlooked some key factors that influence your Downer's behavior in the problem situation. Suppose the late-working husband is in a business where the major work of the day arrives late in the afternoon, and he has to do that work or risk losing business. Although he agreed to his wife's request, clearly he should not have done so. In a case like this, it would be better to find alternative solutions to the wife's Tuesday night problem — for example, to hire a babysitter to cover the period between 5:00 and the time her husband gets home. Never be afraid to reanalyze a problem situation — there is usually more than one way to solve the problem.

Reminder Cues

If you and a Downer find that forgetting promises is a problem, you might want to agree on some way of supplying reminder cues near the time when the new behavior is to be performed. One woman reminded her husband to show more physical affection by smiling at him and saying "Now!' An obese man reminded himself of his resolve not to eat by posting on his refrigerator door two contrasting pictures of himself, one fat and gross, the other slim and handsome.

How might the woman with the late-working mate remind him to leave his office before 5:00 on Tuesdays? She could remind him verbally at breakfast Tuesday; send a note in his Tuesday bag lunch; ask him to record the commitment in his appointment book; mail him a letter which arrives at his office Tuesday afternoon; telephone him at 4:30 Tuesday.

Reminders vary in effectiveness depending on their closeness to the time an action is to be performed. Sometimes it is necessary to use two or more reminders on the same day. But after the desired action has actually occurred in a given situation a few times, it begins to be associated with the situation itself, so your extra cues can be gradually faded out and removed. Eventually, the desired behavior comes to be performed on its own, from habit, without reminders.

Another way to help someone remember a promise or intention is to have the person imagine performing the promised action in the future. To remember to take a book to Julia tomorrow, you can imagine yourself gathering up that book just as you finish breakfast tomorrow and prepare to rush out. If you are to call the electric company tomorrow at 2:00, you can imagine yourself in your office, see the clock hands point to 2:00, and see electrical sparks and lightning bolts shoot out from the clock hands and hit the telephone. By picturing such a scene in your mind you associate the action with the situation so that it comes to mind again when you actually enter the situation. You might suggest that your Downer try this "imaginal preparation" as a help in keeping promises.

What about contracts that call for eliminating an annoying habit? Often, our mannerisms are so thoroughly ingrained that we perform them idly, without thinking. Suppose you are driven to distraction by your Downer's table manners (for instance, chewing noisily) or social mannerisms (for instance, continually pulling on one ear while talking) or other distressing habits (for instance, picking or scratching in unseemly places). Suppose, too, that your Downer understands your annoyance and wholeheartedly agrees to stop — and yet the habit persists.

To deal with this problem, you and your Downer could agree on a signaling system by which you would give the Downer feedback when you notice that the annoying behavior is occurring. Your signal might be the phrase "You're doing *it* again," or "Now," or "Stop!" or some gesture you have mutually decided on as a suitable signal. Remember always, however, that these signals are only a crutch, designed to help the person behave as promised. If they are delivered sharply or with ill humor, they will instead become punishments. So use them gently, discriminately, not in sledgehammer fashion. Your mutual goal is to have the person learn, in time, to behave as promised without reminders, and this is more likely to happen if the behavioral situation has positive rather than negative emotional overtones.

Consider now how you and your Downer can better insure the success of your agreement to change. How much can you expect the Downer to change with just the verbal agreement? How much lapsing or reneging do you anticipate? If you can foresee the need for reminder cues, think out and write below a way of signaling or cueing the person to perform the desired response or to stop doing whatever it is that annoys you. Specify what reminders you will use and with what timing. Keep in mind that if your reminders are to be made in company, they should be unobtrusive so you and others are not embarrassed.

My cueing plan is:

_____

_____

_____

Next, if appropriate, consider how you will "fade out" or gradually eliminate those reminder cues over time, as the Downer's behavior comes closer to what has been agreed on.

My plan for fading out reminders is:

_____

_____

_____

Now add these two elements to your revised DESC script, so that you can discuss them as part of the agreement to change.

A Word About Renegotiation

In the best of all worlds, your Downer will not only agree to the terms of the contract you propose in your DESC script but will follow through and make the behavior change as prescribed. But what happens if you are still not completely satisfied, because you want further changes made? If these are important enough to you, then by all means negotiate another contract for that further behavior change. That will require another script, of course, but there is nothing morally wrong with explicitly changing the terms of a contract over time, or with abandoning one contract to replace it with a new one that is more appropriate to your current goals and interests. People's wants can change, or circumstances can change. There's probably no reason, for example, why a child needs to go to bed as early in the summer as during the school year — so why not change the rules to fit the difference in the situation? There's nothing reprehensible about this and no reason for sticking to rules that are clearly no longer relevant.

To sum up: Good contracts change with the requirements of the situation and the feelings of the people involved. They are tools for improving your life — use them that way!

8

Downer Detours

Even when you're on the right track,
you'll get run over if you just sit there.

UNKNOWN

Earlier chapters in this book have focused on you — what you could say and do in various assertive situations. But your confrontation will not be one continuous *monolog*; rather, it will be a *dialog*. Your Downer is not likely to listen politely and attentively to your DESC spiel, and then acquiesce meekly with "Yes, dear. Where do I sign the contract?" He or she will probably react defensively to some lines of your script. We call these defensive maneuvers "detours," because they can get you off your assertive track. This chapter helps you anticipate your Downer's defensive maneuvers and suggests ways to deal with them.

The best assertive script is short and has been worded in such a reasonable manner that your Downer will feel encouraged to listen and negotiate with you. You try to head off negative reactions to your ideas by making your points without attacking the other person; you avoid insulting or attacking your Downer. In addition, you examine each line of your script to see if it opens you to an effective counterargument or detour. If so, you try to revise it to avoid such reactions.

Of course, even with a "perfect" script, your Downer is going to have some reactions. These might consist only of tagging a simple question to each of your lines. "Is that the way you see me?" "Is that the way you feel?" and so on. To such questions you need only answer "yes" before you go on with your script.

Beyond these mild sociable reactions, however, is a host of defensive detours. For instance, you start out discussing whether to live in an apartment or a college dorm, but your father soon shifts it to criticizing your dating habits. In other examples, your Downer may deny your statements, belittle them or you, argue with your claims, blame the problem on you or someone else, give a lengthy self-explanation, or try to analyze why *you* act the way you do. Such reactions are often meant either to shut you off or to change the issues as you see them. But you can learn how to deal with such maneuvers to get the conversation back on the track.

The following pages describe a number of defensive detours you might provoke with your DESC script. In our experience, none of the maneuvers is exclusively (or even predominantly) a masculine or a feminine tactic. But since we are focusing on one-to-one exchanges, we have for simplicity made an arbitrary choice of "he" or "she" to refer to the Downer described under each heading. You know your Downer's style, and for those illustrations that have a familiar ring, you need only adjust the pronouns to fit.

The detours we discuss are:

Put-Off Detours
Distracting Detours
Denying Detours
Blaming Detours
Verbal-Abusing Detours
Joking Detours
Reinterpreting Detours
Psychoanalyzing Detours
"Poor Me" Detours
Negative-Vibes Detours
Apologizing Detours
Threatening Detours
Debating Detours
Procrastinating Detours
Nonnegotiating Detours

In each case we give examples of assertive counterreplies which could be used. These counterreplies fall into several categories:

PERSIST	Repeat your main point, the object of your assertion (usually this is your SPECIFY line).
DISAGREE	Make a straightforward, direct statement. ("I don't agree.")
EMPHASIZE FEELINGS/THOUGHTS	Stress your feelings or thoughts about the behavior or situation, giving more details or calling attention to their importance. ("This is important to me.")
AGREE . . . BUT	Agree with the other person's right to have certain feelings and draw certain conclusions, but disagree with the

idea that you must hold the same feelings or draw the same conclusions.

DISMISS Ignore the detouring comment completely or — better — quickly deny its relevance to the problem under discussion. ("That's not the point here.")

REDEFINE Don't accept someone's negative label for your behavior; redefine your behavior in positive terms. ("I'm not being nosy; I'm just being naturally curious about a friend.")

ANSWER QUICKLY Sometimes it's best to answer with a simple yes or no or with some other brief, direct reply, so you can get on with your central concern.

ASK A QUESTION Instead of accepting vague criticism, ask for clarification. ("In what ways do you think I'm acting foolishly?")

STIPULATE CONSEQUENCES When pushed to the limit of your tolerance or where you feel threatened, consider promising realistic, negative consequences if the offensive behavior continues. (Beware of this approach, because it may backfire.)

After reading about each detouring tactic in the following pages, imagine how your own Downer might use the maneuver in reaction to your DESC script. If a given detour is a likely response of your Downer, devise an assertive counterreply. In this way you can better prepare for the many detouring defenses your Downer might employ to "keep you in your place."

PUT-OFF DETOURS

The simplest way for your Downer to avoid solution of your mutual problem is to avoid discussing it. If you begin by saying, "I'd like to discuss this problem about budgeting we've been having," she may say "Not now. I'm too tired," or "Let's not go into that now," or "Some other time; I'm busy." All she is really saying is that what she is doing is more important than what you want to discuss. You have two assertive options. First, you can push to have the issue taken up now, saying, "It's important to me that it be settled. [EMPHASIZE FEELINGS] It'll only take a few minutes, since I already have a plan worked out. [PERSIST]" That may whet her appetite to listen. Also, it tells her she doesn't have to do anything but listen. Your second option is to negotiate a specific later time to discuss the problem. You could say, "If not now, then name a specific time today (tomorrow) when you will discuss this issue with me. [PERSIST]" If she gives you a time, repeat it, thank her, then drop the subject. But be sure to keep that appointment.

Put-off detours	*Assertive replies*
"I can't discuss your salary now. I have to prepare for my meeting with J.B."	"Please tell me a specific time when . . . [PERSIST]"
"Not now, I have a lot on my mind and I don't need you hassling me."	"I understand you're under pressure but [AGREE . . . BUT] this matter is important to me. [EMPHASIZE FEELINGS] When could we discuss it? [ASK A QUESTION]"
"I don't have time to waste arguing with you. The matter is closed."	"The matter is not closed because . . . [DISAGREE]" *or* "I don't want to waste time in useless argument but [AGREE . . . BUT] if we don't reach a mutually agreeable solution I will . . . [STIPULATE CONSEQUENCES]"

Suppose your particular Downer tries to put you off when you attempt to deliver your assertive script. Imagine the circumstances as you confront your Downer, and then imagine what she might say to put you off. What are her characteristic put-offs? Think of the exact words she might say and describe the body language she might use. Having done that, jump back into your role and figure out an assertive reply to your Downer's delaying put-offs. Remember, half of negotiating successfully is being prepared to deal positively with your Downer's countermoves.

If your Downer says, "I don't *ever* want to discuss that," you could emphasize your feelings, saying the problem is important to you, and persist by insisting the two of you try to settle it. You can promise brevity and a better relationship to induce her to discuss the problem. If she persists in ignoring you or walks away repeatedly, you have a "nonnegotiator" on your hands. Later we will discuss how you could deal with a nonnegotiator. In general, though, the standard principles of contracting for behavior change apply to encouraging your Downer to "come to the negotiating table." Hopefully, you can get past this hurdle and initiate discussion, so that you can deliver your DESC script.

DISTRACTING DETOURS

Your Downer can divert you from delivering your script by incidental comments about you, your script, or irrelevant questions. These are usually intended to serve as distractions, and one way to deal with them is to refuse to respond to them in longwinded replies.

Distracting detours	*Assertive replies*
"You look beautiful when you're angry."	"That's beside the point. [DISMISS] My point is . . . [PERSIST]"
"Where did you learn that big word?"	"Never mind that now. [DISMISS] My concern is . . . [PERSIST]"
"Don't you have to finish the Jackson account?"	"Yes, but I can take a minute for this. [ANSWER QUICKLY] My point is . . . [PERSIST]"

In each case the replies help you continue with your script and not be sidetracked.

Silence will be distracting to you if you had expected a response from your Downer. So will hostile body language. But such responses deserve separate discussion and you will find this a little further on, under "Negative-Vibes Detours."

Now, anticipate how your Downer might distract you. What are the characteristic remarks he might interject to block or sidetrack you during your assertion? How will you reply to these? Make his imaginary remarks plausible and characteristic, but irrelevant to the topic you want to discuss. Perhaps he might try to beat you to the punch by bringing up a problem he wants to discuss. How would you deal with that?

DENYING DETOURS

An easy defense of a Downer to your DESCRIBE statement is to deny it, or to say that your perspective on the situation is false and distorted. We suggested that the DESCRIBE part of your script refer only to concrete behaviors of your Downer (rather than to her motives) in order to avoid such arguments. Nonetheless, if she denies the behavior, you can simply persist in asserting *your perspective* on the situation. Don't be sidetracked into arguing whose perspective is "correct." Your reply to her denial may be simply to deny her denial. Respond by making your assertion again, perhaps paraphrasing it in other words [PERSIST]. You can note opposing views, but turn them aside temporarily [AGREE . . . BUT]. You say in effect, "That may be *your* opinion, but here is mine." Here are some possible denials to your DESCRIBE line, and some possible replies.

Denying detours	*Assertive replies*
"That's not true."	"I think it is. [DISAGREE] Also, . . . [PERSIST]"
"You don't know what you're talking about."	"That may be what you think, but I am quite sure about this. [AGREE . . . BUT]"

Denying detour	*Assertive reply*
"You're always misreading me."	"I'm describing facts, not reading your motives. [REDEFINE] In any event . . . [PERSIST]"

Make your replies restrained but firm. Don't attack her opinion. Just deflect it, and get on with your assertive plan.

BLAMING DETOURS

When you tell someone about his offensive behavior, he might look for someone to blame it on. He will aim to excuse or rationalize his behavior, and to make you feel guilty. He may automatically interpret a DESCRIBE line as the question "Why are you doing that?" and reach for the nearest reason — you. You could deal with this accusation briefly but firmly, by giving a quick answer to the charge and following it with an EXPRESS sentence or by noting it as a further problem requiring negotiation. Here are some blaming reactions to various DESCRIBE lines with possible assertive replies.

DESCRIBE lines	*Blaming detours*	*Assertive replies*
"You're talking very loudly."	"That's the only way you'll listen to me."	"That's not so. [DISAGREE] I feel . . . [EMPHASIZE FEELINGS]"
"You didn't circulate the memo I had you type."	"No, you didn't tell me to circulate it."	"I want all memos circulated immediately. [ANSWER QUICKLY]"
"You're wearing that wornout sweater."	"That's because you haven't bought me a new one yet."	"I'm not responsible for your clothes. [DISAGREE] I feel . . . [EMPHASIZE FEELINGS]"

Sometimes a Downer's blaming reply might actually point to a desired change in your behavior. As an example, when out in company a husband always dominated the group's conversation, so the wife privately asked him not to talk so much. He blamed her, saying, "You're always so quiet I feel as if I have to keep talking to fill the silence and compensate for your shyness." She admitted she was partly responsible, and agreed to speak up more in company if he would talk less. She contracted to prepare herself with two conversational topics before they went out with their friends, and he agreed to count to ten before trying to fill a conversation lull.

BLAMING DETOUR

A frequent blaming approach is, "I told you so!"; that is, your Downer blames the current problem on your not following his advice. Though this parent-like remark stings bitterly, you should resist counterattacks. The issue is *not* whether he gave good advice in the past; rather, it is his *current* behavior, which you find disagreeable and want changed. You could answer an "I told you so" by simple deflection — "That may be, but my point is . . . [AGREE . . . BUT]" or "I would rather you didn't say 'I told you so' now [EMPHASIZE FEELINGS]; my point is . . . [PERSIST]" That keeps you on the business at hand.

A second form of the blaming detour is to blame others for the offensive behavior. In effect, the Downer says, "I act this way to you because X (parents, boss, etc.) acted mean to me." Suppose your boss frequently comes into your office sullen and angry, criticizing your work unreasonably. You've written a script to let him know how you feel and how you'd like the relationship to change.

DESCRIBE line	*Blaming detour*	*Assertive reply*
"In the past two weeks you have criticized the way I transfer the calls several times."	"I got steamed up because my supervisor has insisted that I move my vacation back six weeks."	"Thanks for telling me, but I feel as if I'm the scapegoat for a problem that isn't mine. [EMPHASIZE FEELINGS]"

Another way a Downer blames others and thereby justifies his offensive behavior is by appealing to group norms: "Everybody does it." You simply indicate that you don't share these norms: "That may be, but the behavior is still offensive to me. [AGREE . . . BUT]"

SPECIFY line	Blaming detour	Assertive reply
"Would you please turn down the radio?"	"You're just too sensitive. All my friends play their radios this loud."	"That may be, but it is definitely too loud for me. [AGREE . . . BUT] I have very good ears. [REDEFINE] Please turn it down. [PERSIST]"

Imagine how you might reply with forceful expressions when your Downer blames you. People are so ingenious at blaming others for their own shortcomings that it is sometimes hard to anticipate and write assertive replies. Basically, keep attention focused on the problem your script is about; don't get sidetracked into new problems of apportioning blame. Keep insisting your Downer has at least half the responsibility for doing something to resolve the issue (changing his behavior), rather than excusing it with blame. Above all, don't blame back!

VERBAL-ABUSING DETOURS

A horror story we tell ourselves is that our Downer will assault us verbally when we speak up. Despite all efforts to eliminate inflammatory words from your DESCRIBE and EXPRESS lines, your Downer may still interpret them as critical and challenging. Her reaction to criticism may be to criticize or attack you.

Verbal abuse is almost unlimited in kind and quality. Generally, the verbal abuser will disparage your views, belittle you, downgrade your ability or personal characteristics, and attack your self-esteem. Verbal abuse includes insults, disapproval, "cussing outs," sarcastic remarks, and put-downs. Most such verbal abuse should simply be ignored as you continue with your assertive plan. Why reward your Downer for the abuse by letting it sidetrack you? (See the Extinction Principle, Appendix A.)

In the examples below, notice that the assertive replies concentrate on staying on the track to solve the initial problem. Avoid counterattacks as they are likely to increase the abuse. Of course, you can acknowledge someone's anger, saying "I can see this makes you angry, but this is important to me." If she screams and hollers at you, you could continue calmly, "It's important that we talk about this, but I can't hear you when you scream." Try to defuse the anger.

If your Downer calls you a dirty name, you can ignore it or perhaps REDEFINE what it means in less emotional terms. You can deflect irrelevant arguments by DISMISS statements, and you can EMPHASIZE FEELINGS as a way of heading back to the issue that matters.

Verbal-abusing detours	*Assertive replies*
"Are you some kind of watchdog?"	"I can observe what you've been doing. [REDEFINE]"
"I don't give a damn about your feelings!"	"Feel any way you wish but right now we have a problem to solve [AGREE . . . BUT and PERSIST] and I think it's an urgent matter to talk about . . . [EMPHASIZE THOUGHTS]"
"Stop dumping on me!"	"You can call it anything you want [DISMISS] but I'm telling you how I feel. [EMPHASIZE FEELINGS]"
"Listen you blundering halfwit, what makes you think you have the right to preach at me?"	"I'm not preaching, only *informing* you that . . . [REDEFINE]"

JOKING DETOURS

Your Downer may respond to your lines by making a joke about them, poking fun at you, or exaggerating your claim in a ridiculous manner. A joke at your expense is a form of ridicule, and you might as well recognize it as such. To deal with the ridicule, you could ignore the humor and simply persist with your serious DESCRIBE and EXPRESS. Nothing extinguishes a jokester's humor as fast as a deadpan audience. Here are some examples of joking detours and how you might reply to them.

DESCRIBE lines	*Joking detours*	*Assertive replies*
"Do you know you have criticized me three times in the past hour?"	"Only three times? I guess I'm off my form tonight."	"That's not funny. [DISAGREE] I feel . . . [EMPHASIZE FEELINGS]"
"You haven't reviewed the committee report as you agreed to do."	"I don't want to wear out my eyeballs."	"Broken promises are not a laughing matter. [REDEFINE] I feel . . . [EMPHASIZE FEELINGS]"

To prepare yourself, imagine a joke or humorous retort your Downer might make to the lines of your DESC script. Considering his brand of humor, which lines of your DESC script are most likely to produce a humorous (or contemptuous) reaction from your Downer? How would you reply? Sarcastic humor is a popular form of put-down in our society, so you may want to prepare some one-line replies for other occasions when you need them.

REINTERPRETING DETOURS

If you express negative feelings about someone's behavior, she may answer by reinterpreting the "meaning" of her actions, saying what she intended (or didn't intend). For example, a person may say she intended you to take her sarcastic remarks in a spirit of light jest, that that is her way of expressing humor. To deal with this strategem you could tell her you can only see what she does, not what she intends; you could say you want her to change her behavior because you dislike sarcastic "compliments" and you would rather she express herself directly, not through some elaborate, sophisticated conventions involving sarcasm.

In some cases you can benefit by seeing how your Downer views the behavior you find offensive. For example, a husband called his wife "honeybunch" when they were out in company. After suffering with this name several years, she asked him to stop it. He was surprised because he thought "honeybunch" showed his warmth and affection for her while with friends. Such misinterpretations are easily cleared up by exchanging opinions.

To repeat, the main way to react when your Downer reinterprets her behavior in the favorable light of her good intentions is to insist you do not see it that way at all, and you want unambiguous behavior change to deal with the matter.

Reinterpreting detours	*Assertive replies*
"I only meant it as a joke."	"That may be, but I didn't think it was appropriate. [AGREE . . . BUT] I felt really hurt. [EMPHASIZE FEELINGS]"
"I only meant to help you out."	"Perhaps . . . but I found it embarrassing to be helped when I already knew how to do that job. [AGREE . . . BUT]"

PSYCHOANALYZING DETOURS

Often we try to find psychological explanations for why people act the way they do. (And we are usually very bad at it!) When your Downer sees you acting assertively, he might play amateur psychoanalyst and divine deep

PSYCHOANALYZING DETOUR

insights into your motivations. Your reply could be either to DISAGREE with the false conclusions (if they *are* false) or to DISMISS his attribution. Essentially you could say, "Your analysis is wrong [DISAGREE] and beside the point. [DISMISS] The problem is your behavior and my reaction to it, so let's work at that level. [REDEFINE]" Here are some examples of psychoanalyzing put-downs and some assertive replies to them. After you've made a quick assertive reply, you can continue with your EXPRESS and SPECIFY messages.

Psychoanalyzing detours	*Assertive replies*
"You're only saying that because you're a castrating female who's hostile to really masculine men."	"That's just not true. I'm not against men. [DISAGREE] I want to say how I feel about *your* behavior . . . [PERSIST and EMPHASIZE FEELINGS]"
"You're just going through a difficult 'stage' now. You'll grow out of it soon."	"This is no stage of mine. [DISAGREE] The problem is the way you've been acting toward me, and my reactions to that. [REDEFINE]"

Psychoanalyzing detour	*Assertive reply*
"You're all uptight because you're afraid I'll get the promotion and not you."	"Don't analyze me. [ANSWER QUICKLY] I know better than you why I act the way I do. [DISAGREE] Are we going to work on *our* problem now? [ASK A QUESTION]"

A person attempting to read your mind and motives is likely to attribute your new assertive actions to your reading this book or attending an assertiveness training course. For example, your mate may ask: "What kind of nonsense has that book been putting into your head?" You could REDEFINE as follows: "It is helping me to express myself." We read self-help books and go to self-improvement courses to change ourselves. So it is no disgrace to admit that your new assertive behavior has come about through the influence of this book or a course. But in becoming assertive you have not fallen under the influence of some fiendish devil; rather, you've gotten better control over yourself! So, speak up openly, honestly, and positively.

"POOR ME" DETOURS

The most common "poor me" detour is for your Downer to try to shut off your assertion by crying and playing the offended martyr. The message conveyed to you is, "You are so *mean*! You hurt me and make me unhappy."

How do you react assertively to a person who habitually cries when criticized? First, don't feel guilty! You have carefully analyzed your needs and your Downer's behavior, and you have carefully chosen your words for the DESC script, so you will have made your most considered and tactful statements. For some people, crying is very easily triggered by even the mildest criticism, and many "criers" don't even want to cry! You might point out to your Downer that you consider her crying to be an attempt to control your behavior by making you feel guilty. You can state that you will not be manipulated by crying in this situation.

If your Downer is listening, go on with your script, through tears and all, and get agreement to the contract. Afterward, refuse to listen to the sob-story of how sad you've made her feel. It will simply make you feel guilty for having requested something which, by your reasoned calculation, you had a perfect right to ask for. Change the topic, leave the room, or go out for a walk. The sobbing and sulking generally wlll soon subside, but the contract for change is now "in force," and you will defeat yourself if you feel guilty about expecting this person to live up to it.

If the Downer's crying prevents communication, then break off the current script-delivery with an appropriate promise. For example, "Your crying is interfering too much, so I'll speak to you again about this at breakfast tomorrow." As with put-off detours, set a time when the Downer will listen. If the crying recurs at that time, you could write your script as a letter or memorandum for your "crier" to read in your absence. Then she can do all the crying she wants as she reads your message. Clearly, one objective could be to get your Downer not to cry when you criticize her. Think of the crying as simply another habit that is controlling you and preventing the two of you from solving problems. The crying is interfering with developing a closer, warmer relationship.

The second type of "poor me" detour is the display of distressing physical symptoms by your Downer when you assert yourself. These symptoms may vary from claims of mild headaches and stomachaches to feigned chest pains, cramps, and dizziness. Symptoms of illness are often a hypochondriac's way of responding to stress. Like crying, such symptoms manipulate people, helping the person escape the problem situation.

Don't debate whether the reported symptom is physical or psychological. Just don't let repeated use of the symptoms keep you from asserting yourself. The facile performance of a symptom "on demand" may indicate that your Downer is using it like tears to forestall your assertions. If so, next time you could try asserting yourself by mail. A letter can be a very useful way to get your assertive message to the hypochondriac without having to listen to complaints about the ailments that you supposedly cause.

NEGATIVE-VIBES DETOURS

Distinct from the physical symptoms of a "poor me" detour is the display of very negative body language. The Downer's face, body, and tone of voice all convey the message that your assertive script is hurting, angering, or boring him. He may glare at you, stare at you, look daggers through you, scowl, squinch up his face, smirk. He may cover his forehead and eyes with his palm, as if to say, "Oh Lord, don't tell me you're going to start on that again!" One reason the Downer will use such negative body language is to punish you for asserting yourself.

You have two basic options for a reply. First, you can explicitly recognize the feelings expressed in your Downer's body message. You can say, "I get the impression this talk upsets you. I can understand why it might. Nonetheless, I still want to persist with the point I began making because this is very important to me. [AGREE . . . BUT]" Such a remark contains only a tentative identification of his feelings empathizes with them somewhat, but allows you to persist with your script after acknowledging the message his body language conveys. As an alternative, you can simply ignore negative body language, and march steadfastly through your script. There is no rule of "proper conversation" which says you must respond to someone's body language. So, just keep delivering your script as though you had a warmly receptive audience. After all, it'll be for only a few minutes.

A particular form of negative body language is total silence from your Downer. He listens to your script, then simply clams up, "stonewalls it," sits in disapproving or despondent silence. He won't agree or disagree with your proposals. What to do?

To deal with silence, you might ask questions as you go along with your DESC script. For example, after your DESCRIBE line you might say "Do you agree with my observations?" After your EXPRESS lines, you might say "Do you hear me when I tell you how I feel?" If you continue to get no response, then you can ignore his silence and interpret it explicitly as his consenting to your proposal. Have your script contract so worded that it requires no discussion from the Downer; state it so that it goes into effect unless he objects explicitly to the terms of the contract. You can say, for clarification, "I consider your silence to be your consent and agreement to the contract as I've stipulated it". Then you can leave the confrontation scene and begin to apply the terms of the contract. If your Downer doesn't like the terms, he'll simply have to break out of his silence and begin negotiating with you. The important point in dealing with the "silent treatment" is to interpret silence as you wish rather than to let it entangle you in the Downer's anger or depression. Remember, the talker usually has the upper hand in structuring the way the interaction goes.

If a negative-vibes reaction is something you have learned to expect, and is in itself a distressing behavior that you'd like to see changed, you might try delivering a separate assertive message on the subject (see the example in Chapter 6, page 121).

APOLOGIZING DETOURS

After describing your Downer's offensive behavior and how you feel about it, you may be interrupted by excessive apologies. Your Downer berates and humbles himself, saying he is to blame for it all, and he promises to stop all offensive behavior. The problem with this detour is to avoid feeling guilty for having caused him to be so apologetic. The tip-off that you've been manipulated by an excessive apologizer is when you notice yourself saying, "Oh, I guess it's okay," or "Really, I'm sorry, I didn't mean to imply you were *that* bad. Don't be so hard on yourself." You really think the person's behavior was offensive, but you are embarrassed by the excessive apology and try to stop it with "okay, okay."

Remind yourself that this encounter began with your feeling that you were the injured party in this relationship. The apologizer's excessive self-recrimination may be a manipulative tactic (like tears) to make you feel sorry. Try to shut it off firmly, then get agreement to the contract in your script. Often you can use a hand gesture that says "Enough!" to stop the apologizer, or just change the subject directly by saying, "Let's talk about X now."

While people who blame themselves excessively and overapologize may resolve to quit their offensive behavior immediately, they may not stick to that resolution. They probably still need the help of the behavior-change contract to stick to their resolution. Don't let your Downer's apologetic resolution preempt and substitute for a definite contract to change a specific offensive behavior.

THREATENING DETOURS

If your assertive lines anger your Downer, she may respond with exaggerated threats. A threat is an "if . . . , then . . ." promise of hurtful punishment: "If you keep on talking this way to me, then I'm going to leave you." In the heat of battle people often threaten far more extreme punishments than they are likely to carry out in the cold light of reason.

If your Downer reacts to your assertion by threatening you with excessive punishment, assess how likely she is to carry out the threat. If you feel her threat is empty, then you can say so briefly and continue on with your script. Or you could say, "No, I don't think you're going to leave me over such a small matter. My point is . . ."

Suppose you think that your Downer's threat is quite realistic. What do you do? Basically, you need a small back-up script aimed at countering and nullifying your Downer's threat behavior in general and the present threat in particular. Think of "threatening" as a behavior that is modifiable and which can be eliminated much as one eliminates other bad habits. How do you do that? You try never to reward your Downer's threatening behavior; don't let the threat "work" so that she shuts you up and gets her own way. A threat is often only a form of manipulative tantrum, and you should refuse to be manipulated by it. However, whereas you can ignore tantrums (and thus, you hope, extinguish them), you can't ignore realistic threats. They are promises of punishment aimed directly at you, and they must be dealt with very carefully and forthrightly.

There are two ways to counter threat behaviors. First, you can verbally criticize the Downer's use of threats as an immature way to deal with a conflict. An accepted cultural ethic is that people should not use force, violence, and coercion in dealing with one another. You appeal to that ethic if you describe your Downer's threatening behavior as barbaric and unreasonable, manipulative or domineering.

Second, you can respond to the threat with a counterthreat, specifying or pointing out negative consequences for your Downer if she carries out her threatened punishment. In some cases you need merely to point out bad consequences that would automatically flow from her own action —

for instance, "If you leave me, you'll just be miserable," or "All our friends would shun you if they heard you call me these names." In other cases you might need to specify counterpunishments you would be willing to carry out if your Downer carries out her threat. Here you are fighting fire with fire; it is dangerous business because it can escalate. Assertive people decide *ahead* of the confrontation exactly how much fire they want to play with. They take responsibility for their counterthreats — they don't shoot from the hip in the heat of battle.

Here are some examples of threats and assertive replies.

Threatening detours	*Assertive replies*
"You keep talking like that to me, and I'm gonna tell your Dad you've been skipping class."	"If you turn me in, I'll turn you in, too [STIPULATE CONSEQUENCES], so we're locked together by that threat . . . I feel terrible when we fight. [EMPHASIZE FEELINGS] Can we solve our disagreement? [PERSIST]"
"Don't talk that way to me or I'll cut off your allowance."	"I feel put down and I think you are overreacting to my request for more independence. [EMPHASIZE FEELINGS] We have a real problem here [EMPHASIZE THOUGHTS] and losing my allowance is only going to make it worse. [STIPULATE CONSEQUENCES]"
"If you complain any more, I won't recommend you for promotion."	"I think my complaint is reasonable [PERSIST] and I feel compelled to oppose inadequate working conditions. [EMPHASIZE FEELINGS] If you continue threatening me, I will go to the Personnel Office to report this unethical threat from a supervisor. [STIPULATE CONSEQUENCES]"

Basically these replies are saying, "My assertion is reasonable and within my rights; your threat is counterproductive and I won't let it deter me, so let's get on with solving the problem that's facing both of us." Remember, try not to let a threat succeed, since it will only encourage your Downer to threaten you the next time you assert yourself. (Even if you decide to give up your assertion goal, don't let it appear that you did so because of the threat.) Try to reward your Downer for resolving conflicts without the use of threats. For instance, you could say, "If we can talk calmly about our budget without your threatening me, then I'll take care of all those errands you've wanted me to do."

Caution. If you think your Downer will react to your assertion with a physical attack on you, then choose a less heated issue for assertiveness. Alternatively, choose a setting that will inhibit violent reactions. For example, you
could deliver your script in a crowded restaurant or over the telephone.
Also, you could include in your script a stipulation to reduce violence in
future negotiations. Be cautious in asserting yourself with people who lose
physical control easily. Seek individual counseling before asserting yourself
with a potentially violent Downer.

If you miscalculate and begin your assertive script only to find your
Downer rising to the verge of violence, leave the scene quickly and stay
away for a while. Anger usually dissipates over time. Anger can also be
dissipated if you get the attacker to think about another topic. If you provoke a physical attack, rethink your scene and script, wait for tempers to
cool, try again, perhaps in a different setting with a different subject or
approach.

DEBATING DETOURS

Some Downers are very analytic, "reasonable" debaters who are quite agile
in arguing against your claims and proposals. One line of the debater's
attack is to ask you lots of questions; a second is to advance counterarguments to your views or proposals. Let's consider these in turn.

Suppose your Downer interrupts your script by a string of "why" questions: "Why do you feel that way?" "Why do you want me to do that?"
"Why" questions require stating the *cause* or *justification* for your action.
You can often answer simply by restating your immediate goal. Some
examples of assertive replies follow.

Debating detours	*Assertive replies*
"Why are you talking about my behavior?"	"I feel compelled to express my feelings about it. [EMPHASIZE FEELINGS]"
"Why are you asking me to change?"	"Because the way you act now in this situation is irritating (or whatever) to me. [EMPHASIZE FEELINGS]"
"Do you really think I need a payoff?"	"Yes. I think it will help you enjoy the change and stick to the agreement. [ANSWER QUICKLY]"

If asked to explain your feelings, you can restate them and elaborate a bit, but
avoid off-the-cuff, inflammatory justifications for your EXPRESS. It is unnecessary and often self-defeating to *explain* feelings. If you do that, you'll
find you are trapped and can rarely regain your composure to think rationally
about solving the immediate problem.

Because debating is a typical reaction to an assertive message, practice answering "why" questions directed at your script lines. Avoid going into detail, since that only provides more material for a debater to argue with. Also, the more impromptu lines you say under stress, the more likely you are to fall back on the negative verbal habits that have defeated you in the past.

If your Downer pushes you with a series of "why" questions, stop them with a simple "feeling premise": "Why? Because I *just feel that way* and I don't have to give any further justification for my feelings." You take a simple stand on what you feel or what you dislike or want; and you state it as the "ground floor" or first premise which for you needs no further justification.

To deal with a counterargument (as opposed to a "why" approach) you will need to repeat or paraphrase your own point or argument until you can get it across. Before rephrasing your point, you may acknowledge the counterargument by noncommittal phrases such as "That may be, but my point is . . ." or "That's your view, but my view is . . ." Your objective here is to contract for behavior change, not to win an intellectual debate according to the rules of logic. Your Downer may have superior logic and eloquence, but you have one overwhelming and undeniable premise on your side, namely, your "feeling premise." You feel upset about the way your Downer has been treating you in a specific situation. He can argue until doomsday without either changing the situation in the future or affecting how you feel about it now. Even if he won't concede that he has treated you unfairly, he cannot deny that you feel unhappy right now. Tell him how you feel at the moment when these intellectual monologs get you down. EMPHASIZE your FEELINGS. Then PERSIST: insist upon some kind of behavior change.

A debater who argues against your every proposal may construct an argument that you don't know how to answer. Here are a few tips: First, if you don't understand a debater's argument, ask him to clarify it for you, to paraphrase or make it more concrete for you. Ask him to clarify emotional terms like "trust," maturity," "irresponsible." Also ask that the logic of his argument be spelled out, and examine it for hidden assumptions that are tipped in his favor. Second, if you need time to think over a statement or counterproposal, ask for it. Take *time out*, then return to the fray. Third, be sure to PERSIST in stating your complaint and what you want your Downer to do about it.

TOUGH CASES: PROCRASTINATING DETOURS AND NONNEGOTIATING DETOURS

So far, you've met only the "lightweight" fighters — Downers who will listen, will probably respond defensively, but will eventually negotiate reasonably with you. Let's now trot out the "heavyweights," the really tough Downers who can put you through the wringer.

Procrastinating Detours — Subtle Form of Nonnegotiation

The Downer who uses procrastinating detours is a misleading strategist who appears to listen and seems ready to agree with your proposed contract, but in fact will do anything to postpone a decision on your proposal. She responds with phrases like, "Very interesting! Let me think about it." "Let me check it out. I'll get back to you." But then she never gets back to you. She simply says, "Wait." Her "research" goes on forever; she never manages to find all the answers. Unlike the simple put-off detour, by which a person puts off having to hear your message, the true procrastinating detour deceives you into thinking you've made progress but then the Downer escapes from making any agreement for change.

Each request for postponement of a contract decision must be judged on its merits. Grant one such request if you're convinced your Downer has a good reason. Otherwise, insist upon reaching an agreement while you have the person there. Failing to force an immediate agreement, you can handle the procrastinating detour in two ways.

First, you can set an early deadline for making a decision without further delay. Contract with your Downer that she will reach an agreement with you by that time; if she doesn't produce any new information, objections, or alternative proposals by then, she forfeits all rights to delay the decision or raise future objections.

A second technique is to insist on a *tentative* immediate agreement along with provisions for further negotiation. You agree now to a contract which will go into force unless she objects or makes new proposals by a given deadline. Your tentative agreement reads, "Unless you get back to me with an alternative plan by next Monday noon, I will interpret your silence to mean that you agree to the proposed contract, so it will go into effect then."

A variation is a "conditional" contract. Suppose a personnel manager wants to delay a decision about your request until she consults the company's labor-relations officer. Anticipate what answers she will receive from the officer in order to plan contract actions you and the manager can make now. A conditional contract would read, "If the labor officer says yes to this question, then Contract #1 will be in force between us; if he says no, then Contract #2 will be in force." As before, you also agree on a specific time when the issue must be finally settled and acknowledged.

Be present at consultations. If the two of you postpone a decision in order to get an authoritative opinion from a consultant, it is assertive to ask to be present at that consultation when the opinion is delivered. Consider the following situations.

- A woman and her husband disagree over plans for raising their children. The wife says she'll present the problem to a child psychologist, who can help them decide how to raise the children. The husband insists (rightly) that he be there to present the problem, listen to, and question the psychologist.
- A supervisor and employee disagree about the employee's job responsibilities. The supervisor agrees to ask her executive officer, and the employee says he will ask his shop steward (labor union manager). They recognize they should arrange a joint meeting of the four — the supervisor, executive officer, employee, and union steward — to decide the question.

You need to be present at such consultations so you can present your view fairly rather than having your Downer present only her version of the facts. Also, you have a right to be there so you can hear the consultant's advice rather than getting it second-hand through your Downer. If necessary, plan a DESC script to present your viewpoint before that consultant.

Nonnegotiating Detours

Suppose after listening to your plan, your Downer flatly rejects it as unacceptable. Although a contract may be unacceptable for many reasons, in most cases either your Downer thinks that his behavior is not offensive at all or he says that the promised rewards or penalties are not big enough to induce him to change. To answer the first argument, that his behavior really is not offensive, repeat and drive home your EXPRESS statement, telling how you feel about his behavior and perhaps elaborating with a specific instance when you felt bad. It is not necessary that he consider his behavior offensive; he must understand, however, that it offends and bothers *you*.

If the contract is unacceptable because the rewards are not rich enough for him, ask him what rewards he would like for that change, or what part of his behavior he would be willing to change. Negotiate back and forth until you reach a mutually satisfactory compromise. This process usually proceeds rapidly. Suppose the Downer states extremely "expensive" terms you are unwilling to pay. (For example your child wants $5 for each hour he studies, your mate wants you to give up smoking to pay him for helping with dishes.) You could try to convince him that he's asked an unfair price, far beyond the value of the "goods" (his behavior change), and you could ask him to reduce his price.

In some cases you may propose several solutions to a problem, all of which your Downer rejects. Then throw the initiative onto his shoulders. Say, "You propose an acceptable solution. I want some kind of reasonable agreement because I won't have this problem continue. If you don't, then I will carry out the consequences I stipulated earlier." The ball is now in his court, and it is his responsibility to propose a new contract. Give him time, perhaps until tomorrow. But set a *definite* time soon when you will listen to his proposal. At that meeting, if he has no new proposal, you might have others to suggest. Assertive people keep on working toward a mutually agreeable solution.

In the the toughest case, your Downer simply refuses to talk about the problem. He listens to your message, says "That's ridiculous!" and stomps out of the room. What now? We suggest that you apply the DESC procedure to his refusals to negotiate. You could describe what he's doing (for example, walking away from you), express how you feel about it (for example, you're discouraged because he won't even discuss a bothersome problem), specify the behavioral change you want (for example, you want him to schedule 30 minutes tonight when he'll discuss it with you), and cite consequences if he doesn't comply (for example, you will cancel out of a dinner party in honor of his boss this weekend).

Let's consider the case of one woman faced with a nonnegotiating partner:

Situation. My husband rarely helped with household chores. Whenever I broached the matter, he responded with a cold shoulder. I wrote this script to get him to negotiate. I delivered it to him in a restaurant on a Friday evening. He wouldn't walk out on a good meal — or me!

> **DESCRIBE**   Essential jobs are not being done around the house.
>
> **EXPRESS**   I feel resentful and I think we need to talk about the mess we're in.
>
> **SPECIFY**   I would like to talk now about who should do what jobs. If not now, how about tomorrow (Saturday) after your golf game?
>
> **CONSEQUENCES**   *Positive:* I'll feel less pressured and uptight if we can agree to talk about our household jobs.
> [*Negative:* If you don't agree, I'll just keep talking about the problem.]

Results. He was surly and withdrawn after I delivered this script. However, I kept talking, reiterating the main points above. He looked at the newspaper to avoid me, but I immediately said, "Don't run away. Give me an answer!" He agreed to listen. Then I went into my original DESC script regarding the sharing of chores around our apartment.

Having devised a script to modify your Downer's refusal to negotiate, you need some way to communicate it to him. If your Downer won't listen now, perhaps he will later, after he's cooled down. If he refuses to listen, leave a note conveying the essence of your "let's negotiate" script on his office desk, or pin a note on his pajamas, or send him a letter. If he ignores this script, apply the negative consequences and send another note. If you still get no answer — if he "stonewalls it" — escalate the consequences to whatever you're willing to risk in solving your original problem.

And speaking of what you'd be willing to risk, consider this tale of a nonnegotiator to whom a strong penalty had to be applied.

Situation. My boyfriend is very hip and attractive, but has a terrifying habit of driving 75 miles per hour and within one yard of the car ahead of us. It scares me to death! Simple pleadings from me had achieved nothing. In exasperation, I used this script *before* we started out on a Saturday adventure. It involves an escalated threat.

> **DESCRIBE** I've told you several times that you drive much too fast and too close to other cars.
>
> **EXPRESS** I am constantly frightened that we'll have an accident. I feel you should be more considerate of my fears.
>
> **SPECIFY** I want you to drive 55 miles an hour and stay at least 60 feet behind the car we're following.
>
> **CONSEQUENCES** *Positive:* If you change and drive slower, then I'll make you the leather belt you want.
> [*Negative:* If you continue, I will refuse to ride with you. I will make you stop and let me out of the car.]

Results. As expected, he paid no attention to my proposal. The first afternoon, I forced him to let me out on the freeway, 60 miles from home. (I had decided hitchhiking was safer than driving with him!) After that big event, he decided I was serious, so he stopped doing the "speed racer" bit while I was in his car.

If stronger penalties fail, you should reanalyze your needs in the original situation and decide how important it is for your Downer to change his behavior. Suppose you decide that the original discomfort is not worth an escalating hassle with your Downer; then reduce your original request or simply drop it. You will at least feel better about yourself for your assertion. But suppose, on the contrary, that the issue is vitally important to you, and yet your Downer refuses to budge. Then you could take your stand; stop arguing and deliver your "power statement." For example, a wife was becoming increasingly antisocial, never wanting to go out or to entertain friends at home. She repeatedly refused to go out with her husband evenings. Finally, in exasperation, he delivered his ultimatum: "Either go out with me once a week or I will go out by myself twice a week." After he had been going out alone for several weeks, his wife compromised and went out with him once a week.

Consider another case: Michael had moved into Cynthia's apartment, promising to pay half the rent, but after three months Cynthia realized that she was paying the entire telephone bill, including his long-distance calls. Her attempts to get him to pay half the phone bill were first met with silence, then with his saying he didn't want a phone in the apartment and wouldn't pay for hers. Her options, to remove the phone or to pay for his calls, seemed equally unacceptable to her. Cynthia then thought up and presented her ultimatum to Michael: either pay half the bill or I'll put a lock on the phone. Michael initially refused to pay. But after two weeks of inconvenience because of the phone lock, Michael realized how much he had been using the phone and reluctantly agreed to pay half the bill.

Ultimatums shouldn't be given without carefully weighing the consequences and your willingness to carry them out because more often than not the nonnegotiator will force you to exercise your power statement before conceding to meet you at the negotiating table. Hopefully, such crises and ultimatums will not become a regular event in your life. Assertive people plan ahead so that conflicts don't escalate to crisis proportions.

SOME SAMPLE DESC SCRIPTS
WITH DOWNER DETOURS

Now that you've seen some detours and possible counterreplies, let's consider two examples of complete DESC scripts in action.

Situation. Your daughter frequently asks you, the Grandmother, to babysit without enough advance notice.

DESCRIBE Over the past several weeks, you have asked me to babysit at the very last minute a number of times.

Downner detour: Sorry about that! I asked you to sit because I thought you liked children. [reinterpreting]

Assertive reply: I love kids. However, I am not talking about whether I like kids, I'm talking about your asking me to babysit on the spur of the minute. [DISAGREE and REDEFINE]

EXPRESS I am inconvenienced and annoyed when you ask me to babysit on such short notice.

Downner detour: That is not true. [denying] I always ask you if you are busy before I leave the kids.

Assertive reply: I know better than you if I'm inconvenienced and annoyed by being asked to babysit at the last minute. [DISAGREE and PERSIST]

SPECIFY I would be happy to keep the kids once or twice a month on week nights if you would give me at least two days advance notice. Will you do that?

Downner detour: I'm *terribly* sorry that I bothered you. [apologizing]

Assertive reply: I accept your apology. [ANSWER QUICKLY] If we can have an agreement, about two days advance notice for two weekdays a month, I will feel much better about babysitting. [PERSIST]

CONSEQUENCES   *Positive:* I would be able to plan for them, and enjoy the sitting.

Downer detour: Well, I *hope* so. I guess you resent having to babysit my kids very much. [psychoanalyzing]

Assertive reply: I like to babysit when it is convenient for me. [REDEFINE]

[*Negative:* Remember, once or twice a month. If you call me more than that, I'll say no.]

Downer detour: I wouldn't *dream* of inconveniencing you. [joking]

Assertive reply: Thanks very much. [DISMISS and ANSWER QUICKLY]

Situation. One of your secretaries is overstepping boundaries when it comes to chatting with her friends on the job. The socializing is interfering with her work.

DESCRIBE   I have noticed that your work is slowing down and I believe it is because your friends frequently stop by your desk to visit.

Downer detour: But they are friends of mine and *they* want to talk to me. [blaming]

Assertive reply: I know you have many friends and I know they want to talk to you — but I think the office is a place to work, not socialize. [AGREE . . . BUT]

EXPRESS   I feel annoyed when your work is not completed.

Downer detour: But my work isn't affected! [denying]

Assertive reply: I know it is. [DISAGREE] Your uncompleted work shows your performance is affected. [PERSIST]

SPECIFY   Starting today I strongly suggest you tell your friends to meet you outside of office hours to chat. Will you do that?

Downer detour: But some of them are on a different break time than mine. [debating]

Assertive reply: That may be the case, but either they will have to adjust their break time, or they'll have to meet you during lunch or after work. [AGREE . . . BUT]

CONSEQUENCES   *Positive:* I'll appreciate a quiet atmosphere for working.
Downer detour: I didn't mean it to get so lively. [reinterpreting]

Assertive reply: That may be, but I feel distracted by so much noise and it is important to me to work in a quiet atmosphere. [AGREE . . . BUT and EMPHASIZE FEELINGS]

[*Negative:* If the visiting continues after now, I'll talk to you again about this matter.]

Downer detour: I don't see why I have to get all the criticism; others visit too. [debating]

Assertive reply: You don't get it all. [DISAGREE] I intend to cut down on everyone's personal visiting on company time. [PERSIST]

YOUR SCRIPT, YOUR DOWNER'S DETOURS, AND YOUR REPLIES

This chapter has considered the diverse ways a Downer can thwart your assertive actions — the gambits, one-uppers, put-offs, and put-downs that Downers use. You have anticipated some reactions your DESC lines might provoke, and have considered counterreplies. Because the human intellect is marvelously inventive, we can't claim to have identified all possible defensive maneuvers or diversionary techniques, or to have prepared you for any and all rejoinders to your assertions. But this chapter has prepared you for most detours.

Normally a domestic conflict (say, getting the plants watered) doesn't get into such elaborate argumentation and arbitration. Most scripts are stated and agreed to in a few seconds or minutes without this hoop-la. The countering techniques are for use with tougher problems, where your Downer may be unsympathetic or hostile to your interests, where you need real courage and rebuttal practice. Courage comes largely from anticipating the other person's arguments and being prepared to reply to them assertively without losing your dignity or your train of thought.

Now it's time to practice assertive replies to your Downer's detours. We suggest that you first review the lists on pages 144 – 145 (names of detours, kinds of replies), and then revise the work you did in Chapter 7 (pages 128 – 129). For convenience, space for rewriting is provided below.

YOUR DESC SCRIPT WITH DETOURS AND ASSERTIVE REPLIES

DESCRIBE _____

_____

_____

_____

Downer detour: _____

_____

Assertive reply: _____

_____

EXPRESS _____

_____

_____

_____

Downer detour: _____

Assertive reply: _____

_____

SPECIFY _____

_____

_____

_____

Downer detour: _____

Assertive reply: _____

_____

CONSEQUENCES *Positive:* _____

_____

Downer detour: _____

Assertive reply: _____

_____

[Negative: _____

_____]

Downer detour: _____

_____

Assertive reply: _____

_____

Note: If you anticipate more than one detouring sentence after any of the DESC steps, prepare your specific replies to those detours on a separate sheet of paper.

If your Downer is likely to take a procrastinating detour, write a mini-script here to ask for tentative agreement on your contract:

DESCRIBE _____
_____
_____
_____

EXPRESS _____
_____
_____

SPECIFY _____
_____

CONSEQUENCES _____
_____
_____

If your Downer is a nonnegotiator, write a mini-script here to get him or her to negotiate with you. Also consider the ultimate consequences you are willing to risk.

DESCRIBE _____
_____
_____
_____

EXPRESS _____
_____
_____

SPECIFY _____
_____

CONSEQUENCES _____
_____
_____

These are the ultimate consequences I am willing to risk to bring about a change in my Downer's behavior:

_____

_____

    With the completion of these exercises you will have put the final touches on your script. You have thought all the way through your problem scene, so now think of other situations in which you feel inadequate or put down. Write DESC scripts for those conflicts, including assertive replies to possible Downer detours.

    Again, practice is important. It may be helpful to work with a buddy (see pages 136–137). Or try recording your script so you can listen to it repeatedly and improve upon the quality and number of your assertive counterreplies. For example, you might record a line of your DESC script, then record an imagined reaction to that line (recorded by you in a voice resembling your Downer's). Then leave a blank space of a minute or less on the tape, and after you've thought of a good counterreply, record it at this spot on the tape. If you think of several replies, record all of them. The tape can then serve as an assertive "model" for your later actions; it allows you to imagine yourself in the conflict scene, to hear your Downer's reactions to you, and to hear your assertive replies in a strong, expressive voice. Your objective is to so engrave these tapes in your memory that your assertive replies will come quickly to mind during a confrontation.

    For more about practicing for an expressive, confident delivery — affecting how you look as well as how you sound — read Chapter 9.

9

Looking and Feeling Assertive

*To feel brave, act as if you were brave . . . and a
courage fit will very likely replace the fit of fear.*

WILLIAM JAMES

Writing the DESC script is a good beginning toward assertive action. But
scripts are written to be delivered to another person. The final step is to
develop assertive speaking patterns, body language, and appearance to
match your script. In this way you continue planning for success. The ability
to plan for success in all details is one mark of an assertive person.

Nonassertive people may say that the language of their script isn't
"natural," that they're not "comfortable" with those sentences. They say "If I
could just get the right *feelings* first, I'd be able to deliver the script with the
right expression and body movements." But for now, it is better to concentrate on assertive *actions,* not feelings. The feelings are likely to follow the
effective actions.

In this chapter, we will focus on the way you stand, look, walk, and talk,
and suggest how these might be improved so that you communicate
strength and affirmation. In effect, we will present a training program for
use in practicing your script. There are nine phases to this training program.

Phase 1: Prepare to Practice
Phase 2: Highlight Your Script
Phase 3: Learn Your Lines
Phase 4: Develop Assertive Body Language
Phase 5: Speak with More Power
Phase 6: Speak with More Clarity
Phase 7: Speak with More Expression
Phase 8: Set the Stage
Phase 9: Look the Part

The exercises illustrate techniques for developing more expressive body language and speech. These techniques can help you translate a good script into meaningful communication with dramatic impact. People who practice them seriously report they begin to feel assertive and confident as a result.

The nine phases generally require practice over at least four or five days. For example, Phases 1—3 might be accomplished in an hour or two the first day. Phases 4—7 take longer, say three or four days, with about a half hour of practice each day. Phase 8 can be accomplished in a few minutes, and Phase 9 in an hour at most. Don't skip steps and don't rush. Practice until assertive speech and body movements seem like second nature to you. After going through all phases with your first script, you can practice later scripts in much less time.

PHASE 1: PREPARE TO PRACTICE

You should now have in hand a script that is worded as carefully as you can make it. So now, do the following.

- Prepare your script in final form, typed or clearly written. Triple-space the writing so you can see it easily and so you will have space for marginal notes. A messy, crowded script will not help you feel assertive!
- Choose a block of time each day for several days when you won't be interrupted. For example, a contractor took his telephone off the hook during the lunch hour so he could practice; a busy supervisor instructed her secretary not to interrupt her the last 20 minutes of her day. Scheduling time for self-improvement is an important assertive act.
- Clear your desk or table of distractions. A busy clubwoman symbolically covered her piles of volunteer projects with a black cloth; an executive turned her paperwork face down on her desk. Signal to yourself that you are preparing to do something quite different from routine, and that you'll allow no interference.
- Assemble these materials and objects: a pack of 3 x 5 cards, three or four colored pens or pencils, a tennis ball.

PHASE 2: HIGHLIGHT YOUR SCRIPT

Familiarize yourself with the flow of your script; select "highlights" or words that carry its main message.

1. Read your script three times *aloud* to hear the overall flow of the steps: DESCRIBE → EXPRESS → SPECIFY → CONSEQUENCES.
2. Write the line or lines for each step on a 3 x 5 card, *one step per card.*
3. Underline with green pen the words that carry the main thought in each sentence. Underline in blue those words that should carry the feeling or emotion of your message. (Or use whatever other colors you have available.)

To illustrate, here is a script a woman wrote, practiced, and delivered. Her significant words are underlined. She wanted to ask her husband to change a Christmas tradition, which included a huge dinner she prepared for her husband's office staff along with the hassle of decorating a 15-foot Christmas tree. She felt sad that their Christmas had become too materialistic and frantic. A single underline denotes her significant thought words and double underlines denote her feeling words.

DESCRIBE You suggested that we spend some time during Christmas vacation at Sunset Beach.

EXPRESS The kids and I really want to spend our Christmas there, too. They're so enthusiastic they offered to give up half their gifts for the opportunity.

SPECIFY I have a tentative hold on the house with a waterbed from Monday, the 23rd through Monday, the 30th. I would like all of us to go. Will you go?

CONSEQUENCES My sister could bring your mother for a few days. That way, our family could be alone together the rest of the week. (To explain: The husband really enjoyed being with his mother as well as his family during Christmas.)

4. Now, read aloud your "green words," those that communicate the idea. Then read aloud the "blue words," those that carry the feeling. Read the words as lists. Don't be afraid you are leaving out the little words, such as "the," "my," or "from." You can remember those little words later, easily and naturally.

5. Next, you may want to make some memory aids to help remember your script. Take four new cards and draw a picture or series of pictures which illustrate your main idea for each step of your script. Use as few pictures as you can. Try to get important (underlined) ideas represented in the picture. Draw a picture for each DESC step. Here are examples for DESCRIBE and EXPRESS using stick figures.

This picture illustrates the DESCRIBE line, "You suggested that we spend some time during Christmas vacation at Sunset Beach."

This picture illustrates the EXPRESS line, "The kids and I really want to spend our Christmas there. They are so enthusiastic that they've offered to give up half their gifts for the opportunity."

Now try drawing pictures — one to a card — for your own script.

PHASE 3: LEARN YOUR LINES

People tend to forget poorly learned scripts when they are under fire emotionally. To prevent this from spoiling your first assertive appearance, learn your script well. Use the pictures you have just drawn. Learn their sequence, and use them to call to mind the most important lines of your script.

- Using the pictures as prompts, say the script aloud five or six times. If you cannot recall the underlined words, redraw the pictures until you have no trouble recalling the words when you look at the pictures.
- Test yourself, seeing the pictures in your imagination as you talk about them. Recall the pictures and try to get the exact words of the associated sentence.

Rehearse the script aloud until it comes easily and spontaneously. The picture method can help people learn faster.

- Now recall your script aloud as you do a small easy task. Select a task that involves only hand movements that come automatically to you, like tying your shoe, sewing on a button, or polishing silver. You are training yourself to recall your script while handling minor distractions.
- Say your script aloud as you do a big job that involves big muscles. Make a bed, wash the car, vacuum a rug, or jump rope as you say your script aloud.

Let the strength in your muscles be reflected in the force of your voice. Feel the energy flow into your voice as you vigorously attack that big job.

- Say your script aloud as you bounce a tennis ball, toss it up and catch it. Try speaking your script with a lilting pitch and volume attuned to the movements of the ball, flipping the ball from side to side, tossing it high then low, bouncing it high then low. Don't be shy about it. Train yourself to think, speak, and move at the same time. The rhythm or phrasing can heighten the enjoyment and show you new ways to express meaning through your voice.

- Practice answering your Downer's objections. Look back at the list you made (page 167) of your Downer's possible objections to your script and your rejoinders. Practice your counterreplies aloud, and then get back on the track with your DESC script.

PHASE 4: DEVELOP ASSERTIVE BODY LANGUAGE

First, discover the nonassertive messages your body sends to others. Read over the following list of nonassertive mannerisms, get them clearly in mind, then observe yourself in a mirror as you deliver your script three successive times. After each run-through, note how often you fall into each

PRACTICING ASSERTIVE EXPRESSION

of these inappropriate mannerisms. At the end of your run-throughs, rate a behavior 3 if you think it occurs far too much; rate it 2 if it is moderately frequent and could definitely be improved; rate it 1 if its frequency is acceptably low. Work to lower the frequency of those nonassertive mannerisms you rated 3 or 2.

One way to eliminate these mannerisms is to observe yourself carefully in the mirror and mentally say, "Stop that!" whenever you catch yourself performing a nonassertive mannerism. In addition, you can practice the specific suggestions given after each bad mannerism.

Eye contact. Practice eliminating these nonassertive behaviors:

_____ *Blinking rapidly.* You can reduce some excessive blinking by closing and relaxing your eyelids. Begin to speak. When ready, open your eyes gently and keep your lids relaxed.

_____ *Staring fixedly.* You can replace staring by shifting your gaze about every few seconds. As you speak, shift your focus about the inner core of your face in the mirror.

_____ *Not looking.* This is "looking away" from the other person's face. To eliminate this, select a spot on your face in the mirror to focus on.

_____ *Shifting your head and eyes excessively.* If necessary, hold your head steady with your hands. If your head constantly moves, stop your speech and begin again. If your eyes constantly flitter about, concentrate on holding fixations for about five seconds before shifting to another part of your "listener's" face.

_____ *Squinting your eyes.* Check for eyestrain and whether you need glasses. Relax the muscles around the eyes, perhaps apply a damp cloth to cool and relax your eyes.

_____ Initial here when you are satisfied with your eye contact.

Facial expression. Practice eliminating these nonassertive behaviors:

_____ *A pursed, tight-lipped, mouth.* Feel your lip muscles with your fingers as you talk. To correct tight lips, pucker up very hard, then let your jaw hang loose, and relax the muscles around your lips.

_____ *Tensing and wrinkling your forehead.* Smooth out your tense forehead by running a hand over "worry wrinkles." Stroke away those lines. Relax your forehead and begin speaking again. To reduce forehead wrinkling, one enterprising student stretched out his forehead with tape; another put on an egg yolk mask which solidified and gave her instant feedback when her forehead wrinkled.

_____ *Swallowing repeatedly.* Place your fingers on your Adam's apple and notice your swallowing. If your swallowing distracts you as you say your script, it is probably noticeable to others and will communicate timidity. To correct this, take a sip of water before speaking. Stop speaking each time you swallow, relax and take a deep breath. Swallow while concentrating on the wave of relaxation that follows the wave of throat tension. Exaggerate and memorize the feeling of an open, relaxed throat. Practice relaxing your throat by recalling that feeling in your throat several times a day.

_____ *Clearing your throat excessively.* Clear your throat or take a drink of water before you begin your script. Relax your throat as above.

_____ *Wetting your lips.* Use chapstick or lipstick for dry lips. Dry lips may indicate fear and tension. To relieve tense lips, first exaggerate lip tension by pursing them into a curled-up, super-kiss position. Hold for 10 seconds, then let go. Feel them relax. Repeat this several times now and throughout the day.

_____ Initial here when you are satisfied with your facial expression.

Gestures and posture. Practice eliminating these nonassertive behaviors:

_____ *Covering your mouth when speaking.* To stop this annoying habit, rehearse your script while holding two objects, one in each hand. The objects will remind you to keep your hands away from your face as you talk. After practicing with the objects a few minutes, lay them aside and practice several trials without them.

_____ *Scratching your head, or rubbing your eye or the back of your neck.* Use the "two objects" exercise above.

_____ *Preening.* Examples are touching your hair, looking at fingernails, curling your mustache, or stroking your beard. To stop it, use the "two objects" exercise.

_____ *Tinkering with jewelry.* Use the "two objects" exercise.

_____ *Adjusting your clothing.* Use the "two objects" exercise.

_____ *Shifting your weight from one foot to another.* To insure standing still, "nail" your feet down with heavy books. When you shift weight, a book slipping off your foot will make you aware of your "shiftiness." Replace the book on the guilty foot and begin your script again.

_____ *Wandering or pacing.* To reduce pacing, put yourself in "prison" by placing two chairs on either side of you, thus hemming yourself in. If you pace in all directions, put chairs in front and in back of you also.

____ *Freezing like a statue.* If you freeze up and are afraid to move, try some moving exercises. First is a comic movement, to show you how *not* to move. (1) Put your weight on your *right* foot, (2) look *left* and *smile,* and then (3) *move right* with your *left foot* while looking left at the same time. That should feel awkward. To move gracefully, try this: (1) put your weight on your *right* foot, (2) look *left* and *smile,* and then (3) *move left* with your *left foot* while looking left at the same time. Here your head and feet move harmoniously and confidently in the same direction at the same time.

____ Initial here when you feel you have eliminated your most distracting body movements and gestures.

Nonassertive mannerisms communicate timidity and distract your listener, who watches you instead of listening to your words. Body language can speak more powerfully than words, so rehearse it at least as carefully as you rehearse your words.

PHASE 5: SPEAK WITH MORE POWER

Your voice is your most effective instrument for expressing your words with power and self-assurance. Like most of us, you can probably benefit from exercises to improve your speaking voice. People's first impressions of us are often dominated by our voice quality. We may characterize a new acquaintance as "friendly" if his or her voice sounds warm and well modulated, but think of the same person as "dull and uninteresting" if it sounds flat and monotonous.

Similarly, while an assertive script communicates rational meaning, its emotional overtones are conveyed by your voice. If you're too loud, you may appear bombastic; if too soft, you may sound timid. Feelings are also communicated by your rate of speaking: too rapid connotes impatience or anger, too slow connotes hesitancy or fear. And the tonal quality of your voice impresses others in varying ways: a nasal voice suggests stupidity, a thin, wispy voice conveys weakness, a lisp suggests immaturity.

The exercises that follow can help you acquire a more assertive voice. We begin here with exercises to help you increase the volume and projection of your voice. The exercises listed under Phases 6 and 7 can help you speak with greater clarity and expressiveness.

If possible, use a tape recorder for the following exercises. As before, there is a checklist for assessing your voice quality initially. Rate yourself on each point as 1 (okay), 2 (suspect), or 3 (terrible — needs improvement), and work to improve your weakest vocal qualities.

Breathing

Because exhaled air initiates voice sounds, forceful speech requires correct breathing and careful use of air. Speakers who breathe improperly literally run out of breath and end up sounding shaky and weak. Here's how you can find out whether you breathe correctly.

_____ Stand erect and put your hand flat against your diaphragm, that large muscle below your rib cage that extends across your front and above your stomach. Take a deep breath without raising your shoulders. If your chest expanded (your diaphragm moved down and your hand went *out*) as you breathed in, then you are probably breathing correctly. But if your hand did not go out as you inhaled, you are probably breathing incorrectly and should correct it.

To acquire better breathing, repeat the following exercise as many times as needed to see and hear improvement. Deliberately push out the area below your ribs as you inhale. When you do this right as you inhale, your hand will be forced out a little. Practice pushing your hand out as you *inhale.* Do this several times a day until you become accustomed to it. Breathe this way as you practice saying your script.

_____ Initial here when you think you are breathing correctly.

Sustaining Power

Now that you are breathing correctly, check how well you can control your use of air to produce sustained sound.

_____ Find a clock with a second-hand to record your time, or count off seconds approximately by thinking "Mississippi 1, Mississippi 2," etc. Now, standing erect, put one hand flat on your diaphragm (below the rib cage); use a finger of the other hand to close one ear. (With one ear closed you can hear the quality of your voice better.) Take a deep breath (push diaphragm *down*), and then say "Ahhhhhh" for as long as your breath lasts. Note the number of seconds you can say "Ahhhhhh" before your voice dies out. Your goal is to produce this sound steadily for at least 45 seconds.

To improve your vocal strength, repeat the above procedure for several short sessions every day. Record your time, and try in each session to exceed your previous time. Record and work to improve your holding times for other vowel sounds in the same manner. The sounds you should produce and record are shown in the following record-keeping chart.

Sound	Longest time held (in seconds):						
	Day 1	Day 2	Day 3	Day 4	Day 5	Day 6	Day 7
ä as in bar							
ă as in pat							
ā as in pay							
ē as in bee							
ī as in pie							
ō as in toe							
ô as in caught							
o͞o as in boot							

_____ Initial here when you are satisfied with your sustaining power.

Projection

The next area to examine is how well you project your voice — that is, how well you make your words carry to the place you want them to go. This is something a little different from loudness alone. It is projection that allows skilled actors to be heard in the far corners of a theater without shouting. To project or "throw" your voice correctly you must focus on the location to which you want your words to carry, and mentally "aim" your words in that direction.

_____ Say your script aloud, looking at yourself in the mirror, and tape record your script. If you would rather talk to someone else, use your buddy or a large picture of your Downer as a target. (Students report that seeing their Downer not talk back to them diminishes their nervousness.) Then listen critically to your recorded voice, or discuss your delivery with your buddy. Does what you say really sound "aimed" toward your listener, or do you seem to be bottling it up, reciting a monolog that you'd be just as happy to keep to yourself?

The following game can help you get the feel of projecting your voice to any desired spot. The game requires a tennis ball and can be played indoors or outdoors. Find a partner who will play the game with you, or throw the ball at a wall or garage door, which will return it to you and serve as a "partner."

Standing five feet from your partner, toss the ball underhand to him or her; at the same time, throw the word "Helllllloooooo," as if it were being carried by the ball. Sustain your "Helllllloooooo" as long as the ball is in the air. Then have your partner toss the ball back to you and project his or her "Helllllloooooo" to you. Repeat two or three throws at a five-foot distance. Next, move farther away from each other, to about ten feet, and repeat the toss with the "Helllllloooooo." Continue backing away at each toss of the ball until you reach about twenty feet. Now reverse the process and begin to move together again, throwing the ball and your "Helllllloooooo" at more closely spaced intervals. Observe how your vocal muscles feel and your voice sounds when you "throw it" differing distances.

_____ Initial here when you are satisfied with your voice projection.

Speaking Distance

How easily can you be heard at differing distances? Ask a couple of friends if they can easily hear you when you are standing (or when sitting) three to eight feet from them. Do they say you speak too softly or too loudly at these distances? At what distance do they say your voice sounds best? Where is it easiest for others to hear you and where is your voice most pleasant for them to listen to you?

_____ feet

If possible, use this information next time you decide to assert yourself.

PHASE 6: SPEAK WITH MORE CLARITY

Articulation is an important factor in the impression you make on others when you speak. Poor articulation comes across as dull, dumb, sloppy, and irritating. The voice gets confused with the personality. This impression can be corrected by changing your articulation; and that comes down to changing the way your tongue and lips move and increasing the amount of air forced through your lips as you speak.

Here are a few suggestions for testing your articulation:

_____ *Plosives.* Hold a light piece of 3 x 4 paper about 6 inches in front of your mouth. Pucker your lips and in your normal speaking voice sound a *p* as in *pet.* The paper should flutter as you sound that *p.* If it doesn't, use more air and a quicker exploding release of the lips. Try other words having *p* in the first position (*potatoes*) or last position (*tap, top*). Try *b* as in *bet* or *boy*; *t* as in *tart, d* as in *dart, g* as in *good, k* as in *could*. Weak plosives give listeners the impression the speaker is lazy and inarticulate. Notice whether some of your plosives are habitually too weak. They can be improved with practice using feedback from the fluttering paper. Look for and correct weak plosives in your assertive script.

_____ *Nasal sounds.* You have good nasal sounds if you hear a full humming quality as you sound the second "m" in "maim," the "n's" in "noon," and the "ng" in "sing." These are sounded through the nose. If these consonant sounds are weak, try forcing more sound through your nose. Practice on words like "humming", "running," "cane," and "name." Good nasal sounds add resonance and depth to your voice.

_____ *Vowel sounds.* Vowels should not be said through the nose since this can make a voice sound unpleasant and irritating. A simple check on proper vowel sounding is whether the words with vowels sound the same when your nose is closed as when your nose is open. If they sound different, you are sounding your vowels improperly through your nose. Test yourself saying *he, bet, ask, butter, buzz, tooth, jaw, watch*. If these words sound different with nose open versus closed, try to direct more air out your mouth and less out your nose as you sound them. The "sameness" test will provide feedback on correcting your nasalized vowels.

_____ *Lisping.* Lisping usually results from inaccurate placement of the tongue. It creates particular distortions in pronunciation of *s* sounds. For example, *sister* comes out "thithter," *soon* comes out "thoon," *yes* comes out "yeath." Almost any listener can tell you whether you lisp. Lisping is difficult to correct by yourself; you may need help from a speech correctionist.

_____ Initial here when you are satisfied with your articulation.

PHASE 7: SPEAK WITH MORE EXPRESSION

Two vocal characteristics determining your expressiveness are the *pitch* and *rhythm* of your speech. Suppose your rhythm is okay — you speak with pauses and at varying rates — but your voice has a steady high pitch. Then people may tend to think of you as being flighty, without depth. On the other hand, if your voice is well pitched, but you don't vary your speaking rate, you probably sound monotonous and boring. Fortunately, there are things you can do to improve matters in either case. The following exercises can help you extend the pitch range and flexibility and the rhythmic variation of your speaking voice.

Your Average Pitch

Measurements of superior speakers have revealed that the average speaking pitch for the male speakers is close to C below middle C, wher .s for the female speakers it is close to G sharp below middle C. Find these notes on a piano or pitch pipe. To locate your own average pitch, say a sustained "Ohhhh" and find the matching key on the piano. If your pitch is no more than two or three tones (notes) away from the ones typical of superior speakers, it is within normal limits. If your pitch is four or more tones lower or higher than that of the superior speakers, you might want to consider having training from a voice teacher. Answer the following:

What is your average pitch? ____

Is it within two or three tones of a superior speaker's? ____

Pitch Range and Flexibility

To increase your expressiveness you may want to increase your pitch variation while speaking. First, assess the upper and lower limits of your pitch range as follows.

Sound your average pitch and play its matching piano key. Sing and play down the scale to the lowest tone you can sing with reasonable purity and audibility; then sing and play up the scale to the highest note you can sing without straining.

How many white keys are there between your lowest and highest tones? ____

That number is your pitch range. To increase your expressiveness, practice *using* more of your pitch range in everyday conversation.

Many people use too little pitch variation so they sound flat, monotonous, and uninteresting. Pitch variations are called inflections. There are three basic inflections — rising, falling, and complex.

Rising: "Who was that?"
Falling: "Always" or "Absolutely not."
Complex: up-down "Really?" (showing disbelief)
          down-up "No-oo." (showing surprise)

You can use different inflections to express different attitudes. Say the words "oh" or "yes" to express either absolute certitude or grave doubt. Then say them to show slight doubt. Try saying other words with different pitch inflections. Note differences in emotions expressed as you alter the pitch, and notice how your message changes when saying one word with different inflections. After a few trials ask a buddy to listen. Can he or she catch your emotional meaning? Practice in your car or in the shower!

Good actors and actresses use a pitch range of 16 notes or more to interpret dramatic material. By varying pitch, they communicate shades of emotional meaning. If you want listeners to "read" your messages accurately, speak expressively. Extend your pitch range and improve your control of pitch variations. Notice what shades of meanings you can communicate.

Speaking Rate

The best speaking rate depends on how complicated your message is and how clearly you articulate your words. The speech rate of many passive people is too slow and that of many aggressive people is too fast, so listeners get either bored or confused. Speech is painfully slow if it is cluttered by long pauses and by disfluencies such as "ah," "anda," "uh" and repetitive fillers like "okay," "you know," "well," "see." To help eliminate such disfluencies from your speech, you can instruct a friend, spouse, or child to signal whenever you utter your own characteristic disfluency.

The following exercises are recommended for changing your rate of speaking.

Read several paragraphs from a newspaper aloud at your normal speaking rate. Then read it at two other rates. Tape record yourself and replay your voice to estimate whether you articulate well (speak clearly) when speaking faster or slower than your "normal" rate. Ask your buddy to help you determine your best speaking rate. This might be faster or slower than your "normal" rate. Read aloud until this optimal rate feels natural for you.

Now substitute your DESC script for the newspaper, reading your script at this optimal rate. Practice delivering your script *from memory* at this optimal rate.

Next, decide how you might deliberately vary your rate of speaking at different points in your script. Analyze and mark your entire script for pauses, words to be stressed, and words to receive pitch inflections. You'll want to pause slightly before or after important words, and slow down for complicated phrases or important words that carry meaning. After marking your script, practice it with a tape recorder, using the pauses, stresses, and inflections chosen. Edit and correct your markings until you get the emotional tone you want.

Monitor your speech rate in conversations and reward yourself for performing fluently. Keep working on improving your speech rate, eliminating unnecessary pauses and disfluencies, learning to move your lips and tongue so as to increase the clarity of your articulation.

PHASE 8: SET THE STAGE

You have now taken inventory of your body language and your voice. Practicing the exercises we have mentioned can help you act and sound more assertive. By acquiring a more assertive voice and body language, you can begin to *feel* more confident and more capable of speaking up appropriately and expressively.

Nevertheless, even with a well-rehearsed script, you must do certain other things to prepare your family, friends, or work colleagues for taking you seriously when you finally assert yourself. First of all, you need to give some thought to the circumstances in which you'll be delivering your script.

When and where is your Downer most likely to negotiate amicably for a desired change in his behavior or in your relationship to each other? You can set the stage for your first negotiation; arrange the environment so it will support and help negotiations with your Downer. Don't allow yourself to be propelled into delivering your script at an unplanned-for time or place. Specifically:

- Note when your Downer is most receptive. For instance, some people are in a better mood after eating than before.
- Plan a special time to talk. Say, for example, "I'd like to spend 15 minutes after supper to discuss our weekend plans. Is that a good time for you?"
- Stop any potential escalation of emotions during talks that occur before you are ready to proceed. Say, for example, "Let's not get into budget talk now. I've done some thinking about that subject and would like to discuss it Saturday morning when we both have some time. How about 10 o'clock?"

Now, keeping in mind the importance of setting the stage, answer these questions:

1. Who is your script directed to? _____

2. When is the Downer's most agreeable time? _____

3. Can you make this a convenient time for you? _____

4. In what setting is your Downer most likely to listen to you? _____

5. What can you do to encourage his or her listening and agreeableness? _____

PHASE 9: LOOK THE PART

As you undoubtedly know, the way you dress can strongly influence the impressions that others have of you. And when you deliver an assertive message, you don't want to wear clothes that alienate your listener. For instance, a group of conservative retired people might not listen sympathetically to you if you appeared dressed in a hippie costume of beads, headband, jeans, and bare feet. It would be difficult to overcome their negative reaction to the symbolic significance of your clothes.

DO YOU LOOK THE PART?...

Unfortunately, there is a conflicting consideration. If you dress in clothes that feel alien to you — for instance, wearing a business suit and tie when you are accustomed to jeans — you may feel uncomfortable and hypocritical. So, what are you to do? The following suggestions should help you decide what to wear when delivering your assertive message. First try answering these questions.

1. Who is the script directed to? _____

2. Describe briefly how he/she is likely to be dressed when you give your script:

   _____

3. What clothes could you wear to make your Downer most sympathetic to your message? For instance, what style of clothes does your Downer most like to see you wear? _____

   _____

4. How important is it that your appearance make an initial positive impression on him or her?

   ___ very important   ___ average importance   ___ little importance

5. Describe temporary changes you could make in your usual style of dress or appearance to positively influence your Downer's attitude toward you. Consider changes in each item of your clothing as well as your hairstyle and general neatness.

_____

_____

_____

The answers to these questions provide some initial guidelines within which to make more specific choices. Now, go through your wardrobe and eliminate from consideration all clothes that make you look or feel like a loser — anything that makes you feel mousey, frumpy, pinched up, dowdy, or uptight. For example, you may discover those neat-looking shoes really don't give you the ankle support you need, or those great walking pants pinch your waist and restrict breathing when you sit. Whether in looks or comfort, be sure your clothes don't work against you.

Next, turn to the positive factors. Color influences some people to feel more assertive. If you know your best colors and know how to wear them, fine. But if you don't know, talk with several friends who have seen you in most of your wardrobe. Ask which colors they think are most attractive and which are least attractive on you. Also ask, "Which outfit do you think makes me look most intelligent, attractive, and in charge of myself?" (Remember that, in trying to look assertive in a business setting, confidence and brainpower must take precedence over sexiness.) Record their opinions and your own below.

ASSERTIVE CLOTHING CHECKLIST

Opinions of:	Your best colors	Your worst colors	Your most assertive outfit
Person 1	_____	_____	_____
	_____	_____	_____
	_____	_____	_____
Person 2	_____	_____	_____
	_____	_____	_____
Yourself	_____	_____	_____
	_____	_____	_____

Finally, put yourself through some "dress rehearsals" — wear your assertive clothes while practicing your script, and become accustomed to the feel of those clothes as you say your lines. Rehearsing in your assertive clothes will allow you to check them for comfort and for tell-tale missing buttons, gravy stains, rips, and wrinkles. Even more important, by looking assertive you will probably begin to feel more assertive. Just as actors and actresses finalize the feeling of their character by putting on their costumes, so can you put on the assertive mood by wearing clothes that make you feel confident and strong.

This chapter completes your preparation for SPEAKING UP. So now, relax, and when you are ready, assert yourself with confidence. You are out to solve a problem, not to win a battle or to lay blame. Make the encounter a humanizing, not a dehumanizing experience. If you do this you will be using your assertive skills to promote a new style of life and to open up new areas for personal growth and fulfillment for yourself and others.

10

Hit-and-Run Downers

Insults are like bad coins; we cannot help their being offered us, but we need not take them.

C. H. SPURGEON

The Hit-and-Run Downer is that person who unexpectedly puts you down in a one-shot or once-only situation. He or she "hits" you — steps on your rights — and then "runs." In these episodes you have little power to exert long-term pressure for change. One-shot put-downs are what Jules Feiffer called "little murders" — the numerous affronts and insults that are inflicted on all of us daily. The accumulated psychological assaults add up to the murder of one's rights and self-esteem. Practically everyone wants help in asserting themselves with Hit-and-Run Downers.

WHO'S GOT THE POWER?

One-shot situations may be classified according to the Downer's power versus yours. This is determined by who needs the other's help or support the most. Your social power is greater when you are the "buyer" and the other person is selling you some service, as occurs with repairmen, service station attendants, taxi drivers, salesclerks, bellhops, waiters, and so on. The other person is paid specifically to provide satisfactory service to you, the customer. If you receive unsatisfactory or offensive service, the implicit contract has been broken and you have a legitimate right to complain. Whether you complain to the serviceman or his boss (or both) depends on whom you see as the cause of your unsatisfactory service.

In a second class of one-shot situations, you and your Downer have equal status. Someone cuts into a line ahead of you. A couple seated behind you at the theatre makes so much noise you cannot concentrate on the movie. A smoker annoys you in a stuffy room. These situations carry implicit social contracts. Service lines are supposed to be run on a "first come, first serve" basis, and breach of that contract is cause for complaint. In public gatherings people are expected to behave in ways that do not diminish the pleasure of others, and you invoke this implicit "golden rule" when you complain to the noisemakers or smokers.

The third class of one-shot situations — those in which the other person has more social power than you — is the most frustrating. Examples arise with authorities in law, business, or government, in dealings with judges, policemen, congressmen, teachers, impersonal corporations, dentists, doctors, and hospital personnel. Often, there is an implicit social service contract: the judge, the policeman, the social worker, the probation officer are paid to be of service to the public (that's you) and if they treat you unjustly, you have a right to complain. Similarly, the doctor, the hospital, the retirement home staff presumably aim to serve their clients. Their greater power is due to the heavy demand for their services. Doctors, dentists, and hospitals find themselves in a "sellers' market"; more people require their services than they have time to take care of. Consequently, buyers put up with poor service (for instance, waiting weeks for a dental appointment) because they think they have relatively little power to control the service. The ultimate punishment you can deal out, namely, to quit a doctor or dentist, has relatively little sting for him since there are always plenty of other patients

A ONE-SHOT DOWNER

to be drawn among the anonymous masses. Only in a very small town do you have some power, because there you can persuade patients away from a doctor or dentist you dislike.

Although congressmen or local politicians are presumably your servants, you as an individual have relatively little influence over their decisions. You can write letters of complaint about zoning laws, real estate assessments, or national political issues. But the more power the officeholder has — that is, the larger his "constituency" — the less he will be influenced by a single appeal or complaining letter. Politicians try to strike a representative average of their constituency on any given issue of importance. A single letter from you can always be discounted, if necessary, as unrepresentative or from a crackpot. That's why people with a particular political axe to grind enlist others to their cause, forming neighborhood groups, or county taxpayers' associations, or state and national lobby groups. Such political associations unite voices (and votes!) behind common complaints and proposals. By so uniting, they have an impact upon political decisions far beyond what they could have achieved by individual, uncoordinated attempts at influence.

HOW PREVALENT IS THE PASSIVE VICTIM?

People often ask us whether they are atypical in putting up with the offensive stranger, in not asserting themselves with the Hit-and-Run Downer. A recent study by Thomas Moriarty, called "A Nation of Willing Victims,"[1] shows that on the contrary, nonassertiveness is all too common. Moriarty and his psychology students studied the willingness of people in New York City to stand up for themselves in several "little murder" scenes in which their rights were stepped on. The scenes were staged in such manner that the real subjects did not know that their "assertive resistance" was being observed.

The investigators found that college students were loath to ask another student to turn off loud rock music which annoyed them as they were working on a complex and important mental task. Eighty percent of the students said nothing to the noisemaker, just tolerating what they later admitted was a very annoying distraction. Although 15 percent asked the noisemaker to turn down the music so they could work, they didn't repeat the request when the offensive person gave them a mild put-off. Only 5 percent (1 out of 20!) of the subjects actually asked twice and thus got the offensive person to quiet down. These results are surprising. 80 to 95 percent of the people tested had no "assertive resistance"; they simply put up with "little murders," becoming passive victims.

The same pattern emerged in other situations. For instance, students studying in a library seemed reluctant to ask two nearby loud talkers to

LITTLE MURDERS

quiet down. Although 23 percent of the subjects got up and moved away from the talkers, only 2 percent actually asked the talkers to be quiet. The other 75 percent simply endured the noise. Similarly when loud conversation was staged behind subjects in a movie house, most people simply tolerated the annoyance.

Moriarty went even further in his investigation when he arranged an experiment in which innocent persons would be practically accused of stealing. The experimental aide would stand behind an adult businessman making a call in a phone booth in Grand Central Station; when the call was completed, the aide would play out the following script: "Excuse me, I was here a few minutes ago and I left my ring on the counter under the phone. Did you find it?" Of course, all subjects replied "No." The aide would then say, "I've got to find it. Are you sure you didn't see it? Sometimes people pick things up without thinking about it." Again, subjects would deny having seen the ring. Then the aide would ask, "Would you empty your pockets?" The investigators wondered how many people would comply with such an overbearing request, one which amounts to an allegation of petty thievery. Again the compliance rate was 80 percent: four of every five adult males essentially submitted to a search by emptying their pockets. The percentages were even higher in laboratory experiments. And even when a "disinterested bystander" said to the aide, "You've got no right to ask him to empty his pockets," the subjects still complied.

Such studies show how prevalent passivity is. It is alarming that so few people are willing to stand up for their rights when they are being put upon and clearly annoyed. Apparently, most of us would rather not get into a hassle about anything, especially with a stranger. The slogan is: Don't make waves.

RATIONALIZATIONS OF NONRESISTERS
(NICE PASSIVE FOLKS)

The nonresisting, nonassertive person has many excuses for reacting passively to one-shot put-downs. Let's consider a few so you can identify them and eliminate them from your thinking.

"Oh well, I don't want to make a mountain out of a molehill." One reason people don't react assertively is that they are not sure whether to judge the other person's behavior as annoying, offensive, or unreasonable. For instance, in the Moriarty studies, many put-upon subjects who were clearly annoyed nonetheless denied feeling that way when questioned. They felt uncertain of their right to have negative reactions! The best antidote here is to tune in to your "discomfort level," and admit rather than deny your negative reactions to other people's behavior.

"But he's got rights, too." The nonassertor will excuse the loud music player by saying, "Everybody should be allowed to do his own thing." But that holds true only if his thing doesn't infringe upon your rights and pleasures. Another excuse of the nonassertor is, "He was upset, so he had the right to ask me to empty my pockets. Besides, I knew I was innocent and didn't have the ring." But strangers (or friends, for that matter) do not have the right to accuse us of theft and ask to search us. Freedom from arbitrary search is secured in the American Bill of Rights.

"Oh well, it's just this once." Since you will soon be out of this discomforting scene, and may never see the other person again, why bother about it? Why get yourself worked up into an emotional scene with the other person when it will be over and done with in a few minutes?

There are two answers to this argument. First, consider your self-esteem, whether you respect yourself and your ability to speak up for your rights. If you feel dissatisfied, wronged, put-upon, and then do nothing about it, your memory is simply going to record another failure experience. If you are ever to become assertive, you simply cannot permit failure experiences to accumulate and erode your confidence. Although you may forget the failure as soon as you escape from the unpleasantness, that failure pattern nonetheless persists as a habit recurring repeatedly in the future. "Laws that are not enforced cease to be laws: and rights not defended may wither away."² Putting up with a nonassertive failure now is practically the same as committing yourself to more such failures in the future. Therefore, view one-shot put-downs as challenges to your self-respect rather than as minor annoyances that you will soon be rid of.

Second, asserting yourself in one-shot situations shows your concern for the benefit of your fellow citizens. It is a fraternal gesture to change a Downer's behavior so other community members do not suffer similar offenses. It improves the quality of life. Think of your assertion as "community work" for your brothers and sisters; you are helping clean up pollution in the social life of the community.

"I don't want to make a scene." Often you draw attention to yourself when you complain in public about something. Your children or mate may feel embarrassed if you complain to the waiter or restaurant manager about receiving poor service. But why do people feel embarrassed when they (or their companions) complain?

Probing, we find that all kinds of worries go through people's minds. They think that since they are creating some unpleasantness for the Downer (the waiter), he will dislike them; they imagine that their complaint will arouse disapproving whispers or snickers from others nearby; they are afraid the management will not give them good service if they return there.

You can negate and dispell the force of these "horror show" images by changing the way you talk to yourself about your relation to the Downer (the waiter, in this example) and by changing the way you make your complaint. First, review your wants or priorities. Ask, "Why did I come into this place of business?" Notice the answer is *not* "To please the waiter" but rather something like "To buy a good meal served satisfactorily." Few people would patronize a restaurant whose ads read, "You can come in here only if you don't displease the waiters." Recognize this simple priority: you are paying for the pleasure of being served a good meal. Tell yourself, "I am paying for good service, not for just the goodwill of the waiter." With this attitude, you should be properly concerned that you receive value as contracted, namely, a good meal well served, rather than a poor meal served badly.

Displays of displeasure may upset an occasional onlooker, and you should recognize that possibility. Assert yourself firmly but gently with the waiter or the manager. If you make your complaint in a restrained manner, people nearby will not even notice the complaint. And if they do hear, think of your assertion as producing an indirect benefit for them, namely, a little better service from this waiter.

"He'll call me a name." Some people do not speak up for their rights because they expect to be called a name by the Downer. They are afraid of being called a troublemaker, a fussbudget, or a whiner.

Name-calling is a device for controlling someone through disapproval. But a negative label makes an impact on you only if you let it. You could desensitize yourself (Chapter 3) to all the dirty names in slang books if you wanted to take the time for it. However, we hope you don't need such treatment and can already see name-calling for what it is, a simple form of venting frustration and anger.

If your complaint is restrained, you'll probably not provoke an attack. In customer situations, you'll probably receive an apology and better service. If the Downer swears at you, you can always walk out. If people in a library make too much noise, you can complain repeatedly, then call an authority to enforce your demand for quiet.

"But nobody else has complained." When you lodge a complaint about some unsatisfactory service or condition, the first defensive maneuver of your Downer may be to deny the validity of the complaint. He may say something like, "Nobody else has complained about that. Don't you think you're being oversensitive?" This remark attempts to place the blame for the problem on your "oversensitive" character rather than on the external condition or situation. You are the "guilty deviant," whereas he is blameless. Some other examples:

- At a school function, you think the hotdogs aren't cooked enough. You complain and are told, "Everyone else seems to like them."

- At a pro football game, the person behind you has his portable radio blaring loudly, tuned to the station that is broadcasting the game. When you ask him to turn off the radio, he says, "All the other people seated around here seem to want to hear it."

- At a cocktail lounge, you complain about the chauvinistic cartoons on the napkins, which depict women as either nags or sexpots. The bartender says, "You're the first person who's ever complained about it. Aren't you going overboard on that 'women's lib' stuff?"

Reply by questioning whether you represent a minority view. Refuse to be labeled as a deviant freak. If the situation irritates you, it probably irritates others, but they are too shy to speak up. Because silence is interpreted as consent, each says to himself, "Since the others don't seem to mind the radio, I guess I'd better not make a scene." But silence does not mean agreement; it probably connotes the timidity of the silent majority.

When you complain, emphasize this silently suffering majority. Say, "If you took a poll, you would see most people feel as I do. They've just been hoping someone else would speak up. Well, I've nominated myself to speak for all of us." Such a reply is difficult to counter since it appeals to a silent majority (in the surrounding crowd) who allegedly support your assertion. Your Downer will feel some group pressure to comply and probably won't test your claim about the group's opinion. If he wants to test it, pose the question in such a way that "no action" by neighbors means support for your complaint. For instance, you could ask, "Who here wants to listen to this loud radio?" Do not feel guilty about persisting with your complaint; noisy, offensive people and practices should be squelched. They violate your rights.

"That's life — you can't change it." To conclude, probably the main reason most of us fail to complain about put-down situations is that we do not specifically identify the situation as one calling for assertiveness. We are aware of mild irritation or discomfort but we don't stop to think that we are being taken advantage of and that there is something we could do to remedy the scene. Throughout countless hours of poor service, assaults, insults, and frustrations in modern society, we have learned to tolerate a lot of annoyance and irritation because "That's the way the system is." We adapt to the noise, the littering, the intrusions, the delays, the offensive acts of some strangers. We rationalize with "There's always a few bad apples in every barrel." After a while, we habituate to the point where these assaults don't bother us so much. But by keeping quiet, by going along, we lose our rights and with them our self-esteem.

Blind acceptance of the "system" has done much harm in the past. It sometimes takes mass social movements to make us aware of demeaning conventions and unsettling conditions that we previously tolerated. For instance, "consciousness-raising" literature in the women's liberation movement identifies accommodations women have made to "get along"; it also notes how these accommodations have kept women resigned to an oppressed status in society. The same is true of the literature supporting the "Black Power" movement or the American Indian movement.

We have learned to resign ourselves to being "had," frustrated, and exploited in many standard situations (for instance, waiting at a welfare office or a doctor's office). It has become so habitual and expected that we hardly notice the situation or think it cause for alarm. But we'd like you to question your discomforting situations, and ask "How irritating is this?" "Does it have to be this way?" "What can I do to change it or at least make my needs known?" Asking these questions, you become more aware of your feelings, more sensitive to violations of your human rights, and more willing to alter the situation by your assertive actions.

WHEN SHOULD YOU BE ASSERTIVE?

As with other problems, consider the risks of being assertive in a one-shot situation. Obviously, you do not speak up if you are at the mercy of a powerful Downer who controls your fate — for example, someone who has your life or job under his control. During a job interview, an applicant probably should not tell the interviewer his questions are annoyingly inappropriate. During doctorate exams, a student would be ill advised to tell a teacher that he asks confusing or irrelevant questions. In any situation of this nature all you can do is to stay task-oriented and salvage whatever self-respect you can from the ordeal.

But we are only rarely under such fate-control. The more likely put-down situation involves co-equals (for example, the line-jumper) or employee-customer relations (for example, the nasty salesclerk). Work on becoming assertive in these settings. Such one-shots make easy practice fields for assertiveness. Compared with threatening put-downs from a mate, boss, or friend, customer-service situations are brief, you have relative power, and you won't be hurt by your assertion. That why it's a good idea to start practicing assertiveness when necessary and appropriate with repairmen, storekeepers, salesmen, station attendants, waiters, telephone operators, or whoever causes you to feel discomforted.

Another good exercise is to write letters (composed according to DESC) to public officials, politicians, newspapers, or business firms. In the letters you can outline a problem or complaint and perhaps propose a solution. Or you can simply support or oppose a legislative bill or policy currently under consideration. One woman wrote to a national chain of furniture stores complaining about sexism in their TV advertising; she convinced them to stop playing the offensive ad immediately and to take steps to avoid sexism in future ads. Writing letters is a low-threat act of assertion, but every little bit helps you.

Assertiveness isn't only for consumers; service people have rights as well. Specifically, a clerk or repairman has a right not to be bullied and abused by the customer. His job is to give courteous service, but the customers shouldn't expect subservience, meekness, and tolerance for any abuse they wish to dish out. Consider some cases in which the service person might be assertive with overbearing customers:

- After trying on ten pairs of shoes, a customer seemed no closer to a decision. The assertive salesman said, "Excuse me. I have other customers to wait on. Please look over these pairs again, and let me know if you want any of them."

- The clerk running the menswear section of a large department store was bothered by three teenage boys who took many pairs of trousers to the dressing rooms to try them on; amid great laughter, each accumulated a pile of mussed-up trousers. The clerk challenged them, asking which boy (if any) intended to buy trousers. When they continued to sass and mock him, he telephoned the store's security guards and insisted the boys be removed from the store.

These are simple but clearly necessary assertive acts by clerks. Customers do *not* have all the rights: clerks have rights, as well. Clerks might wish to assert themselves when their rights are being infringed upon by an overbearing customer. Of course, it is best if this can be done gently without alienating the customer. But when a situation requires remedying, then a clerk and the boss can decide if they are willing to risk angering and losing a customer; if the risks outweigh negative repercussions, the clerk might simply accept the risk and follow through with the assertion.

SOME RULES FOR COMPLAINING

An easy way to compose a complaint is according to the DESC procedure discussed in previous chapters: DESCRIBE, EXPRESS, SPECIFY, and CONSEQUENCES. Your script will often be abbreviated and invariably impromptu or given with only a few seconds' planning time. Here are a few additional rules to follow when making a complaint.[3]

- *Select the correct person.* Deliver your assertive script to the person who is truly responsible for your poor service. If you receive sloppy service in a restaurant, complain to the waitress; if you receive poorly cooked food, send the complaint (via the waitress or manager) to the cook; if you receive very slow service during a heavy rush of lunch hour, do not complain to your waitress (who is running her legs off) but to the manager for not hiring more help to deal with the rush-hour overloads. If there are not enough checkout clerks to handle the rush lines at the grocery store, complain to the manager, not the clerk. If you do not receive enough police protection, complain to the precinct captain, not the patrolman on the beat. Unless you're only rehearsing, don't waste time complaining to your companions about another person.

- *Lodge the complaint privately.* If possible, talk to the responsible person in private. Hardly anyone can tolerate criticism in public, so you will get better results if you complain in private. If criticized in public, most people feel compelled to defend themselves, to "save face."

- *Do it soon after you notice the problem.* Discuss your complaint while the problematic incident is fresh in mind, before your memory is likely to garble the events. The longer you wait, the more your recollection of events will differ from your Downer's. Moreover, if you wait too long you will forget that indignant feeling which motivates assertive acts. So assert yourself as soon as you can.

- *Make only one complaint at a time.* Complain only about the immediate problem, and don't bring up older complaints regarding other issues with this Downer. That is, don't overwhelm him with criticism.

- *Don't build up defensiveness.* Don't begin your complaint by saying how terrible it is: "There's something really terrible happening here. It's really getting me mad. What I mean is . . ." Such prefaces make the Downer defensive. If you need a preface, just say, "I'd like to speak to you about something I've noticed."

- *Don't apologize for your complaint.* Do not apologize or say you are "sorry to be raising a fuss" when you complain. That suggests you are at fault for being overly sensitive. It lessens the impact of your assertion. One student phrased it, "Don't say 'I'm sorry' unless you really feel sorrowful!"

- *Avoid generalizing words like "always" or "never."* Recall the rules for DE-SCRIBE; don't use these generalizing words for emphasis; they endanger the accuracy of your statements and allow the Downer to refute them. Just describe the specific incident in question.
- *Complain only about actions which you think can be changed.* If you think a service person is doing the best he can, given the size of his job, you don't help matters by complaining to him that it is inadequate. For example, prices in a chain store or nationally owned gas station are set regionally and the local manager has no say in it, so don't criticize him for high prices. You don't complain that a cripple takes longer to get across an intersection. Be realistic in assessing the other person's options.
- *Try to compliment something about the other person.* No one likes to hear only criticism. Therefore you should figure out something complimentary to say when your Downer listens to your complaint. A good way to slip in such compliments in a customer service complaint is at the beginning, as a sort of preface to your complaint, and at the end. You might say, "I like to shop here because you are usually so responsive to customers needs" or "I like the unique atmosphere and the really outstanding food you have here." The compliment rewards the person for listening and perhaps agreeing to your proposed solution to the problem.

Review these rules when preparing a complaint. Use them to supplement the DESC rules for preparing assertive messages. That is, continue to apply the DESC rules with only slight modifications to the one-shot complaint situations. Let's consider some applications now.

ABBREVIATED DESC SCRIPTS FOR ONE-SHOT SITUATIONS

By their nature, one-shot situations cannot be anticipated and planned for in every detail. However, you can plan and write scripts for the *general class* of one-shots. The steps of the DESC procedure help you compose your "complaint script" on the spur of the moment. That is, you first DESCRIBE to your Downer what the problem is, what he has just done or failed to do. Specify concrete acts, avoiding labels or motives. Second, EXPRESS your feelings about the situation, keeping restrained and brief. Third, SPECIFY what you want him to do or stop doing. Fourth, spell out or merely imply CONSEQUENCES if he changes as suggested. In the examples below, negative consequences are given in brackets and might not be said the first time.

Situation A woman took her car in for repair. She could not describe very precisely what was the matter with it. The mechanic made a few grunts, snickers, and facial expressions (rolling eyes and head) which she interpreted as ridiculing her ignorance. Her impromptu script follows.

DESCRIBE The tone of your remarks and the way you roll your eyes suggests to me that you are poking fun at me for my ignorance of cars.

EXPRESS This offends me and I feel dumb. However, if I knew how to repair cars, I would not be here now paying you.

SPECIFY Please repair my car without further snide remarks or insinuations about "stupid women drivers."

CONSEQUENCES *Positive:* If you are helpful, I'll tell my friends to bring their cars here for repair.
[*Negative:* However, if you continue your insinuations, I will take my business elsewhere and tell my friends to avoid this place.]

Situation. An old man was bothered by having to walk from his house to the edge of his lawn to pick up his morning newspaper. He wanted it delivered to his front door, whereas the newspaper boy rode by on a bicycle and merely tossed the papers onto the lawns on either side of the street. The next time the boy came to collect for the paper, the man gave the following script:

DESCRIBE You often toss the paper at the far edge of my lawn so that I have to walk about 100 feet to fetch it into the house.

EXPRESS With my arthritis, I find it painful to walk that distance to get my paper.

SPECIFY Will you deliver the paper all the way up to my front porch?

CONSEQUENCES *Positive:* If you do this, I'll really appreciate your efforts.
[*Negative:* But if you don't, I'll switch to a paper delivered by someone who will deliver it to my door.]

Situation. A college student goes jogging nearly every night around his neighborhood. One night as he jogs a large boxer dog comes barking and snarling at him, and nips him on the ankle. The dog's owner comes out and apologizes to the jogger, saying; "Sorry, but old Fido can't resist chasing joggers." The student gives the following one-shot script.

DESCRIBE That dog chases me and other joggers in a very aggressive way, biting at our ankles and snarling.

EXPRESS I feel it is unfair to let him run loose, harassing and injuring joggers, and it is certainly illegal.

SPECIFY Please tie him up with a leash.

CONSEQUENCES *Positive:* I appreciate your helping me with my jogging exercises!
[*Negative:* If he chases me again, I will report your dog to the sheriff's office.]

Impromptu scripts have many variations. Their "consequences" are typically punitive, saying, "I'll take my business elsewhere" or "I'll report you to your supervisor." However, try to include rewards, as when you say, "I'll tell my friends to shop here" or "I'll praise you to your supervisor" (and then do so). In restaurants, the size of your tip can tell how much you appreciated the service received.

After deciding on an appropriate payoff or penalty, be prepared to escalate it if the initial amount isn't enough. You escalate a reward by promising more money, more praise, more support. The way to escalate punishment varies with circumstances. In many businesses, there is a chain of command or hierarchy, and you can buck your complaint up to higher levels of that hierarchy. If complaining to a gas station attendant gets you nowhere, you may try his boss; if he gives no response, then you can try the district manager of that chain. If you are sure of your claim, you can complain to the Better Business Bureau or send a critical letter about the business to the editor of the town newspaper.

Suppose your complaint to a business elicits no satisfactory response. What leverage do you have? It depends on whether the complaint surrounds misrepresentation by the business about something you bought (false or misleading advertising), or whether it involves defective goods or products (an appliance or spoiled food). If you feel you were misled about what you were buying, then help is available from the Consumer Protection Division of your County District Attorney's office. (The Real Estate Commission deals with real estate frauds.) Laws protect consumers against misrepresentation, so call the D. A. if you think you've been bilked.

If your complaint concerns the quality of a purchased product (say, a defective TV, auto, or appliance), you address it to the local firm; and then, if not satisfied, address the manufacturer. If you get no satisfaction from these, have an independent expert (say, an electrician or repairman) certify in writing the defective nature of the item; then threaten to file suit against the manufacturer and the local firm in small claims court. If they don't react to the threat, then take them to court. Small claims courts cost almost no money (you don't hire a lawyer); businesses loathe small claims suits because they usually lose, or else they spend more money for legal counsel than the cost of the claim. The disadvantage of small claims court is that there is a low ceiling on the amount of damages you can claim. To collect larger damages, you must go to a trial; the lawyer's fees for that can be expensive and you have to decide whether it is worthwhile. If such legal options fail, you won't get your money back but if impelled you could still protest the business practices by picketing it with "Unfair to Consumers" signs. Only you can decide whether your grievance is worth the time and effort to follow up with such punitive consequences.

Finally, consider asserting yourself with a service person — a doctor, for example — who really doesn't need your business. Many doctors (or receptionists) are inept at scheduling and sticking to their appointments. They might schedule one patient every 15 minutes, while the average patient requires, say, 20 minutes. The result by late morning or late afternoon is a backlog of appointments, each patient being required to wait for 30 to 60 minutes beyond his appointed time. The doctor, knowing "Time is money," typically wants to see as many patients as possible, so his schedule is set up to reduce his waiting time between patients. The existence of waiting rooms is testament to the doctor's belief that his time is more valuable than that of the collection of patients sitting there. But you need not accept that assumption; you can complain about it and assert your rights.

In one instance, after two delayed appointments with a former dentist, one man told the dentist that his time was money, too, and at his hourly-pay scale a half-hour delay caused the real cost of his appointment to double. He made three suggestions: (1) schedule his appointments when the dentist was most likely to be on time, or (2) let him show up routinely a half hour after the nominally scheduled time, or (3) allow him to deduct $2 from the dentist's fee for every 5 minutes of delay beyond their agreed-upon appointment time. The explicitly stated consequence was that if the dentist failed to agree, the man would find himself another dentist who valued his patients' time as well as his own. The dentist opted for alternative 1 and his receptionist listed some ghastly hours; still when the man visited him at the recommended hour, he had to wait again. He complained, quit that dentist, and searched out a more agreeable one.

The example demonstrates that you can assert your rights even in unequal-status situations in which the cultural habit is to resign oneself to being "had" or exploited. You don't always succeed in changing unfair practices, but at least you'll feel better for having stood up for your rights.

Some Practice

For practice, respond to the public annoyances described below that require a one-shot assertion. Fill in a possible assertive script (be brief) for each situation. For comparison, we have recorded a possible script. For maximum benefit, write in your script before you read the suggested one.

Situation. A salesman has rung your doorbell to sell you brushes (or whatever). He is very persistent. How do you say no assertively?

Your script: _____

_____

_____

Possible Script. "I don't care to see your samples since I do not want any brushes, and will buy none. You cannot spend your time profitably here. Good day."

Situation. You're a woman sitting with a girlfriend at a nightclub while waiting for the show to begin. Two uninvited men come to your table and sit down with you. Thinking you want to be picked up, they impose themselves obnoxiously. You and your friend want them to leave you alone. What assertive message can you deliver?

Your script: _____

_____

_____

Possible script. "We are not here to be picked up. We are here to enjoy each other's company and the show, so please leave. If you don't, I will call the manager."

Situation. At a movie theater, the mother behind you has a 4-year-old child with a persistent noisy cough. The child's coughing is disturbing you, although his mother seems unperturbed by his commotion. What can you do?

Your script: _____

_____

_____

Possible script. "Your son's coughing is interfering with my enjoyment of the movie. I would appreciate it if you would move or take him out. Thank you."

Situation. You are waiting in your car for another car to pull out of a parking space you want to take. You have to move a bit forward to let the other car out of the space. As he exits, a third car flashes in behind him, taking the parking space you've been waiting for. What do you do?

Your script: _____

_____

_____

Possible script. (getting out of your car, if necessary) "I was waiting for this space so I could park in it. Since you came later, I am entitled to this spot. Please move to another spot."

Situation. Your small child falls while playing and hits her forehead, causing it to swell painfully. Fearing a skull fracture, you race to the emergency room of the local hospital. While you hold a bleeding, unconscious child, scared out of your wits, a very slow receiving clerk checks in the patient ahead of you. Then, turning to your case, she starts asking you a long series of questions to fill out her insurance form. Exasperated by her questions while you fear for your child's life, what do you say?

Your script: _____

_____

_____

Possible script. "Nurse, this is taking too long and I feel my child needs *immediate* medical attention. I have an emergency here, so let me see a doctor right now. I will fill out your forms later."

Situation. You have waited in a movie line for 20 minutes only to learn at the door that you are in the wrong line, one for people who have already purchased tickets and are just waiting to go in. You are told to go to the end of the other line to buy a ticket. You know you'll never get in if you do that. What do you say and to whom?

Your script: _____

_____

_____

Possible script. *To the ticket taker:* "I'd like to see the manager." *To the manager:* "You have no signs or ushers informing people where to line up for what. I've waited here 20 minutes and I am angry to learn I'm in the wrong line. Sell me a ticket and let me in right away. If you don't, I'll write to the owner of this movie house and complain about your poor management in servicing the public."

Situation. Your insurance agent calls you at dinner time and you are annoyed at being pestered in the middle of your meal.

Your script: _____

_____

_____

Possible script. "We are eating now. I'd appreciate not being interrupted before 7:00. Please call me after 7:00. That way you will find me more ready to discuss insurance."

Situation. You are waiting at a drive-up bank window while a slow cashier gets some traveler's checks which you requested. The person in the car behind embarrasses you by honking his horn repeatedly. What can you do?

Your script: _____

_____

_____

Possible script. (getting out of your car and going to the person) "The cashier is doing the best he can, and your honking at me is unnecessary and embarrassing. Please stop honking your horn. If you're in such a rush, you can park and walk into the bank."

After working on these exercises, review this chapter for suggested practice opportunities. Try overtly practicing assertiveness in one-shot situations. Contract with yourself to be on the look-out for Hit-and-Run Downers and be ready to speak up for your rights. This chapter is only worth the assertive actions it persuades you to perform.

11

Developing Friendships

Many a friendship is lost for lack of speaking.

ARISTOTLE

As a rule, nonassertive people are shy. They feel uncomfortable with people because they lack the social skills that would enable them to start and keep friendships. But nonassertive people can learn how to make new acquaintances and how to change a casual acquaintance to a deep or loving friendship. This chapter contains some suggestions that can help you do this.

The formation of a friendship generally follows a series of stages. Two people meet each other; then they get to know each other better, usually by doing some things together. As they spend more time together, the relationship develops in one of several directions, or it wanes. If there is mutual liking and further opportunity for interaction, there is an increase in trust, love, and dependency; if liking is not mutual, conflicts will occur increasingly over time spent together, until there is little desire to see each other, and the relationship will fade.

INCREASING YOUR LIKABILITY

We all wonder at times whether we could be more effective in making friends with the people we are attracted to. Some people seem to move into friendships with ease and grace, whereas others have grave difficulties. The successful ones just seem more likable. But what makes a person likable to others? Is there something you can do to increase your likability without diminishing your assertiveness and self-esteem?

This topic has been researched by social scientists for years. They have studied what factors influence our judging another person as likable or "socially attractive." Such researchers[1] have found that we tend to like others who (1) are similar to us in basic beliefs, interests, and values; (2) are talented at some intellectual, social, or athletic skill we value; (3) have "admirable" or pleasing personal qualities such as honesty, kindness, loyalty, tolerance; and (4) like us in return. These factors all fit into a general "reward basis" of mutual liking: we generally like people who reward us, and whose rewards "mean something of value" to us. For instance, we like people who agree with us because they provide consensual validation for our beliefs; they make us feel our opinions are "correct." We like pleasant, cooperative people because they reward us for our actions.

How might we become more likable? Dale Carnegie proposed six rules to follow in making friends.[2]

1. Become genuinely interested in other people.
2. Smile.
3. Remember that a man's name is to him the sweetest and most important sound in the English language.
4. Be a good listener. Encourage others to talk about themselves.
5. Talk in terms of the other person's interest.
6. Make the other person feel important — and do it sincerely.

These may be interpreted as rules for rewarding the other person's approaches to you.

An important factor is missing from the "Carnegie list," however; Carnegie's rules emphasize the passive role of the pleasant listener, and ignore the positive presentation of yourself. Friendship involves a sharing or mutual exchange in which both of you disclose something of yourselves. Friendly conversation, or intimacy-producing dialog, is neither an interview nor a one-way stream of flattery. Rather, it consists of interlocking give-and-takes, with each person taking turns providing information about himself and showing genuine concern for the other person.

Passive people are often recluses; they stay at home, in their apartment or house, watching TV or reading. That's no way to make friends. To make new acquaintances or deepen superficial acquaintances, you need to contact people, give yourself a chance.

Getting out of your shell and making more friends takes time. Thus the exercises below take time, occasionally a lot. You have to decide whether having more close friends is worth the time and effort. Some people really *prefer* to be alone — having struggled all day under social stress, they prefer to spend their leisure hours quietly reading, painting, or resting. They want quietude rather than the bustle of the social scene. That's okay so long as they act that way by choice. This chapter is for people who are alone not by preference but because of fears and poor social skills.

DEEPENING OLD ACQUAINTANCES

The first step in forming closer friendships is for you to initiate more activities with the acquaintances you already have. Set a series of social goals each week which you contract with yourself to accomplish. These behavioral objectives are designed to get you moving socially, out of your shell.

As a first contract with yourself, agree to call up at least two acquaintances of either sex this week just for a friendly chat. (Conversational skills are discussed later.) The idea is to let them know you feel friendly toward them. You should also try to arrange further contacts with these people if the chats go well.

Write below the names and phone numbers of two acquaintances you will telephone this week. Also list two or three conversational topics you could bring up with each person. (These could be the same topics for both people.) Here is an example:

Person 1: Bill Richards. 339-4270

Topics: (1) The note I saw about his alma mater; (2) the new job-assignment our section is receiving from his department; (3) whether he still sees Sally.

Person 1: _____

Topics: _____

_____

_____

Person 2: _____

Topics: _____

_____

Now, contract with yourself to telephone these people on particular nights in the coming week. The call need not be lengthy — 5 to 10 minutes is enough. Some people use the phone only for business or making specific requests, so they may wonder what is the point of your call. For such people announce early that you are contacting them simply for social interest and the pleasure of their company.

After completing each phone assignment, reward yourself with some pleasure. Continue telephoning for 4 to 8 weeks, increasing the number of calls per week, and expanding the number of different people you telephone.

A second exercise for enhancing your "connections" is to invite at least two acquaintances a week to join you in some activity. Restaurant meals or picnics provide easy occasions for friendly conversations. So do movies, concerts, sporting events, museums, hikes, and cookouts. Don't imply you have something big to talk about with the other person. Again, simply stress your desire to get to know them better. If one person is "all booked up" call others until you get two.

Write below the names of the two people you intend to invite to do something with you this week. Also note what the activity will be and where you will go.

Person 1: _____

Activity and place: _____

Person 2: _____

Activity and place: _____

Reward yourself for actually setting up these engagements. Continue to carry out this socializing for 4 to 8 weeks. Try each week to increase the number of different acquaintances (of both sexes) that you know well.

MEETING NEW PEOPLE

When you are ready to add new people to your list of acquaintances, we suggest that you focus initially on the sheer numbers of new people you can meet rather than on the quality of the relationships or the joy you get from them. But how can you go about meeting new people?

You can ask your current friends to introduce you to their friends. For example, invite your friend and his friend to go to dinner or the movies with you. Friendships often spread out in concentric social circles.

Another way to meet new friends is to go to places where people congregate. You can meet new people in hotel or dormitory lounges; in elevators, buses or trains; at concerts, plays, dances, parties, movies, athletic events, public lectures, church services; in classes, student unions, hiking clubs, sailing clubs, bridge clubs, nature clubs; in a dining hall or restaurant; or in a singles bar. You can become acquainted with shop clerks, waitresses, gas station attendants, bartenders, teachers, students, and so on.

Follow your interests in choosing places or events to meet compatible people, whether that be birdwatching, historical societies, rock concerts, bowling, or art shows. At such places, you will meet kindred souls, so you have a topic of conversation of guaranteed interest. You can attend such gatherings alone or with a companion, whichever is more conducive to your meeting new people.

Once in such a setting, you must find an opportunity to initiate conversation with a specific target person or group. Select someone whom you think you'd like to meet and who appears at least moderately approachable. We have all learned social conventions regarding when it is proper or improper to "break into" someone's space with our acquainting overtures. For instance, we don't interrupt people while they are doing something which they probably prefer to talking to us. If we try, we are likely to be rebuffed. A shy boy would not succeed in initiating acquaintance talk with an unknown girl engrossed in a symphony or her boyfriend's conversation. So you should wait for an appropriate opening pause.

A large part of the impression you make on the other person will be determined within the first few minutes of your contact. Why are the first impressions formed so fast? Because he or she is trying to figure out what type of person you are in order to decide whether to encourage or discourage further conversation.

These "fast judgments" are largely about your surface features — your physical appearance, body language, and self-assurance. Experiments on interpersonal attraction show clearly that simple physical beauty and appearance play a large role in inspiring postive initial feelings. Therefore, you should make every effort to look as good as you can (in whatever style suits you) when meeting people to be friends with. The better you look, the easier it is to strike up conversations with strangers. Not that you are sure to lose if you're not a handsome man or beautiful woman, but you may have to work harder to make initial contacts and sustain them.

Your body language is another quick indicator of your personality. Get a large mirror and practice looking friendly, warm, interested, and outgoing. Look into the other person's eyes frequently as you and he talk, lean toward him, and smile whenever you can. Such behaviors communicate "I like you. I'm interested in you. I'm enjoying meeting you." As an exercise, you could go out tomorrow and smile at several strangers you pass in the street. Record the reactions you noted.

Besides smiling, practice looking confident and self-assured. Stand up straight, head upright, hands at rest, mouth and face relaxed, without nervous twitches, jitter, or agitation. Breathe slowly and deeply. Identify nervous mannerisms in your mirror, or with the help of your buddy, and work to eliminate them while increasing more attractive behaviors. Such efforts can pay off in making you a more attractive person.

DEVELOPING CONVERSATIONAL SKILLS

Although you may think of difficulty in conversation as just another proof of shyness, the fact is that conversational skills can be learned, and the more you try out your skills the easier it becomes.

Openers

Once you have selected a person to speak to, and waited for an appropriate pause, the next step is to make some opening remarks. An "opener" is the first line you utter, the small "foot in the door," permitting the two of you to begin developing conversation if you want. It doesn't have to be a pithy remark loaded with humor and intelligence. Its sole function is to draw positive attention and provide an opportunity to start a conversation. The opener is often a hackneyed expression, one we have heard a thousand times, but that doesn't make it any less necessary or useful in opening conversations.

- "Which way is the Skillings building?"
- "Do you have a match?"
- "Haven't I seen you somewhere before?"
- "You're new around here, aren't you?"
- "How do you like that great sunset?"
- "How do you like the music?" (the movie, the painting, etc.)
- "Do you think Tommy is a cute baby?"
- "How do you like this rain?"

Other openers offer help, as when you open a door for someone, light her cigarette, offer him part of your newspaper to read, help her pick up spilled groceries, pick him up from a bicycle spill.

Men or women who want to be easily approachable can carry some striking or unusual object — a "hooker" — which gives others an opportunity to open conversation by commenting on it. For example, you could carry a copy of a controversial book such as Karl Marx's *Das Capital,* Hitler's *Mein Kampf,* Masters and Johnson's *Human Sexual Response,* or any book likely to provoke comment. Of course you should have at least one remark prepared to say about the book!

Other openers are pets, musical instruments, art supplies, a sketch pad, and striking clothing that in some way is "remark-able." One college man got a puppy from the humane society and tried to give it away to coeds on his campus; a coed bought a crate of apples and sold them outside the student union.

While openers are ways to begin conversing with a stranger, they can also be used to strike up conversation with casual acquaintances. By knowing something about the person, you can plan good questions as openers. Use your imagination. For instance:

- "Hi. We're in the same Biology class. Could you tell me what our assignment is for next Tuesday?"
- "You're in the Accounting Division, aren't you? I've been trying to get a pay-order through there for two weeks. Could you tell me . . ."

- "I understand you're in the Civil Service. I'm thinking of going into that and I wondered about the ranking system. How does that work?"

According to what you already know about the person, he or she should be able to answer your question. This answer provides you with more material to elaborate into a conversation.

Following Up Openers

The problem with simple openers like "Do you have a light?" or "Nice day, isn't it?" is they provide only a very brief opportunity to come up with an appropriate conversation igniter. That is why you should have two or three remarks planned in advance; then a brief "Yes" from the target person does not leave you speechless. Here are a few example "backup" sequences.

- "Sure is a bad rain! The street vendors are going to lose business, huh? Have you got far to go in this mess? Do you want to share an umbrella with me?"
- "Could I have a light? Thanks. I have a zippo but it doesn't work . . . Seems like most mechanical contraptions don't work these days . . . Do you have a lighter?"
- (On elevator). "You live on the third floor, huh? I live on the sixth. How's the view from your apartment? . . . Isn't this elevator an oldie? . . ."

OPENERS FOR CONVERSATION

- "Change for a dollar? . . . You look like one of those well organized people who plan your life to keep change on hand. Is that right? . . ."
- "Haven't we met before? . . . You look like a girl who was in my Political Science class. She was wild about political discussions. Are you nuts about politics? . . . No; well, you and the rest of the American people! What kinds of classes do you like?"

Try to have a sketchy outline of such a conversational series before you deliver your opener. Accompany such remarks with a smile and good eye contact. The point of such a series is to search for a topic of common interest permitting the two of you to "take off" in conversation. This is a "feeling out" period. Think of yourself as quickly scanning over a "topics" list, trying to click with a topic the other person will enjoy.

You can estimate how much the other person wants to converse with you by how much "free information" he gives about himself in response to your questions. Free information is personal information given in elaborating or going beyond a simple factual answer to your question. You ask, "Do you like the play?" and she answers "Yes; I like nearly all of Brecht's plays"; her second clause is "free information" about her tastes and preferences. Free information provides strong clues about someone's interests, so you know better what questions will get her or him to talk further. You reply, "Yes, I think Brecht is a brilliant craftsman of modern dramatic forms. Which of his plays have you seen? How did you feel about them?"

During the opener and the moments of conversational scanning that follow, the two of you are sizing each other up, trying to decide whether you want to continue the conversation. If a person doesn't want to converse, he or she gives off any of several signals: he or she will look away, not smile, give short, perfunctory answers or none at all, go on busily with his or her work, and generally appear to be cool and indifferent to you. You can decide whether to withdraw with a "Thank you" or continue the pursuit and search for a conversation topic that will engage him or her.

You can make two kinds of social mistakes at this decision stage: first, you can continue to pursue when the other person really wants you to leave; second, you can stop and retreat when the other person really wants you to persist but temporarily can't think of how to help you. In trying to initiate conversation, shy people usually make the second mistake, retreating when the other person wouldn't mind if they continued their opening conversation. So the best advice for a shy person, particularly in starting conversation with another shy person, is to continue scanning for interesting conversation topics until either you succeed or the other person clearly signals that he or she does not want to talk now. In other words, assume you are welcome until you are clearly told otherwise. An assertive way to find out where you stand is to comment on the other person's behavior. For example, you might say, "I see you are busy now" or "I get the feeling you don't really want to talk about the Brecht productions you've seen."

In the following exercise, think up an opening line plus two follow-up sentences you could say to four specific people. The people will be two same-sex and two opposite-sex persons, one of whom is a total stranger, the other of whom you know very slightly and want to get to know better. Imagine a specific past occasion in which you were in such a situation with such a person, then write your opener and two plausible follow-ups.

Same sex, familiar person

Situation: _____

Opener: _____

Follow-up lines: _____

_____

Opposite sex, familiar person

Situation: _____

Opener: _____

Follow-up lines: _____

_____

Same sex, stranger

Situation: _____

Opener: _____

Follow-up lines: _____

_____

Opposite sex, stranger

Situation: _____

Opener: _____

Follow-up lines: _____

_____

Keeping Conversations Going

Let us suppose you have delivered your opener and its follow-ups, and you have the other person actively participating. He or she has communicated, "This conversation is pleasant so far. Let's see what develops." You keep a conversation going by encouraging or prompting the other person to talk about himself or herself while you interject frequent remarks about yourself. Listen in particular for the free information that other people supply about themselves, their likes, feelings, background, or character. You use such information to make a comparable statement about your own values or experiences on that topic, elaborating or giving specific experiences when possible. You can also use the free information to ask a question. If someone answers your question with "I don't know the next class assignment. I went skiing on the day of the last class meeting," comment on the free information. For instance, "Sounds great. I like skiing myself. I was at Dodge Ridge about 4 weeks ago, where the snow was very fast. Where did you go? How was it?"

In the examples below, identify the free information in the other person's answer and use it to frame an elaborative comment or question.

You: Where did you get your tan?

She: At Fort Lauderdale. I went there for my spring break.

You: _____

_____

You: Where do you shop?

He: At the Super Duper market. They have a great organic food section.

You: _____

_____

You: How did you vote in the last campaign?

He: I didn't. I'm totally indifferent to politics.

You: _____

_____

In elaborating upon the other person's remark, you should also give free information about yourself before ending with some kind of question. The information given about yourself and your interests should be specific, so the other person can easily continue the conversation with you. Most people are slightly anxious to keep a conversation going with a newly met person. So help the other person as much as you can, supplying lots of free, elaborative information about your experiences, values, and opinions. If you don't do this, the other person may conclude you aren't interested in the conversation.

The simplest way to get another person to talk is to ask appropriate questions. Let's divide questions into three classes.

1. Factual questions about external events which you could, in principle, look up in a newspaper or encyclopedia. Examples would be "How did the Dodgers do yesterday?" or "When does the show begin?"
2. Questions about the other person which are factual and only slightly personal. Examples would be "What's your major?" or "Where are you from?" and "Are you married or engaged?"
3. Questions which ask about personal feelings, reasons, motives, and emotions, eliciting answers that are subjective and personal. Examples would be, "How do you feel about school?" or "Why are you interested in dreams?" or "I can understand your rage at the draft. Did you feel like a slave?"

Learn to identify and to ask these three types of questions. The first and second types of question will elicit background information, but won't promote feelings of close friendship, whereas questions of the third type promote closer intimacy. "Feelings" questions express your concern for the other person. In trying to understand someone else's feelings, you are saying you value that person and are interested in him or her. When conveyed clearly, such sentiments are likely to be returned; the other person becomes interested in what you have to say.

Here are some further instances of questions.[3] Decide what types of questions they are (1, 2, or 3). Write your answer beside each question.

____ Do you have any brothers or sisters?

____ How do you feel about your parents?

____ What did the President do yesterday in Geneva?

____ Where are you from?

____ What kinds of things really scare you?

____ Did that make you very depressed?

____ Your mother was a cripple?

____ How do you feel about drugs?

____ What work did your father do?

____ Who's teaching your physics course?

[Answers: 2, 3, 1, 2, 3, 3, 3, 3, 2, 1]

The way you get to know someone well is by eliciting and sharing the "feeling" information given by Type 3 questions. The degree of intimacy of a conversation is rated by observers to correspond directly with the number of Type 3 questions occurring. Therefore, to deepen a friendship, concentrate on moving a conversation from Types 1 and 2 to Type 3 questions. That can give you both a sense of growing intimacy.

Open and Closed Questions

Learn to ask "open" questions, ones calling for the other person to describe a situation in detail, when appropriate. These may be contrasted to "closed" questions, which tend to be answered briefly, with a single word, perhaps a yes or no. Because of their wording, open questions elicit longer, more elaborative answers, more details and statements about motives, feelings, and intentions. Open questions might begin with phrases like "Could you tell me more about . . .?" or "How did you happen to . . .?" or "How did you feel about . . .?" or "In what way do you see . . .?" From the free information in the response, you can select an interesting item to help you with formulating your next comment, self-disclosure, or question.

Here are some examples illustrating open versus closed questions. As you read them, see how much you would have to say to answer the two types of queries.

Closed questions	*Open questions*
"You're from Chicago, aren't you?"	"What are your memories of Chicago?"
"Did you feel scared?"	"Tell me how you felt."
"When did you serve in Vietnam?"	"How did you feel about fighting in the Vietnam war?"
"Do you like science fiction?"	"Who are your favorite authors? What do you like about their stories?"

Note that closed questions are basically of Types 1 and 2, and elicit some information. The open questions build on such information by probing for details, feelings, reasons, and perspectives.

Now, let's generate open and closed questions for some hypothetical situations:

Situation. You are standing in a line to get into an Ingmar Bergman film. You strike up a conversation with the person ahead of you in the line. He says "I've been looking forward to seeing this film." You reply with:

Closed question: _____

_____

Open question 1: _____

_____

Open question 2: _____

_____

Situation. At a singles bar, you are dancing with a person you've not met before. To your opener, he or she replies, "I work as a certified public accountant." You reply with:

Closed question: _____

_____

Open question 1: _____

_____

Open question 2: _____

_____

Situation. You join a church choir because you like to sing. You're attracted to another person in the choir. After a rehearsal, you ask her how long she has been singing in this choir. She answers "Nearly six months now." You follow up with:

Closed question: _____

_____

Open question 1: _____

_____

Open question 2: _____

_____

What's the use of all these questions about personal feelings and values? They serve several functions. First, they tell other people you are interested in and care for them. Second, people often enjoy answering such questions since they like to talk about themselves and topics that interest them. Your honest attention communicates that you're a very appealing and interesting person yourself. Third, their answers tell you about their likes, dislikes, and goals. You learn what topics or events interest them, and what you can do to please them. Such knowledge is useful for encouraging budding friendships.

Sharing Through Self-Disclosure

Good conversations develop according to step-by-step reactions to self-disclosures by each party. You gain closer friendship and intimacy by telling the other person about your feelings, tastes, fantasies, deep-seated desires, long-range goals, or historical background relevant to your current goals or hang-ups. By disclosing yourself to the other person, he or she feels you are *sharing* your feelings and intimacy with him or her. Therefore, when appropriate, help out a budding conversation by providing lots of free information about yourself, especially about your feelings and attitudes.

Occasionally, after listening to this advice, a shy person will ask, "But what kinds of self-disclosures produce intimacy? What topics?" Surely you can't produce intimacy by disclosing guarded secrets about your halitosis, dandruff, and constipation. But there are hundreds of topics concerning "deeply held personal beliefs" that, with gentle inquiry, can be intimacy-producing. A possible list of topics might include opinions about the follow-ing:[4] your parents, brothers and sisters; your home town and up-bringing; your life style; your future plans; your views on marriage and having children; your violence and hatreds; your personal fears; your feelings about growing old; your view of God; your view of death; your use of drugs; your failures and triumphs; your ex-loves and jealousies; your times of sorrow. Nearly everyone can talk for several minutes or more on such basic personal subjects.

A word of caution here: Intimacy cannot be rushed. Usually, a person will want to spend quite some time alone with you before being willing to disclose feelings or personal facts that he or she considers embarrassing. The cultural convention is to wear an amiable mask and to confine early social exchanges to nonembarrassing themes and disclosures. At this stage, a person will be puzzled if you rush him or her with a fountain of purple self-disclosures of a most intimate kind. The reaction is, "He doesn't know me well enough yet to be telling me this kind of heavy stuff." Shy people are unlikely to have this problem of overwhelming a casual acquaintance with "too much, too soon." Nonetheless, it is a danger worth watching out for.

We also do not want to leave the impression that intimate friends talk only about their psychodynamics — their feelings, hang-ups, and motiva-tions. Intimates exchange an enormous amount of small talk and do so comfortably. But after a few meetings, they have usually explored in depth the feelings, values, and opinions of one another on issues vital to them. It is the ease with which they can talk comfortably about such matters of deep concern that identifies intimate friends. Therefore, in developing intimacy, "heavy, feeling talk" should be used judiciously, mixed in with lots of small talk and simple information exchanges. A friendship is not for nonstop psychoanalysis, but for enjoyment.

Dead Ends

Conversation topics like the weather, inflation, and the movie you both saw can usually be sustained for only a few minutes. You eventually run into a "dead end" where neither of you has any more to say about it. Dead ends are usually recognizable by a long pause after a "speech" and before a "reaction" comes to it. When a topic seems to have run dry for the mo-ment, try to come to the rescue quickly. The first type of rescue is to explicitly return to an earlier topic of this conversation or a previous one. Use some "returning" remark such as "Okay. Say, I'd like to go back to a point you made a while ago about X. Could you tell me how you came to that conclusion?" The second type of rescue from a dead end uses a transition sentence which simply leads into a new topic you are introducing into the conversation. After the dead end pause, you can say:

- "Right. I was just wondering a little while ago about . . ."
- "Okay. Well, if you liked *that,* then you will probably also be planning to see . . ."
- "Yes. Let's try to get our minds off that heavy subject and save it for later. To get back to the mundane, I wonder what you think about . . ."

These begin with an interjection like "Okay" or "So," which signals a distinct break-point in the conversation. You then relate your new topic either to an earlier one or to one suggested by what you know about this person. Unless you or your partner can supply such transitions, you will either terminate the conversation or meander aimlessly around the dead-end topic. It is always advantageous to be prepared with a couple of topics which you can call to mind in such emergencies.

Listening

To become a good conversationalist, you have to become a good listener. It is surprising how many people are terrible listeners. They give the impression we are boring them and that they are only waiting for a chance to interrupt us with some precious point that has crossed their minds.

Although you may think of listening as a passive behavior, it has its assertive aspect. Your active listening shows concern for others, and since it provides you with a wealth of free information about the other person it is a necessary and welcome element in the total interaction between you and the other person.

To become a good listener, follow at least a couple of rules. The first rule concerns your body language; it should communicate that you are attending fully to the speaker and are interested in or pleased with what he or she is saying. (Recall the body language exercises in Chapter 4, page 80.) The second rule is not to interrupt the speaker unless you think he is being unusually offensive, longwinded, or a boor. People whose friendship you want to cultivate will repay your courtesy with similar attention when you are expressing your own ideas.

Closers

Conversations don't go on forever. In fact, it is far better to have a brief, "meaty" conversation than a prolonged one filled with lots of dead air-time, yawning, and frantic searching for another topic. You will seek out again the former conversationalist but not the latter.

How do you terminate a conversation? It is very instructive for you to observe for several days the many conversations that happen around you, looking in particular for the cues or "tip-offs" people use to communicate that they are about to terminate a conversation.

A typical conversation, say between a supervisor and employee at the office, begins with a rush of remarks about a specific problem and the way to deal with it. As that topic runs out, the last speaker says something like, "So I'll handle that as agreed. Okay?" The "okay," given with rising inflection, is an implicit question which asks "Is there anything else? If not, this conversation is closed." The listener understands that implicit communication. If he replies "Okay" with a tone of finality (falling inflection), then the conversation is effectively over except possibly for perfunctory good-byes. If the listener wants to introduce another topic, he has to jump in with it quite soon after the first speaker's "Okay?" If he lets the moment pass, and the conversation appears to be ending, he can reopen it only by some apology such as "Oh, yes, I forgot. There was this other point . . ."

The "Okay?" is a conversation "closer." There are several others such as "Right?" "That's all?" "Anything else?" or "Is that it?" Here are some other things people do to signal the end of the conversation:

- Summarize. ("So I'll get this out by Friday.")
- Legitimize leaving. ("I have to get to X now.")
- Indicate support. ("Well, it's been nice meeting you.")
- Indicate continuance. ("I hope I see you again soon.")

People also send messages in body language when they're about to terminate a conversation. They break eye contact, stand up (if sitting before), sigh (release breath loudly), smile and shake hands, or begin to fidget — rocking on their feet or wringing their hands.

People excuse themselves from a conversation because they have to go to work, to their home, to the library, to the bathroom, to dinner, to study, to sleep, to the dentist, to get their drink refreshed, to keep an appointment, or to circulate and talk to others. Conversational etiquette dictates that when people introduce such a closer, it is impolite for you to challenge their reasons or to detain them further.

When developing a friendship, as you prepare to leave it's usual to mention an interest in future interaction. It may be general, as in "I'll look around here for you next weekend," or specific, "Let's meet here tomorrow for lunch." In the beginning, you may only indicate a general interest in meeting again; once greater intimacy has developed, a specific time and place for the next meeting could be set. Alternatively, the conversation may end with a promise to telephone one another to make such arrangements.

SOCIALIZING EXERCISES

If you consider yourself shy, practice the following activities[5] to get over it. Use your assertiveness diary to keep a daily record of your accomplishments in several tasks. Record what you observed, how you felt about it, and how the other person reacted. Have your buddy help you with these exercises.

Note first that these activities are listed in random order, not according to their difficulty. Read them over and rank them in the order of subjective difficulty you would experience doing them. Discard any exercise that can't be done in your social setting. Place a 1 beside the easiest exercise for you, and larger numbers beside progressively more difficult ones.

_____ Introduce yourself to a new person in your office building, the grocery store, or in a class.

_____ Invite someone who is going your way to walk with you.

_____ Ask to join the next game or bull session you see in progress. If you're in an office, join a coffee-break talk group.

_____ Conduct a personal opinion survey. Ask 10 people their opinions on a current topic. Ask one question about their opinions.

_____ Ask someone you don't know if you can borrow ten cents for a phone call. Arrange to pay them back!

_____ Find out the name of someone (opposite sex) in your office or class or social club. Call him or her on the phone and ask about the latest work issue, class assignment, or upcoming event.

_____ Go to a coffee house. Smile and nod at the first three people who look at you. Strike up a conversation with at least one person of the same sex.

_____ Stand in a line at a grocery, bank, or movie. Strike up a conversation about the line with whoever is near you.

_____ Converse with the gas station attendant as he is filling the tank with gas and checking the oil.

_____ Sit down beside a person of the opposite sex who looks interesting (in a bus, lounge, class, movie). Make some sort of opening commentary.

_____ Ask three persons for directions. Shift at least one of them into general conversation for a brief minute or two.

_____ Go to a jogging track, beach, or swimming pool. Converse with two or three strangers you come close to there.

_____ Notice someone who needs help in your neighborhood or class or office. Offer to help.

_____ Carry a copy of a controversial book with you for one day. Count how many people you can get to start a conversation over it.

_____ Organize and throw a small party (say 3-5 people). Invite at least one person you don't know well.

_____ The next time you have a problem, find someone in your dorm, office, or neighborhood who is not close to you, and ask his or her advice.

_____ Invite someone to go eat with you — someone you have not eaten with before.

_____ Practice your openers and follow-up statements before a mirror and tape record yourself. Listen to yourself, then do it again, trying repeatedly for improvement in the liveliness and enthusiasm of your voice.

_____ Say "Hi" to five new people today whom you would not usually greet. Try to provoke a smile and return "Hi" from them.

Now contract with yourself to begin work on the easiest exercise. Some exercises can be done in one day's session, others will require several days. Complete each exercise, reward yourself, then move on to the next harder exercise the next day. Observe the effect of your social behaviors on others and on yourself. Record your observations each evening in your daily assertiveness diary, and mentally rehearse at that time the positive social experiences you had that day.

ON MAKING DATES

One of the most anxiety-provoking situations for the shy is asking another person for a date. But it is a mistake to think of a first (or later) date as a gigantic production with elegant dining and expensive entertainment. Some of the more sociable dates are made for very casual activities like walks, sailing, a coffee break, tennis, studying together, lunch, shopping, a movie, a lecture, a dance, or some small event. It needn't be "heavy" or expensive to foster a friendship; relationships develop according to the quality of the interaction, not the cost of the activity.

Among single people today, it's not unusual for a woman to take the dating initiative, especially for the more casual, low-cost activities. Nevertheless, many people feel uncomfortable with this idea, and the traditional pattern is still the most common. So our comments about making a first date are phrased in terms of a man approaching a woman. What we say can be equally well applied by a woman, of course.

Many dates are made by telephone, so here are a few useful tips to follow.[6] First of all, *be prepared:* have some specific event or activity in mind for the date, one which you think the two of you will enjoy. If it's a play, concert, or other public event, be sure tickets are available, and know the times, days, and places for the event. Second, when you reach the person by telephone, identify yourself clearly: tell her your name, where you met her, remind her of some incident that may jog her memory about you. Third, don't beat around the bush but go directly to the point: say you enjoyed meeting her last time and you would like to meet again. Fourth, relate the specific activity (or activities) you had in mind, say you think it will be fun for the two of you, and ask whether she would like to go with you. Fifth, if the answer is yes, then set a specific day, time, and place where you will meet.

TALKING STRAIGHT AND GETTING CLEAR

If the answer is no, assess tactfully whether it's because she's tied up but interested or whether she's simply not interested. You may be able to assess this by suggesting an alternative activity or alternative time, or asking if you can call again soon. If any of these are accepted, fine: make the date as specified. But if she rejects or hedges on all suggestions, you can infer she isn't interested in going out with you now. Get as much clarity as you can about whether your assessment is correct. Despite the discomfort you feel in confronting a possible rejection, it is far better to get a clear message instead of worrying over all the possible negative interpretations of an ambiguous message. After several no's, you can say, "I get the feeling that maybe you don't want to go out with me. That would disappoint me but I'd rather not push you into something you don't care to do. Am I perceiving things correctly?" Your goal is to get as clear an answer as the person is willing (or able) to supply, yet let her know a no will not crush you. You can suggest casual friendship meetings rather than dates with romantic prospects. All varieties and levels of friendship arrangements are possible.

If you do get rejected, don't embarrass the other person further by demanding an explanation. The situation is already uncomfortable; don't intensify it. It is entirely probable that the negative response is no fault of yours; it may be due to an overfull schedule, to a relationship that has developed with someone else, to the need for time to recover from a recent bad experience, or even to shyness more severe than your own. Any of these probable explanations allows you to save your self-esteem despite the rejection. Look upon the rejection as a clear signal that you should pursue other "candidates" as more likely to yield rewarding company for you.

For the timid, setting dates requires careful planning, particularly for initial dates. We suggest you write out and rehearse a script requesting a date in a confident voice, anticipating the other person's reactions to your proposals, and planning how you will react. Write several different scenarios that develop to the point at which the other person says yes or consistently says no.

The fully planned "date request script" is appropriate for only the first date or two. Thereafter, most dates are made by arrangement near the end of each date. Before each date, you might have thought about what further events or activities you might both enjoy, so you are prepared to ask the other person for ideas but you also have suggestions about the next date. As a couple becomes more intimate, they plan things jointly, of course, with each person sharing and making suggestions for dates.

What about rejecting someone else's request for a date with you? Nonassertive people have a hard time saying no because they don't want to hurt the other person's feelings. But don't let your guilt feelings outweigh your assertive right to go out only with people you find appealing. When an unwanted person asks you out or makes advances, express polite appreciation but say clearly and firmly that "I don't want to go out with you now." If you have a socially acceptable reason, such as another live romantic interest, simply say that, to save the self-esteem of the rejected caller. But if you can think of no good reason besides your lack of attraction or interest in the other, simply stand firmly behind a statement of "I don't care to spend more time with you." You owe no one an explanation, and you need not supply one beyond your "I don't want to." The goal is not to hurt but to clarify in order to gain freedom for yourself and the other person. After all, the other person didn't explain why he called you, beyond saying "I wanted to!"

COPING WITH SOCIAL ANXIETIES

While tips about meeting strangers, conversing, and making dates may be useful, perhaps they do not go to the heart of your problem, which may be extreme social anxiety or fear of rejection. For example, very shy people are often terrified of calling up someone they barely know to ask for a date. If this applies to you, you must first work on reducing your fear of approaching others. In this section we suggest how you might apply the procedures of "systematic desensitization" (Chapter 3) to the social actions of "speaking up" that you have planned.

To begin with, focus on only one action, one you are mildly afraid to perform. This might be calling up someone for a date, asking someone to dance, or telling a story to a group at a party. Break the action down into a series of small steps, so that you produce an anxiety hierarchy as described on pages 52–55. Now, turn on your relaxation tape, get fully relaxed, and imagine yourself carrying out successfully each of the small steps of your social action while remaining completely calm and relaxed. Imagine the first step in vivid detail for 10–20 seconds while keeping relaxed. After imagining this step, switch immediately to imagining a very pleasurable experience such as lying in the sun, swimming, gliding, eating ice cream, getting a massage. The point is to reinforce yourself in your imagination for having successfully climbed one rung up your social-fear ladder. After imagining the pleasurable activity for about 10 seconds, relax and let your mind go blank for about 20 seconds. If you felt tension during the first scene, go through that scene again before moving on. Then repeat the sequence: imagine yourself performing the next step in your fear hierarchy for 10–20 seconds while remaining relaxed, and follow it by imagining the reinforcing scene. After you have completed the entire hierarchy several times, you may feel ready to contract with yourself to perform the action in real life.

Here is an example of the steps in telephoning a woman for a date.

1. In my room, thinking about telephoning Sally for a date. Remaining calm.
2. I pick up my "script" to use in asking her for a date. Keeping calm.
3. I walk over to the telephone and sit down comfortably. Remaining relaxed.
4. I lift the receiver and hear the dial-tone. Staying unafraid.
5. I dial the number, and hear her telephone ringing. Breathing freely, relaxed.
6. She lifts her receiver, and I hear her say hello. Staying calm.
7. I say hello and identify myself, using my prepared script. Keeping relaxed.
8. I ask Sally for a date using my script. Staying unafraid.
9. She says she's busy that evening. Remaining calm and relaxed.
10. I ask her out for the alternative event, as planned. Keeping calm.
11. She accepts delightedly. Hurray!

Here is another example in which an older woman imagines getting acquainted with an attractive older man at a church potluck.

1. I am sitting at the table watching the others eating. Remaining relaxed.
2. I notice two men eating cake at another table. One seems especially pleasant. Staying calm.

3. I see another woman approach him and say a few words. Calm.
4. I watch him react to her conversation. He is friendly and outgoing. Keeping calm.
5. After the other woman leaves, he starts to clean up the table. Remaining calm.
6. I decide to introduce myself. Keeping relaxed.
7. I get up and walk directly toward the table, getting closer and closer. Staying relaxed and calm.
8. He and the other man are conversing. They stop and look at me as I arrive at their table. Continue feeling relaxed.
9. I look at him and say, "Can I help you clean up?" Remaining calm.
10. He smiles and says, "Of course," and hands me a cloth. Staying relaxed and unafraid.
11. We start cleaning the table as we exchange names and small talk. Remaining calm.

If you are afraid to approach someone, make up a similar hierarchy for your situation. Desensitize yourself to it in your imagination several times, and then perform the action if you choose to do so. Finally, just before and during the actual performance, use the stress-coping internal monologs suggested in Chapter 3, pages 59–63; these can help you keep your fear to a manageable level as you begin asserting yourself to find new friends.

CONCLUSION

Throughout this book, we have presented information to help you deal with situations in which you might feel inadequate or put down. We have designed exercises and examples so that you can acquire specific assertive skills: building self-esteem, coping with stress, learning to write and deliver effective DESC scripts, answering detouring remarks assertively, developing assertive body language and speech, dealing with one-shot situations, and making new friends. We hope that by now, some of these positive skills have become a part of your everyday behavior. It takes careful practice and perseverance, but it's worth the trouble. You *can* feel better about yourself and others. And now is the time to start!

Appendix A
Principles of Behavior Change*

This book uses ideas from behavior-change psychology to help you change your behavior. People are often curious about the principles that underlie the procedures we recommend. So, in this appendix, we have summarized some of the more important principles used throughout this book.

The principles can be applied to changing your own behavior (including your thoughts and images) as well as the behavior of those around you. The emphasis is on changing specific responses, not nebulous attitudes or traits.

A. To strengthen or teach a new behavior

1. *Positive Reinforcement Principle.* To improve or increase performance of a certain activity, provide a reward immediately after each correct performance.

   The "reward" is something the person likes; it may be a material incentive (money, cookies), social praise (compliments, approval), or opportunity to engage in a pleasant activity (watching TV, enjoying dinner out, reading). The timing is "response-then-reward" (or "work-then-play"), with a specific requirement that the "play" isn't available unless the desired behavior occurs first.

---

*The statements of these behavior change principles are quoted, with adaptation and selection, from pages 232–233 of *Changing Children's Behavior* by John D. Krumboltz and Helen B. Krumboltz (Englewood Cliffs, N.J.: Prentice-Hall, 1972), and are used here by permission of the authors and publisher.

2. *Token or Point Reward Principle.* A neutral stimulus or event can serve as a reward if it is convertible into (exchangeable for) a basic reward.

Paper money is a token, with its worth established by convention as convertible into so many ounces of gold. Similarly, in assertiveness training, you can set up a token or point system whereby you contract to receive and record so many points for each assertive exercise practiced, and you can "cash in" the points accumulated over several days for some particularly desirable pleasure, whether it be attending a play or movie, visiting a Chinese restaurant, or taking an afternoon nap. The point system gives you immediate small rewards for the many little jobs you do in working toward your larger goal.

B. To develop new behavior

3. *Successive Approximations Principle.* To teach a behavior that someone has seldom or never before displayed, reward each small successive step toward the final behavior.

This is the old adage that you must learn to crawl before you walk and to walk before you run. A new skier starts on the beginner's slopes, then moves on to slopes of intermediate difficulty before attempting the very steep slopes that challenge the advanced skier. The same idea applies to learning to assert yourself in progressively more stressful situations.

4. *Modeling Principle.* One way to teach a new way of behaving is to show how an effective (or prestigeful) person performs the desired behavior.

This is the old idea that we "learn by example," by seeing how someone else does the job successfully. In our assertiveness training, for instance, one exercise asks you to think about an assertive friend (or actor) and to behave the way he or she would behave in specific situations.

C. To stop inappropriate behavior

5. *Extinction Principle.* To stop someone from acting in a undesirable way, try to arrange conditions so that he or she consistently receives no rewards following the undesired act.

When you say no to unreasonable demands on your time and energy (for instance, from volunteer organizations), you are extinguishing the habit of the requester to call upon you whenever a chore is to be done.

6. *Alternative Behavior Principle.* To stop someone from acting in a particular way, you may reward an alternative or substitute action that is inconsistent with or cannot be performed at the same time as the undesired act.

Nonassertive people often tell themselves negative, self-defeating things, such as, "I'm no good, I'm hopeless, weak, stupid." You can acquire a more positive self-concept if you think about and dwell upon your good attributes as often as you can. The "good" thoughts drive out the "bad."

7. *Relief Principle.* To stop someone from acting in a particular way you may arrange to terminate a mildly unpleasant situation in exchange for improvement in that behavior.

This principle was applied by a working mother who received no help with household chores from her family. She simply refused to do any dishes or laundry for several days until her family finally agreed to discuss a contract for sharing household duties.

8. *Fear Reduction Principle.* To help someone overcome fear of a particular situation, start by providing a minimal exposure to the feared situation while the person is otherwise comfortable, relaxed, secure, or rewarded, and gradually increase the exposure.

In assertiveness training, you can use this principle to help you overcome your fear of asserting yourself and to control your anxiety in a variety of confrontation situations.

Appendix B
*Progressive Relaxation**

Instructions Either record these words into a tape recorder or memorize the sequence of the exercises. The phrases at the side are not for recording; they are printed here to help you visualize the progression from one muscle group to another. [*Note:* People with physical problems should consult their doctor about these exercises.]

PROGRESSIVE RELAXATION EXERCISES

Now is the time to relax. Find a nice comfortable position on a bed or on a floor mat and try to relax as much as you can right now. I am going to ask you to tighten certain muscles and study the sensations that come from these muscles while they're tense, and then notice what happens when you relax them and continue to relax them further and further.

HANDS AND To start with, clench your right fist and try to keep all the other
FOREARMS muscles in your body relaxed. Your forearm will be down flat (holding it up makes some tension in your upper arm). Study the feelings of tension in your forearm. Notice the location of the muscles and how they feel when they're tensed. [Pause for tensing] . . . . . . Relax now, all at once — don't ease off — let everything go all at once and then study the sensations in that muscle group as muscles relax further and further. [*Pause for relaxing*] . . . .

---

*Adapted by permission, from a tape recording for teaching relaxation, produced by John Marquis, Ph. D., Self Management Schools, Los Altos, Ca.

Now, of course, it goes more quickly if you can do it with both fists at once — so this time clench both fists. Once more study the sensations in these tense muscles — and as they begin to get a little tired locate them very clearly and specifically. [*Pause for tensing*] . . . . And again, let go all at once without easing off — relax. Now study the sensations as these muscles relax further and further. [*Pause for relaxing*] . . . .

UPPER ARMS Now pull your forearms up against your upper arms as far as you can, keeping your forearms relaxed — you can tell they're relaxed when your wrists are limp. Fold them up right now and feel your biceps work and study the pattern of tension in your biceps — locate these muscles in your upper arms. [*Pause for tensing*] . . . . And relax. Let your arm flop and each time notice the contrast between how the muscles feel when they're tense and when they're relaxed. [*Pause for relaxing*] . . . .

Now straighten your arms out — completely straight — and try to turn your elbows inside out. Feel the muscles work up the back of your upper arms — study the feeling of tension in this muscle. [*Pause for tensing*] . . . . Relax now. [*Pause for relaxing*] . . . . And a final word about the thing that you do in order to relax the muscle — *enjoy* the *good feeling* as the tension gradually goes off more and more. [*Pause for relaxing*] . . . .

Now raise your arms out to the side. You have nothing to push against so it will take a little more time before the muscles get tired enough for you to feel the tension in them. These will be the muscles up across the tops of your upper arms and the muscles from the points of your shoulders up to the back of your neck. [*Pause for tensing*] . . . . And now relax and study the sensations as these muscles relax. [*Pause for relaxing*] . . . .

FOREHEAD Now raise your eyebrows and pull your scalp down to meet your eyebrows so that you can feel the tension in your forehead and up across the top of your skull. Study the pattern of tension. Don't worry if you can't feel your scalp — lots of people can't. [*Pause for tensing*] . . . . And relax now and just feel your forehead smoothing out and enjoy the good kind of creeping sensation as the muscles in your forehead and scalp relax. [*Pause for relaxing*] . . . .

Once more raise your eyebrows and feel the muscles work up there. [*Pause for tensing*] . . . . And relax. [*Pause for relaxing*] . . . .

This time instead of letting everything go, try to let go approximately half the tension in your forehead and try to keep it in a disciplined way at that level — stamping out the fluctuations so that the level remains constant. [*Pause*] . . . . Then let half of that go and once more try to keep it at that level without letting it vary upward or downward. [*Pause*] . . . . And half of that. [*Pause*] . . . . And half of that. Try to maintain just a tiny level of tension so that you can become aware of it when your forehead begins to tighten up just a little bit. [*Pause*] . . . . And relax now — let it all go and just enjoy the good feeling as your forehead relaxes and smooths out — gradually lets go and relaxes. [*Pause for relaxing*] . . . .

Now frown — pull your eyebrows together across the top of your nose — feel the muscles work there? Almost makes you feel angry, doesn't it? [*Pause for tensing*] . . . . . . Then relax. Let it go. [*Pause for relaxing*] . . . .

EYES Now close your eyes tightly — this will perhaps use a little bit of your frowning muscles. You can feel the circular muscles that go all around your eye and your eyelids and maybe a little of your muscle that wrinkles your nose is there. [*Pause for tensing*] . . . . . . Then relax — let all the tension go out and let your upper lids rest very gently on your lower lids. [*Pause for relaxing*] . . . .

Now as we continue through the rest of these muscles I want you to leave your eyes closed so that you'll be able to attend more easily to the sensations that are coming from your muscles without the interference of seeing things around you. If you find it uncomfortable to keep your eyes closed, open them for just a second and then close them again as soon as you can comfortably do it. Now, keeping your eyes closed, roll your eyes in a large circle and feel the muscles work as you move your eyes to the right — now notice those muscles that move your eyes downward — to the left — and up — and around — don't work them too hard because it's easy to strain your eyes. [*Pause for moving eyes in circle*] . . . . . . Then relax. Study the sensations as the tension goes out of these muscles that move your eyeballs about — think of looking at nothing and just let all those muscles go. [*Pause for relaxing*] . . . .

MOUTH Now act as if you were going to brush your upper teeth and retract your upper lip. You will find the two muscles that you use to do this — one that pulls up the middle of your upper lip and the other that pulls up the corners of your mouth — like when you smile. Now feel these muscles work. [*Pause for tensing*] . . . . . . And relax now — each time noticing what you do to relax and just observing for a moment the sensations those relaxed muscles give rise to. [*Pause for relaxing*] . . . .

Now pucker your mouth — feel the circular muscle around your mouth work. [*Pause for tensing*] . . . . . . And relax now. [*Pause for relaxing*] . . . .

JAWS Clench your teeth — but try to leave your lips relaxed — clench your teeth and feel the muscles work there and in the corners of your jaw and on up to your temples. If you can't feel them in your temples, reach your finger up to your temple and feel them work there. Study the sensation of tension in these powerful muscles that close your jaw. [*Pause for tensing*] . . . . . . Relax now and just let your jaw hang slack and let all the tension go out of it. [*Pause for relaxing*] . . . .

TONGUE Now push your tongue forward against your teeth and feel the muscles work. Now pull your tongue back and feel the muscles work there. [*Pause for tensing*] . . . . And relax now — just let your tongue lie very passively in the front of your mouth. [*Pause for relaxing*] . . . .

THROAT Now push the back of your tongue upwards and feel your voice box move with it. Once more, if you have trouble feeling this, put your fingers on your Adams apple — feel it move — now push the back of your tongue down and feel your voice box go down and feel the tension go in the upper part of your throat. [*Pause for tensing*] . . . . And relax now. Let your tongue relax, as well as muscles that operate your tongue in the upper part of your throat. Pretend that you are going to clear your throat and feel your throat close. Feel it — hold it — study it — let go. Relax now. [*Pause for relaxing*] . . . .

Now swallow and observe what happens — notice the wave of relaxation that follows the wave of tension down your throat. Try swallowing now and note the wave of relaxation that follows it. And next, elaborate that wave of relaxation — just let your throat open up and relax. [*Pause for relaxing*] . . . . Now, swallow and stop in the middle with your throat contracted. Study the tension pattern. [*Pause*] . . . . Then relax it. Just enjoy the good feeling as your throat opens up and relaxes. [*Pause for relaxing*] . . . .

Now think of humming a high note. Feel the tensions in the muscles that tighten your vocal cords. [*Pause*] . . . . Relax now by singing the scales downward — feeling the changes in the level of tension in the muscles and finally ending up by picturing yourself forming a very low restful note as your vocal cords relax. [*Pause for relaxing*] . . . .

SHOULDERS Now move the points of your shoulders forward and together. Feel the muscles work from the points of your shoulders down to your breastbone. These are your pectoral muscles. [*Pause for tensing*] . . . . Now relax a minute. [*Pause for relaxing*] . . . .

Now pull your shoulders back as if you were trying to touch the points of your shoulders behind your back. Feel the muscles work in *between* your shoulder blades and *around* your shoulder blades. [*Pause for tensing*] . . . . And relax now — and just feel the relaxation spreading all around your shoulders, all the muscles around your shoulder blades and upper back muscles and over the top of your chest — just let your shoulders droop and sag. [*Pause for relaxing*] . . . .

NECK Now move your chin as you try touching your chin to your chest. Feel the tension [*Pause for tensing*] . . . . Now try to move your head to the right and to the left at the *same* time. Now, holding your neck stiffly, study the tension [*Pause for tensing*] . . . . And let all the muscles in your neck relax — just let them all go at once. Let them relax so deeply that if a breeze came along it would blow your head from one side to the other, almost as if you had no bones in your neck at all. Take no responsibility for the position of your head. Don't worry about its position — just let it be carried passively. [*Pause for relaxing*] . . . .

BACK AND PELVIS Now, leaving your neck relaxed and working just from your shoulders down to your pelvis, arch your back gently — raise your back up. Arch it and feel the muscles work, the two great columns of muscles down your spine. [*Pause for tensing*] . . . . And relax. [*Pause for relaxing*] . . . .

Now rock a little bit — just rock your pelvis from side to side and feel a little more tension in one of these muscles and then in the other [*Pause for tensing*] . . . . Now relax and just lie still and feel yourself sinking deeper and deeper into the bed [floor] as your muscles let go and relax more and more. Each time notice what you do in order to relax the muscles so that you can use this later. [*Pause for relaxing*] . . . .

BUTTOCKS Now tighten your buttocks. [*Pause for tensing*] . . . . This should be easy to feel because this includes the largest muscle in your body along with a couple of others. Now relax and just sink back into the bed [floor]. [*Pause for relaxing*] . . . .

THIGHS Now tighten all the muscles in your thighs. In order to do this, tighten the muscles that would move your knees together and at the *same* time the muscles that would move your knees apart — and at the *same* time the muscles that would push down and would raise your thighs — and then, to top it off, think of crossing your right leg over your left, similarly your left leg over your right. Study the pattern of tension. [*Pause for tensing*] . . . . And relax now and just let all these muscles lengthen and smooth out — relax. Feel the muscles let go as they gradually lengthen and expand. [*Pause for relaxing*] . . . .

LOWER LEGS Now point your toes downward so that they are in a direct line with your legs. Feel the muscles working in your calves — study the pattern of tension there. [*Pause for tensing*] . . . . And relax now. [*Pause for relaxing*] . . . .

Pull your toes toward you and feel your muscles work up your shin. [*Pause for tensing*] . . . . And relax now. [*Pause for relaxing*] . . . .

FEET On the next one you have to be rather careful because it is easy to cramp these muscles. Try this with your toes. Curl your toes under — feel the muscles work up under your arch [*Pause for tensing*] . . . . And relax now. [*Pause for relaxing*] . . . .

Feel all your muscles smoothing out and relaxing so that you are completely relaxed now from the top of your head to the tip of your toes and that you continue to let all these muscles relax more and more. After being good and tight when you have tensed them, the muscles can continue to be more and more deeply relaxed for as long as 20 minutes.

ABDOMEN Now, harden your abdominal muscles as if somebody were going to hit you in the stomach. [*Pause for tensing*] . . . . . . And relax. [*Pause for relaxing*] . . . .

Now harden your abdominal muscles again and study the pattern of tension — perhaps adding a little bit of an *attempt* to sit up. [*Pause for tensing*] . . . . . . And relax now. [*Pause for relaxing*] . . . . . .

Okay — once more — tighten these stomach muscles. This time pull your stomach in and tense [*Pause for tensing*] . . . . . . Now push it out — and in — and out — and relax. [*Pause for relaxing*] . . . . . .

CHEST Now, take about three-quarters of a deep breath, hold your breath and at the same time *try* to breathe in. Feel the muscles work — now, *try* to breathe out — feel the muscles work [*Pause for tensing*] . . . . . . And relax now. [*Pause for relaxing*] . . . . . . Now, as you did that perhaps you noticed that as you tried to breathe in you could feel your diaphragm flatten and then as you tried to breathe out you could feel it arch up. So let's try this once more — three-quarters of a deep breath — hold it — keeping your throat closed, *try* to breathe in some more. [*Pause*] . . . . . . Then *try* to breathe out [*Pause*] . . . . . . In . . . . . . Out . . . . . . In . . . . . . Out . . . . . . Feel your muscles work in your chest and diaphragm. They are powerful muscles which can help you to breathe correctly without running out of air.

Now, practice a different kind of breathing than usual. Breathe in — only leave your abdominal muscles relaxed while you raise your chest to breathe in. Using only your chest to breathe in, breathe in a little more deeply and a little more slowly than usual and then let everything go each time you reach the top of a breath. Breathe in deeply and slowly and then let it out. Breathe in slowly now by using your chest muscles. Hold it . . . . . . Let go. Again: breathe in slowly . . . . . . Hold it . . . . . . Let go . . . . . . This time when you reach the top of your breath, just let these muscles go for a few seconds *so that you don't have to do any work with any muscles in your body while you exhale. Let this be a signal to relax every other muscle in your body a little bit more and drift down gradually deeper and deeper* each time you breathe out. Again, breathe a little more slowly and a little more deeply than usual . . . . . . Hold it . . . . . . And then let go. Make no positive effort whatever when you are breathing out — just let the natural elasticity of your chest pour the air from your lungs. [*Pause for relaxing*] . . . . . . As you continue breathing, relax a little more slowly and a little bit more deeply, letting everything go, so that each time you breathe out it's like a sigh of relief.

Now, just continue relaxing like that for awhile now — deeper and deeper — without concentrating, because concentrating usually involves a little eyestrain. Attend to the sensations which are coming from your muscles. If any muscle has a little bit of residual tension left in it then you should be able to feel this tension — it will kind of "stick out" above the others. Lie quietly and passively and feel these sensations coming from your muscles along with the good feelings that come from your muscles as they relax further and further — perhaps finding one that sticks out a little bit. [*Pause for only three or four more breaths and sighs of relief*] . . . .

Now, relax from the tip of your toes to your head. Relax consciously, now your toes [3 – 5 second pause between parts of the body] . . . . feet . . . . ankles . . . . calves . . . . thighs . . . . pelvis . . . . stomach . . . . chest . . . . shoulders . . . . arms . . . . wrists . . . . fingers . . . . throat . . . . neck . . . . mouth . . . . eyes . . . . eybrows . . . .

If you notice any little bit of residual tension, just try to find the source of that muscle and turn it off — don't try to relax by moving because you always have to shorten a muscle in order to move. It will take longer to relax the muscle if you move it. Just take the muscles where you find them and let them go down from there.

Now, in order to impress your overall feeling of relaxation, start counting backwards from 10 to 1. With each count, see if you can become a little bit more relaxed and perhaps get a little more of a drowsy, sleepy feeling. 10 . . . 9 . . . 8 . . . 7 . . . 6 . . . 5 . . . 4 . . . 3 . . . 2 . . . 1 . . . .Now continue relaxing like that — deeper . . . . and deeper . . . . Just let the chemicals of relaxation do you all the good they can. Relax for 10 to 20 minutes — or simply go to sleep. When you are ready to arouse yourself, gently move a hand, then an arm, a foot, then a leg. Open your eyes gradually. Treat yourself to a quiet, relaxed arousal!

Appendix C
Rules of Contracting*

It helps to have some guidelines for thinking up behavioral contracts and for using them. Some rules were formulated by Tosti, Loehr, and Homme, three psychologists intimately involved in behavioral change contracts. Their rules are paraphrased below.

Rule 1. *At first, ask for and reward small changes.*

Don't request too much of the learner initially. Divide the overall task into manageable components.

Rule 2. *Use immediate reinforcement.*

Write your contract so that you reward the desired behavior as soon as it occurs; don't delay. Adhere to the "first work, then play" principle, and don't reverse the order.

Rule 3. *At first, reinforce often, then gradually less often.*

Reinforce nearly every response at first in order to get a behavior going; you can keep it going while reinforcing progressively less frequently.

Rule 4. *Be systematic in applying the contracting method.*

Once a contract is agreed to, stick to it rather than suspending it for all sorts of special occasions or mitigating circumstances. Try to extend explicit contracting to various problems you have with an individual.

---

*The rules are paraphrased and quoted with permission from D. T. Tosti, J. G. Loehr, and L. Homme, "Behavior mediation in individual and group counseling for rehabilitation." *Training Manual,* Marin County Probation Department, 1975.

Rule 5.   *Ask for and reward a specific accomplishment rather than general obedi-ence or good intentions.*

Specify the behavior you want positively. Don't specify it in terms of "Obey anything I ask you to do." Don't accept a statement of good intentions in place of positive behavior change.

Rule 6.   *Ask for high-quality performance.*

Ask for excellent performance standards and don't reinforce sloppy or shoddy performances that could be improved.

Rule 7.   *Contract for active, not passive, behavior.*

Emphasize the reward for desirable behaviors rather than the punish-ment for undesirable responses. Whenever possible, say "Do this" rather than "Stop doing that."

Rule 8.   *Make sure the terms of the contract are clear.*

Specify the expected behaviors and rewards in explicit, concrete terms.

Rule 9.   *Be fair and honest in fulfilling the contract.*

The reward should be worth the "effort" or difficulty of the new behavior being requested. Also, hold up your end of the agreement. Do what you've promised as soon as you can.

Rule 10.   *Try to shift most of the control of the contract to the person as soon as practical.*

Self-management is easier and increases the person's feelings of self-worth and dignity.

These are good rules to review periodically as you contract for behavior change with the people around you. In Chapters 5 through 8 we apply various facets of these rules.

Notes

Introduction

1. See "The social disease called shyness" by P. Zimbardo, P. Pilkonis, and R. Norwood in *Psychology Today*, May, 1975.

Chapter 1

1. The list of assertive behaviors is adapted from Andrew Salter, *Conditioned Reflex Therapy* (New York: Farrar, Straus, 1949) and from S. A. Rathaus, "An experimental investigation of assertive training in a group setting," *Journal of Behavior Therapy and Experimental Psychology* (Pergamon Press), 3, 81–86, 1972.
2. Sharon routinely teaches classes entitled "Self-Control of Speaking Anxiety" which use behavior-change methods to extinguish students' phobia about public speaking and which train them to prepare and deliver organized talks.

Chapter 2

1. "You" exercise, by Kathy Huguenin, appears in an Instructor's Manual to J. V. Baldridge, *Sociology: A Critical Approach to Power, Conflict, and Change* (New York: Wiley, 1975). Further adaptation by Sharon Bower.
2. This exercise is adapted from Jane L. Anton's doctoral dissertation entitled "An experimental analysis of training the anticipation and performance of reinforcement activities in the treatment of depression," Stanford University, 1974.

Chapter 3

1. The discussion of progressive relaxation has been adapted partly from the article "How to relax without pills," by Leavitt A. Knight, Jr., *Reader's Digest*, February 1971, 139–141.
2. A standard reference is Edmund Jacobson, *Progressive Relaxation* (Chicago: University of Chicago Press, 1938).
3. The systematic desensitization technique is usually ascribed to Joseph Wolpe, in his *Psychotherapy by Reciprocal Inhibition* (Stanford, Calif.: Stanford University Press, 1958).
4. The efficacy of this technique was demonstrated in research by Patricia L. Garfield (nee Darwin), "Effect of greater subject activity and increased scene duration on rate of desensitization," unpublished doctoral dissertation, Temple University, 1968. (See *Dissertation Abstracts*, Vol. XXX, No. 3, 1969.)
5. From "Modifying what clients say to themselves," by Donald Meinchenbaum and Roy Cameron, in *Self-Control: Power to the Person*, by Michael J. Mahoney and Carl E. Thoresen. Copyright © 1974 by Wadsworth Publishing Company, Inc. Reprinted by permission of the publisher, Brooks/Cole Publishing Company, Monterey, California, and by permission of the authors.

Chapter 5

1. From Sharon Anthony Bower, "Assertiveness training for women," in *Counseling Methods*, edited by John D. Krumboltz and Carl E. Thoresen, Copyright © 1976 by Holt, Rinehart and Winston. Reprinted by permission of Holt, Rinehart and Winston.

Chapter 6

1. See Leonard Berkowitz, "The case for bottling up rage," in *Psychology Today*, July 1973, pp. 24–31.

Chapter 10

1. See Thomas Moriarty, "A nation of willing victims," *Psychology Today*, April 1975, pp. 43–50.
2. The quotation is from the Moriarty article.
3. These points about lodging a complaint are adapted from George Weinberg, "How to make a complaint" in *The Action Approach* (New York: St. Martin's Press, 1969).

Chapter 11

1. See Elliott Aronson, "Attraction: why people like each other," in his book *The Social Animal* (San Francisco, Freeman, 1972).

2. From Dale Carnegie, *How to Win Friends and Influence People,* Copyright ©️ 1936 by Dale Carnegie, renewed ©️ 1964 by Dorothy Carnegie. Reprinted by permission of Simon & Schuster, Inc.
3. Adapted from R. N. Bale, Jr., "The effect of discrimination training, guided practice, and role-playing in modeling treatments designed to increase bidirectional verbal behavior in socially withdrawn males," unpublished doctoral dissertation, Stanford University, 1971.
4. Adapted from R. N. Bale, Jr., as cited in Note 4.
5. Adapted from Peggy H. Smith's unpublished doctoral dissertation, "A comparative study of friendship behaviors: increasing interpersonal contacts," Stanford University, 1974.
6. This material on dating is adapted from that presented in *Assert Yourself: You Deserve It,* unpublished manuscript by Terry Paulson, North Hollywood, Calif.

Suggestions for Further Reading

OTHER BOOKS ON ASSERTIVENESS

Robert E. Alberti and Michael L. Emmons, *Your Perfect Right,* rev. ed. (San Luis Obispo, Calif.: Impact Press, 1974).

George Bach and Herb Goldberg, *Creative Aggression* (New York: Doubleday, 1974).

Lynn Z. Bloom, Karen Coburn, and Joan Pearlman, *The New Assertive Woman* (New York: Delacorte Press, 1975).

Herbert Fensterheim and Jean Baer, *Don't Say Yes When You Want to Say No* (New York: David McKay, 1975).

Susan Osborn and Gloria Harris, *Assertive Training for Women* (Springfield, Ill.: Charles C Thomas, 1975).

Stanlee Phelps and Nancy Austin, *The Assertive Woman* (San Luis Obispo, Calif.: Impact Press, 1975).

Manuel J. Smith, *When I Say No, I Feel Guilty* (New York: Dial, 1975).

OTHER SELF-HELP BOOKS ON SOCIAL SKILLS, NEGOTIATING, RELAXATION, BODY LANGUAGE

Louis M. Savary, *Passages* (New York: Harper & Row, 1972).

George R. Bach and Ronald M. Deutsch, *Pairing* (New York: Avon, 1971).

Albert Ellis and Robert A. Harper, *A Guide to Rational Living* (North Hollywood, Calif.: Wilshire, 1961).

Julius Fast, *Body Language* (New York: Pocket Books, 1971).

Haim Ginott, *Between Parent and Child* (New York: Avon, 1965).

Haim Ginott, *Between Parent and Teenager* (New York: Avon, 1969).

Laura A. Huxley, *You Are Not the Target* (North Hollywood, Calif.: Wilshire, 1963).

Chester L. Karrass, *Give and Take: The Complete Guide to Negotiating Strategies and Tactics* (New York: Thomas Y. Crowell, 1974).

Kent Keyes, Jr., *Handbook to Higher Consciousness* (Berkeley, Calif.: Living Love Center, 1973).

Maxwell Maltz, *Psycho-Cybernetics* (New York: Pocket Books, 1970).

Gerald I. Nierenberg and Henry H. Calero, *How to Read a Person Like a Book* (New York: Pocket Books, 1973).

Albert Scheflen, with Alice Scheflen, *Body Language and the Social Order: Communications as Behavioral Control* (Englewood Cliffs, N. J.: Prentice-Hall, 1973).

Martin E. P. Seligman, *Helplessness: On Development, Depression, and Death* (San Francisco: Freeman, 1975).

C. Eugene Walker, *Learn to Relax* (Englewood Cliffs, N. J.: Prentice-Hall, 1975).

Barbara Walters, *How to Talk with Practically Anybody About Practically Anything* (New York: Dell, 1971).

George Weinberg, *The Action Approach* (New York: St. Martin's Press, 1969).

Leonard Zunin, with Natalie Zunin, *Contact: The First Four Minutes* (New York: Ballantine Books, 1973).

TEXTBOOKS ON BEHAVIOR MODIFICATION

Albert Bandura, *Principles of Behavior Modification* (New York: Holt, Rinehart and Winston, 1969).

John D. Krumboltz and Helen B. Krumboltz, *Changing Children's Behavior* (Englewood Cliffs, N. J.: Prentice-Hall, 1972).

John D. Krumboltz and Carl E. Thoresen (eds.), *Counseling Methods* (New York: Holt, Rinehart and Winston, 1976).

Michael J. Mahoney and Carl E. Thoresen, *Self-Control: Power to the Person* (Monterey, Calif.: Brooks/Cole, 1974).

K. Daniel O'Leary and G. Terence Wilson, *Behavior Therapy: Application and Outcome* (Englewood Cliffs, N.J.: Prentice-Hall, 1975).

David C. Rimm and John C. Masters, *Behavior Therapy: Techniques and Empirical Findings* (New York: Academic Press, 1974).